OPTIONS TRADING

THIS BOOK INCLUDES:
OPTIONS TRADING FOR BEGINNERS AND STRATEGIES.
FIND HERE THE BEST TIPS TO INVEST IN THE STOCK
MARKET AND TO MAKE AN INCOME OUT OF IT.

MATTHEW MORRIS

OPTIONS TRADING

FOR BEGINNERS

THE COMPLETE GUIDE ON HOW TO INCREASE YOUR INCOME WITH OPTIONS TRADING. LEARN HOW TO MAKE A LIVING WITH THE HELP OF THESE TECHNICAL STRATEGIES

MATTHEW MORRIS

TABLE OF CONTENTS

INTRODUCTION

If you were to find an investor and ask to look at their portfolio, you will be able to see that they have a large variety of investments that they are working on. They don't just put all their money on one company all the time. Instead, they have many different types of investments they can work with, such as bonds, stocks, mutual funds, and more. In addition, there are times when a portfolio will include options, but it is not as likely to be there as some of the others.

This is like getting a key where once you use that key to open the front door of a house, then it belongs to you. You may not technically own the house because you have the key, but you can use that key whenever you would like and if you choose, you could purchase the house later on.

Options are set up so that they cost you a certain fixed price for so much time. This length will change based on the option that you are working with. Sometimes you will have an option that only lasts for a day and then there are some that you may hold onto for a few years. You will know how long it is going to last before you make the purchase.

They are nothing new. It's a well-known term in trading, and even though it might be overwhelming for some people to think about, options are not really hard to understand.

It can be considered as an investment that gives you more "options."

But that does not mean that there are no risks involved. Almost every investment entails a multitude of risks. The same goes for it. An investor ought to know of these risks before proceeding with trade.

Options are a part of the group of securities called derivatives. The term derivative is many a time associated with huge risks and volatile performance. Warren Buffett once called derivatives "weapons of mass destruction," which is a little too much.

Also it is a kind of derivative. Investors are often talking about different derivatives. Options derive their value from an underlying stock or security. In fact, options belong to the class of securities known as derivatives. For a long time, people associated derivatives with high-risk investments. This notion is not really true.

Derivatives obtain their value from an underlying security. Think about wine, for instance. Wine is produced from grapes. We also have ketchup, which is derived from tomatoes. This is basically how derivatives function.

One can gain a real advantage in the market if they know how options work and can use them properly since you can put the cards in your favor if you can use options correctly. The great thing about options is that you can use them according to your style. If you're a speculative person, earn through speculation. If not, earn without speculating. You should know how options work even if you decide never to use them because other companies you invest in might use options.

Options are an attractive investment tool. They have a risk/reward framework, which is unlike any other. They can be used in a multitude of combinations that make them very versatile. The risk factor involved can be diluted by using these options with other financial instruments or other option contracts, and at the same time, opening more avenues for profits. While many investments have an unbound quantum of risk attached, options' trading, on the other hand, has defined risks, which the buyers know about.

Now, several choices will work when you are dealing with options. Some of the ones that you will come across regularly include:

Bonds: This is going to be a debt investment where the investor is able to loan out their money to the government or company. Then, this money will be used for a variety of projects by the second party. But, at some time, usually determined, when the money is given over, it will be paid back along with some interest. Most of the time, you will work with a government bond that you can even found on the public exchange.

Commodity: It's another choice that you can make when you are working with options. These will be any basic goods that will be used in commerce and can include some choices like beef, oil, and grain. When you trade these, there will be a minimum of quality that they must meet. These are popular because commodities are considered tangible, which means that they represent something real.

Currency: It's going to talk about any type of money accepted by the government like coins and paper money. Of course, cryptocurrency and Bitcoin are starting to join the market as well. The exchange rate of these currencies, especially when it comes to the digital currencies, will change quite a bit in very little time, so it is important to be careful with these.

Futures: These are going to be similar to what you found with commodities, but they have some different guidelines on how they can be delivered, the quantity and quality, and more.

Index: It's going to be a group of securities that are imaginary and will symbolize the statistical measurement of how those will do in the market.

Stock: You can own a certain percentage of the share, but instead of running that company, you will let other management do that while you make some profits each quarter when the company does well.

Options may sound complex but are pretty easy to understand if you pay keen attention. You will come across numerous traders' profiles with different security types including, bonds, stocks, mutual funds, ETFs, and even options.

Options are another asset class. If applied correctly, they will offer numerous benefits that all other assets on their own cannot. For instance, you can use options to hedge against negative outcomes like a declining stock market or falling oil prices. You can use options to generate recurrent income and for speculative purposes like wagering on the movement of a stock.

As an investor, you will have many opportunities to use options. However, there is a truly beneficial number. Here is a brief look at them.

Options buy you time if you need to sit back and watch things develop.

You require very little funds to invest in options compared to buying shares.

Options will offer you protection from losses because they lock in price but without the obligation to buy.

Always keep in mind that options offer no free ride or a free lunch. Trading in options carries some risks due to their predictive nature. Any prediction will turn out one way or another. The good news here is that any losses that you incur will only be equivalent to the cost of setting up the option. This cost is significantly lower than buying the underlying security.

There are several parties involved in a trade. It isn't possible to trade directly with everyone, and it isn't even practical. This is why, for the sake of convenience, stock exchanges were formed. This is a channel where all the stocks are being traded.

You cannot work directly with the stock exchange, as this would create great confusion. It would mean too many people making deals at the same time. This is where brokers come into play.

Brokers work as the mediators between you and the exchange. They charge a commission for their service. In the stock exchange industry's early stages, most of the transactions were carried out by the brokers on behalf of their clients. Brokers nowadays are still doing it, but the clients now have the option to manage their accounts easily. You will have to open a trading account with a broker, and they will give you access.

Currently, several software have been successfully developed where you can directly trade on stock exchanges. The program recommendation, as well as the access credentials, will be provided by the brokerage firm you'll choose.

Like a bond or stock, an option is a tradable security. You can purchase or sell options to a foreign broker or trade them on an exchange within the United States. An option may allow you to leverage your cash, though it may be high risk because it eventually expires (expiration date). For stock options, each option contract represents 100 shares.

An instance of an option is if you want to buy a car/house, but for any reason, you do not have immediate cash for it, but you will get it next month. You can now buy the asset at the agreed price and sell it for a profit. The value of the asset may also depreciate perhaps when the house develops plumbing problems or any other, or in the case of a vehicle, gets into an accident. If you decide not to buy the asset and let your purchase option expire, you lose your initial investment, the $2,500 you placed for the option.

This is the general concept of how option trading happens; however, in reality, option trading is a lot more complex and involves more risks.

CHAPTER - 1

The Basic of Options Trading

First of all, what is an option? You must be familiar with financial market instruments such as stocks, bonds, FX, etc. In addition to this, it is the third type of instrument called a derivative. A derivative isn't a type of instrument as much as it is a separate class of instrument. You see, derivatives don't have any value of their own. They derive their value from an underlying instrument.

What does this mean, practically speaking? Well, when you buy an option, you're buying a contract that gives you a choice. You can either buy or sell a particular stock (or FX pair, but we're sticking with stocks in this book) at certain terms. Here are the terms that are stipulated within the contract:

1. Whether you can buy or sell that stock.

2. When the contract expires.

3. The price at which you can buy or sell the stock.

4. The price of the contract called the premium.

Let's look at this one by one. The first point, whether you can buy or sell the stock, determines what type of contract you're buying. If you have the option to buy, the contract is a call. If you have the option to sell, the option is a put. Next, we have the expiry date of the contract.

This is the time until which the option is valid. You can choose to exercise this option (i.e. buy or sell the underlying stock) at any time until this date. This is how American options work. European options can be exercised only ON the expiry date. We'll deal only with American options since they're traded heavily.

The third point stipulates the price at which the underlying stock may be bought or sold. This is called the strike price. So if you exercise the contract, this is the price which you will pay when you buy or sell the stock. Lastly, the contract itself has a price, which is called the premium ("Options Terms," 2019).

The premium is comprised of three elements that determine its value: intrinsic value, time value, and volatility factor. The intrinsic value is simply the difference between the current market price of the stock and the option's strike price. For example, a call that has a strike price of $10 and if the market price is $15, the intrinsic value is $5. Similarly, a put with a strike price at $20 will have an intrinsic value of $5 for the same market price.

A call will have intrinsic value only if its strike price is lesser than the market price. Why is this? Well, you cannot make money on a call when the market price is lower. For example, if you exercise a call with a strike price of 20, but with the market at 15, you're paying $20 for something worth $15.

A put will have intrinsic value when the market price is below the strike price. It is also like shorting a stock in anticipation of its price moving lower. Hence, if the market price is above the strike price, the put has zero intrinsic value.

Any options contract, be it a put or a call, is said to be in the money when it has intrinsic value. If the strike price equals market price, it is said to be at the money. When it has negative intrinsic value (basically none), it is said to be out of the money. I'm throwing a lot of terms at you, so take the time to memorize them. Understanding these concepts inside out is necessary to put the strategies in this book into play.

So that's intrinsic value. Next, we have the time value. This is pretty simple to understand. The further away from the expiry dates of the option, the more time value it has. Time decay refers to the reduction of the time value as the option gets closer to its expiry date. The last factor is the volatility adjustment. This one doesn't have a practical use for you, but you should know about it nonetheless.

Volatility refers to how far and violently a stock will move. A stock which fluctuates in a given direction, or both, by ten points per hour, is more volatile than a stock that moves just two. As such, the options for the high volatility stock will have higher premiums than the ones for the lower volatility stock.

How are these volatility adjustments calculated? Well, this is where the Black-Scholes model comes in and this involves a whole bunch of math, which is pointless for our purposes. If you are curious, I suggest reading about it. There's enough literature out there. I mean, the pair who invented this model won the Nobel Prize (Kenton, 2019).

So, these three factors, the intrinsic value, time value, and volatility adjustment, determine the premium option. When you pay for an option, you will lose the premium no matter what happens to the underlying. So even if your option moves into the money, you're not going to get the premium back.

What happens if your option doesn't move into the money by the expiry date? Nothing. It expires worthless and your loss is limited to what you paid for the contract. Also, a single options contract represents control over 100 shares. Premiums are quoted on a per-share basis, so you need to multiply the price by 100 to arrive at the total price.

Now that we've established all that, let's look at how to trade them.

What is Options Trading?

There are two major ways you can trade options. The first involves buying the option itself and speculating on the price of the premium. The price of the premium is going to fluctuate based on how the underlying stock moves so you can profit from these movements. For example, if you think a stock is going to go up, you can buy an in the money call and as the stock rises, the intrinsic value rises as well.

Thus, you benefit from the rise in the overall premium value. With a put, as the stock falls, the intrinsic value of the put rises and so does its premium. Remember, you're buying a put in order to benefit from the price drop (you're not selling a put). The second method of speculating in options is to not pay as much attention to the premium but to the underlying.

What I mean is that you're not concerned with the price rise in the underlying, you're far more concerned with exercising the option. This involves an additional step, but if you aim to own the stock, then this could be a better method for you to deploy. Generally speaking, a lot of options traders don't bother exercising the contract since the premium tends to capture the intrinsic value change pretty well.

Pretty straightforward so far, isn't it? You can swing or day trade options like you would a common stock, but these methods will need you to develop a directional bias in the markets. As we've seen, this increases your risk and is no different from usual trading activity. The point is, you don't need options to trade this way. So how one trade does options intelligently?

Well, the best method to do this is to use the structure of the contracts themselves to isolate yourself from major market risk factors such as volatility. Often when swing or day trading, traders will use what is called a stop-loss order to limit their downside. This is a safety net only on paper since the market is liable to simply jump the stop loss level during times of high volatility.

So the trader is faced with larger than expected losses and in some cases, such volatility might wipeout their entire account as well. Options avoid all this drama since you will only pay the premium upfront, thereby limiting your initial investment greatly. Next, you will be using ironclad contracts to protect your downside and therefore, there is no possibility of the market jumping the price. Even if it does, your contract specifies the price, so you will always receive the price as stated on it.

This being said, there are a few risks to options trading you should be aware of.

The Risks of Options Trading

Thus far, I've only been mentioning the trading of options concerning the underlying stock's movements. If you think it's going to rise, you buy a call. If you think it's going to fall, buy a put. Well, can you short call or a put? Yes, you can, and this is precisely where the risks inherent to options trading enter the picture.

When you buy an options contract, your risk is limited to the terms of the contract. The person who sold you the contract receives the premium in exchange for selling it to you. They keep this premium no matter what. The seller of the option is generally called the writer.

Option writing has its advantages. For one, the majority of options traded tend to expire out of the money. Hence, the writer keeps the premium on the option and usually doesn't have to worry about the contract being exercised. If the contract does get exercised, this leads to a whole world of trouble. Think about this scenario: if you've written a call (that is, you sold it), and if it moves into the money, your downside is unlimited.

Remember, when you're writing a call, you're betting that the underlying stock will not rise. Well, if it does rise, it can rise to infinite levels. What if your call's strike price is at $10 and before the expiry date, the stock rises to $10,000? Unlikely, I know, but theoretically possible. The loss will easily exceed your account's equity.

Writing a put doesn't have an unlimited downside, but it does have a large one nonetheless. If the strike price of the put you wrote is at $50, your downside is a total of $50 per-share (since the stock can decline only till 0). This is why writing options need to be carried out carefully.

So if the risks are this huge, why do people write options in the first place? Well, aside from the fact that option writing usually results in a profit (via earning the premium), most option writers cover their downside by covering their option positions. So if someone writes a call, they buy the underlying stock first. Another option is to buy a put at a lower strike price since this covers their downside.

You must understand the differences between writing naked options and writing them when covered. Naked option writing is the riskiest thing that you can do and in fact, your broker will not allow you to do this. Covered writing is perfectly fine and no broker is going to stop you doing this.

In case you're wondering, once you write an option, you can buy it back at a lower price before the expiry date. In other words, you can short an option like you would a stock. Generally, with the strategies in this book, you won't need to do this unless you adjust your trades.

Options have leverage inherent in them and you should be aware of this fact. Every contract represents control over 100 shares of the underlying stock, so everything that happens is magnified by a 100x multiple. This makes it even more crucial that you execute your strategies perfectly.

Other than this, options don't present any risks. In fact, they reduce your risk of trading in the market thanks to minimizing the effects of volatility. Volatility is both a blessing and a curse for directional traders. On one hand, it makes them money via massive swings. However, it's not so much fun when the swings go the other way and wipe them out.

CHAPTER - 2

The Types of Options Trading

There are, of course, only two ways a stock can move, and so there are two types of options. These are:

- A call: this is a bet that the stock will rise in price on the ending date of the contract or before.

- A put: this is a bet that the stock will decline in price on the ending date of the contract or before.

For a call, the condition that the contract is based on is that the price of a share of stock will go up past an agreed-upon price per-share, which is called the strike price. When it does, the buyer of the option can exercise their right to buy the shares of stock from the seller (or writer as they are called) of the call option. That is, they can "call it in."

This is true, no matter how high the stock price has risen. So, let's suppose that the strike price for ABC stock was set at $67 when the contract was entered into by the two parties. Second, we'll assume that at that time the share price was $65. If the share price rises to $68 a share, the owner of the shares must sell them if the buyer wants to exercise their option (to buy the shares). This is also true if the share price rises to $100.

The seller of the contract takes a bit of risk. They can't lose money, but they might miss out on a big move in the share price of the stock, and hence miss out on a big profit they could have had.

Why bother? The reason is that the buyer can buy the shares at the strike price. If the shares have risen to $100 a share, the buyer can buy the shares from the seller of the options contract at $68 per-share, and then immediately turn around and sell them for $100 a share, making a quick profit of $32 per-share! Of course, that is a quote of gross revenue, there are some fees involved and a commission to the broker, but in the end, the buyer would make a substantial profit in this scenario.

Now you may be wondering why the person selling the contract would bother. He can charge a non-refundable fee for entering into the contract. This fee is called the premium. If you're selling calls, you get to keep the premium no matter what. In many cases, the share price will never exceed the strike price, so they get to keep the premium and the shares. If it does exceed the strike price, they get to keep the premium, and even though they may have missed out on some profit they could have had, they will probably earn a bit of profit on the shares they sold anyway. For the seller, it's a win-win deal. This kind of option contract is known as a covered call.

Covered calls provide one option strategy, which is to generate income from your shares.

Premiums are small, as compared to the price of the underlying stock. The risk to the buyer of the call is relatively small, and they get the chance to control shares of stock for a certain time without actually owning them. Of course, to exercise your option, you will have to have the capital on hand or access to the capital to buy the shares making your quick profit. Many people, however, don't even do that and they simply trade options (that is, you get the contract, and then, sell it on the options markets before the expiry).

Options contracts are for 100 shares each. Premiums will usually be pretty small, so say $1 per-share, so you can buy the options contract for 100 shares for $100. If it doesn't work out for the buyer, they lose a relatively small amount of money, as compared to the large funds that would be involved actually buying the stock. From the buyers' perspective, it gives them the ability to speculate on the markets for relatively small sums of money and without actually owning the stock. Then, if their speculation proves right, they can exercise their options and buy and sell the shares of stock.

When you read about options, they are typically described in some fancy-sounding language. It will make sense now that you've seen how a covered call works. For a call, an option is a contract giving the owner the right, but not the obligation, to buy shares of stock at a fixed price over a specific, limited time period. Typically, options contracts last a few months, but you can also buy weeklies, which last a week on Fridays. There are also quarterly which expire the last business day at the end of each quarter. Also, for long term considerations, you can buy LEAPS which is typically a time period over a few years.

Now let's take a look at the other type of options contract, which is known as a put. A put gives the buyer the right to sell the underlying stock at an agreed-upon price on or before the expiration date. Again, the put contract is sold for a premium and the pre-agreed upon share price is known as the strike price. When a trader buys a put, the bet is that the price of the stock will go below the strike price over the lifetime of the contract. Let's illustrate you with an example.

Joe buys a put contract for XYZ Company. At the time that he buys the put contract, XYZ is trading at $100 a share. The premium for the contract is $2, so he buys it for $200. The strike price is $90.

Joe believes or has heard that some bad news will come out about XYZ, or maybe he is simply bearish about the market at large. Then before the contract expires, the bad news does come out. The share price drops to $60. Now Joe can exercise his right in the contract.

He buys 100 shares on the stock market at $60 a share. The seller of the put contract must buy the shares from Joe–at the strike price. So, the seller buys 100 shares of XYZ stock at $90 a share, and Joe walks away with a $30 per-share profit (less the premium fee and brokerage commission).

The seller of the put got a raw deal, they probably doubted the news would drive the stock price that low, and so made a bet it wouldn't in order to get the income from the premium. Even though they lost their bet, they get to keep the premium. So, they aren't totally out. They also have the 100 shares of XYZ, and who knows, maybe things will turn around in the future.

These are dramatic examples designed for illustration. Most of the time, stock probably won't move that much, although options traders try to look for volatile stocks that are moving a lot. Sellers will probably try and sell more stable stocks, so they won't risk as much.

If the share price of stock never goes above the strike price in the case of a call or goes below the share price in the case of a put by the expiration date, the option expires worthless. The seller of the option walks away with their premium and, in the case of the call, keeps their shares, and in the case of a put, has no obligation to buy shares. The buyer of the option loses only the premium when the option expires worthless (note that the buyer never gets the premium back under any circumstances).

A call is an option for a long position. So, you'll buy a call option if you believe that the market price of the stock will rise above the strike price. In that case, you'll get a bargain price for the shares. Let's say that you are bullish on XYZ stock, which is trading at $50 a share. You buy a call with a strike price of $55. The price of the call is the premium, which we'll say is $5, so the total cost of the call is $5 x 100 = $500. Your analysis holds true, and XYZ spikes in price 30 days after you've bought the option contract to $70 a share after XYZ announces a snazzy new smartphone. The seller of the call must sell you 100 shares of XYZ at $55 a share, so you're "in the money" at $70 a share. You buy the shares for $55 and then, you can sell them immediately for $70 a share. Your profit per-share is the sales price minus the strike price minus the premium:

$70 - $55 -$5 = $10 per-share

Of course, you'd have to pay a commission to the broker for the trades as well.

The seller of the call didn't do all that badly. Even though they didn't get the benefit of being able to sell at $70 a share, they were able to sell the shares at $55 and make a profit as compared to the $50 a share they were trading at when you entered the contract. However, the main reason the seller of the call would go for a deal like this is to get the premium, which is a way to leverage your stocks to get income. When you write a call contract and its stock that you currently own, that is called a covered call.

You can write a call on stocks you don't own. That's a naked call. However, if the buyer exercises their right to buy the shares, you've got to come up with them. In the scenario described here, you'd be in serious trouble. Since you didn't own the shares, you'd have to buy shares at $70 a share and sell them to the buyer of the call for $55 a share since that was the agreed-upon strike price. In other words, you'd lose $15 x 100 = $1,500. Your loss would be partially offset by the $500 premium.

Now let's look at puts. This is an option to sell a stock. ABC is trading at $50 a share, but you're bearish on the stock. You buy a put for $5 a share, with a strike price of $40. Before the contract expires, the stock crashes on bad news to $20. So, you buy 100 shares at $20 a share. The seller of the put contract has to meet their obligation. So, they are forced to buy the shares from you at the strike price, which was $40 a share. Therefore, on a per-share basis, you made (not including commissions):

$40 - $20 - $5 = $15 per-share

To summarize, you pay a premium for the right but not the obligation to buy stocks when you buy a call. Or you pay a premium for the right but not the obligation to sell stocks when you buy a put.

All options contracts have an expiration date, which is typically the third Friday of the month. You can look at options tickers to see what the expiration date is. An option has more value, the further it is from the expiration date, and it loses value the closer, the contract gets to the expiration. The reason is that if the stock price hasn't passed the strike price. Then, the less time there is remaining on the contract, the less time is available for the stock to move in order for the option to be exercised. The value of the option and the time remaining until the expiration date is captured in the concept of time value.

CHAPTER - 3

Options Contracts for Beginners

Options contracts are nothing less than an enigma for the beginners. They look so hard to understand, because there are a lot of uncertainties involved that determine its price.

Some people fear that options contracts are similar to betting, as there is a risk of the total investment getting zero.

You must understand that options are speculative in nature, but dealing in options is not gambling. There is a lot of science behind options, and it is a great tool to earn money in the securities market.

In the options contract, your risk is limited, but your rewards can be very high.

Your exposure is limited, and you get enough chances to cover your positions. There are several strategies through which you can minimize your risk even further.

Options are contracts to buy or sell assets at a set

price in a future period.

Let us try to understand the options contracts with the help of an example.

Suppose you are a trader, and you deal with gift products.

Your specialty is superhero characters.

You have a good network through which you can sell these toys in the upcoming Christmas season.

There are several big-budget movies to come in a short period based on those characters.

If those movies perform well in the box office, the demand for those toys will be huge.

You want to buy those toys in good volume so that when the demand picks up, you have the goods to sell at a good price.

You also know that as the demand rises, the prices would also rise, and you may not get the toys in the required volume as other traders would also come looking for them from the same manufacturer.

Yet, you are skeptical about buying those toys in advance, as the popularity of those toys would depend on the public reception of the movies based on those characters.

If the movie doesn't perform well, the demand may not be that big, and you may not be able to sell them at a higher price.

You are in a dilemma.

However, you also don't want to miss the bus when the movie becomes a huge success.

You have a few important things clear in your mind:

- If the movie based on those characters turns out to be a success, there would be a huge demand for those toys in the market.

- This would mean that the prices of those characters would go up. You may also face difficulty in getting the toys based on them in the required quantity.

- There is also a possibility that the movie tanks and doesn't get the required attention. In that case, your total investment can get blocked, and you may not get the price you are expecting.

- You will also have to store the toys for a long period.

- Your total investment will also get locked for several months.

- The results are uncertain.

You don't want such a big risk but would like to have a stake in the profit when the tide is in your favor.

You think you can sell 1 million toys in the season if the movie works well. This can mean a great profit.

You go to the manufacturer and suggest a contract:

Suppose the price of the toys at the moment is $5.

You suggest the manufacturer enter into a contract to sell you 1 million toys at $5 per piece on 30th November.

The manufacturer will have to give you the toys at this price, and the prices cannot be raised.

However, in case the movie doesn't work, you want to reserve the right to not buy those toys.

This might look like a bad deal for the manufacturer. But this isn't.

The manufacturer puts some condition:

He says that you will have to pay 10 cents per toy upfront.

This is the cost of locking the price of the goods to be bought at a future date.

This price is non-adjustable in the cost of the toys when you buy it.

In case you decide against buying the toys by the given date, the contract would expire, and he would be free to sell it at the current market price.

The meat of the deal for the manufacturer is the additional 10 cents value per toy that he is going to get irrespective of the fact that you buy the toys on the said date or not.

The manufacturer has all the reasons to believe that he will be able to sell the toys to various traders across the country, even if you don't buy them.

This means that this contract has a benefit for both parties. The manufacturer is going to get 10 cents extra on each toy irrespective of the fact that they get sold or not.

You will get the surety to buy the toys at a fixed price irrespective of the fact that the prices may get very high after the success of the movie. In fact, the higher the prices go, the greater would be your profit.

If the movie tanks, you will be under no obligation to buy those toys, and you can simply forgo your right to buy those toys.

- You will not have to invest $5 million upfront.

- You will not have to store the toys in your facility.

- You will have no risk of all your money getting stuck in a losing venture.

- You will have complete freedom to walk out of the deal.

An options contract is a Choice and not an obligation to buy or sell a product or a service by a predetermined date at a predetermined price.

- You have to pay only a small amount as the token money to reserve the right to buy or sell the product or service at a reserved price by a predetermined date.

- By the predetermined date, you can exercise your right to buy or sell.

- If the deal is lucrative at this point, you can choose to buy at the decided price.

- If the deal has lost its attractiveness by this point, you can decide to walk out of the deal without any obligation.

You can see that there is a certain degree of speculation involved. You are speculating that the trade would remain profitable soon; however, you are not committing serious money to the trade.

By investing only a token amount, you are buying the right to exercise the option to buy or sell in the future at the price fixed at this moment.

You will have to judge the prospects.

We all judge things, whether we like to admit it or not, but we all do it regularly, continuously, and religiously.

In fact, the whole world runs on the judgment.

People are judged based on their looks, their intelligence, their wealth, their behavior, and their social circle. This judgment keeps pushing them to improve continuously.

This is one aspect of judgment.

We also judge things to secure our interests.

We judge things before buying them. We want to ensure that they justify their cost.

We judge properties based on the value they may give in the future.

Similarly, we judge our investments in order to speculate the returns they might fetch.

Investment in stocks and commodities is also a part of that value judgment.

Judgment is a part of the bread and butter of every trader.

For instance, if you own a manufacturing unit and you feel that the prices of the raw material in your unit are going to rise, your natural instinct would be to buy as much as possible so to prevent yourself from the pain of inflation.

This is a value judgment that can help you in saving a lot of money on the raw material cost, and you will also be able to sell things at a competitive price when the prices of the raw material go up. This would happen because you made a wise decision to buy things at a cheaper price.

The same happens with stocks. We all want to buy stocks when they are a really low price and then expect them to rise phenomenally.

You can take the example of real estate investing too. You invest your money in properties that hold real value. If you feel that the property which you are going to buy will have interesting projects coming up in the vicinity in the future, the prices of that property will go up. This will give you a great profit.

Therefore, you see that our judgment of the value of an asset is a part of our lives. We do it all the time. There is nothing abnormal or unnatural in it.

However, in most of the judgments made above, your risk is very high.

You bought the raw material expecting the prices to go up.

• You invested a lot of money beforehand.

• Stored it at your warehouse.

• Lost interest on your money.

But, if the prices of that raw material come down, your losses would be substantial.

You locked your capital in an asset that you will be using slowly.

You lost on the opportunities that might have presented themselves if you had free capital.

The prices will also not remain competitive as you have bought it at a higher price.

The same thing happens with stocks.

People invest their money in stocks expecting the prices to go up.

There are times when stocks underperform. In that case, your money can get locked in that asset. Selling the stocks at a lower price would mean substantial losses. Keeping that stock can mean the prices may go further down, and your money would also remain locked in an underperforming asset.

Many people lose a fortune due to this.

The story of real estate investing is also no different.

People invested a lot of money in the real estate sector before the subprime crisis. Everyone was buying property, and hence the prices of properties were going higher and higher. This was propelling more and more people to invest in properties, then came the recession in the property segment after the subprime crisis.

The money invested in the properties got stuck.

The prices of properties went down substantially.

People didn't even get the actual amount they had originally invested leave aside any kind of profit.

In all these investments, there was one central problem. They needed fixed commitments.

You invest your money in raw material, stocks, real estate speculating a rise in their valuation.

If the prices fall, you lose your money and a substantial amount of it. If the prices rise, you gain money on your investment. But, in any case, your investment is substantial, and there is no way you can get out of it easily.

What if there was a way to speculate without having to invest heavily?

A way in which you can bet on the prices or value of something rising and falling, and when that happens, you get the profit in the same way as you would have got if you had invested.

This facility is called an Options Contract.

CHAPTER - 4

The Components of an Options Contract

The Role of the Underlying Stock

It's vital to understand that stocks do play a fundamental role in options trading, even though they are not what you are buying and selling. Bear in mind that an option is only a piece of paper that gives you the right to buy or sell that stock– without the stock, you would have nothing to buy or sell.

You might say that the stock is Oz behind the curtain, changing and moving while your attention is fixed elsewhere. Letting Oz get up to his tricks without you is a bad idea–you need to be keeping an eye on your stocks just as much as you do the options themselves.

Not every stock is allowed its options to be traded on an options exchange. In total, you'll find somewhere in the region 3600 stocks spread across 12 different exchanges, though this number changes all the time.

What does this mean? Well, the exchanges have in place some very solid rules that dictate which stocks may and may not participate in options trading. You'll find some of the biggest business names on the planet there, and you'll also find what are known as "penny stocks," which buy and sell for less than $3.

In general, the latter won't do you much good for options trading. There simply isn't enough liquidity in such a small number for you to bother with the effort required to trade on them.

Instead, I would recommend sticking with the big names–the recognizable companies, such as Microsoft, Apple, Google, and McDonald's.

Another point to bear in mind is that there is a fixed relationship between options trading and its underlying stock. One option contract will always equal a hundred stock shares.

In other words, a single contract will give you the right to buy or sell 100 shares (or one stock). Multiply the number of contracts involved in a trade by 100 and you'll know how many shares are also involved.

A third factor of that relationship between an option and its underlying stock: whenever the stock goes up or down, in most cases, so too will the option contract.

Because the two are so inextricably linked, you will need to study the stock market in detail to be whizzing at options trading. You will need to be able to predict which stocks are going to head in which direction and when–only if you get this right will your trading be truly successful.

For that reason, a lot of options traders started with the stock market itself, giving themselves the experience of its whims before taking a step up to the next level. If you haven't done this, it will be worth spending a month or three trading on the stock market, even a theoretical portfolio that you manage in a folder rather than on your own desktop and never pay a penny to invest in is a helpful step.

Doing this will allow you to get a sense of how the market functions overall and will familiarize you with some of the stocks you might be interested in trading on with options. The best options traders have almost a sixth sense of how an underlying stock is going to perform. The only way to develop that uncanny ability is through exposure, research, and experience.

Understanding the Strike Price

The strike price is the fixed price at which the underlying stock can be either sold or bought. When you purchase a call option, what you are purchasing is the right to buy that stock at this price, while selling a call option means that you are selling the right for your buyer to purchase the stock at that price.

The strike price is an aspect of every options trade that you will want to hone in on every time–it's that important. Never forget that, if the underlying stock never reaches that strike price, the trade is worthless because the option will simply expire on the deadline.

The difference between the current market price of the stock and the strike price of the option also represents the profit-per-share you can expect to make.

Let's say, for example, that you find two trades on a stock that is currently worth $150. One has a strike price of $125 and the other has a strike price of $100.

In the first trade, the stock price will need to drop to $125 before you have the right to buy or sell it (depending on whether the option is a call or a buy). In the second, it will need to drop to $100 before you get that right.

The value of the option is simple to calculate: it's the difference between the strike price and the current worth of the stock. In the first of these examples, the trade has a potential worth of $25; in the second, the potential worth is $50.

At first glance, it would seem to mean that the second option is the one to go for, because its value is so much higher. However, you also need to bear in mind that you cannot dictate what the market does.

This is where the risk comes in. How confident are you, in this example, that the stock will plummet $50 before the expiration date of the option? If you're as certain as it's possible to be, it's a great investment. If you're not, you stand to lose the premium you paid for the option, because it will never reach the price at which you have the right to realize the trade.

The trade that has a strike price of $25 is, therefore, a sure bet–it's always going to be more likely that a stock will rise or fall by the smaller amount than the larger one. The trade-off, as you can see, is that you won't make nearly the profit you would on the riskier option, so you have to ask yourself whether the premium you'd be paying is worthwhile.

Strategy for Selling Covered Calls

We've covered the process, but what about the strategy behind it? We looked at the absolute basics of that strategy, but an experienced trader knows there's always going to be more to an option than meets the eye.

There's a whole list of considerations that you will eventually want to bear in mind as you expand your knowledge and develop your own personal strategy. Every trader has a different attitude towards what works and what doesn't–there are plenty of ways to make selling a covered call work, but you'll probably find yourself preferring one or two strategies.

We'll take a look now at those considerations in more detail to guide you as you delve into the covered call more deeply:

The Market Environment

You are no doubt aware that traders of stocks and shares are happy in a bull market and disgruntled in a bear market. You may also know that such traders hate a flat market most of all because very little is happening and there aren't many big profits to be made. For you, as a seller of covered calls, the opposite is true. I highly recommend waiting for the market to temporarily flatten before embarking on a spate of covered call sales. This is because you're only really interested in small changes to your share prices–if they are skyrocketing, you're losing more money on your contract. There also isn't as much danger of the bottom falling out of the market and your stock prices plummeting at the same time, which would be problematic.

Your Underlying Stock

There is nothing more important to your success than choosing the right stocks to invest in the first place. I cannot stress strongly enough that your success will be heightened if you pick stocks that move up very slowly. You don't want stocks that rise and fall very quickly, especially as a beginner, because they have a habit of making surprising moves that ruin your strategy. If they drop too far, you stand to lose a lot of money in the sale; if they rise too high, you lose the money you could have made if you'd sold them at that price. Traders who deal at risk often enjoy these stocks because they have higher premiums and a chance for huge profits, but that goes against the idea of selling covered calls: you're looking for a steady income that will underpin your riskier strategies elsewhere. By all means, go for the riskier stock elsewhere in your strategy, but avoid it like the plague for this particular function.

The Premium

Always remember that the premium is your guaranteed profit. Whatever else happens, you're going to walk away with that cash. When you factor in the cost to list the option and any commission you will lose to your broker, you'll be able to calculate the actual profit you'll make on that premium. Set yourself a minimum premium–a number that you consider to be enough to provide a profit you'll be happy with, on the assumption that it's the only profit you make. When you move ahead on setting the strike price, you'll likely adjust this base figure up or down based on what you think the underlying stock is going to do before the expiration date. Remember that the premium is only one component of the overall profit you will make–if you then set a strike price that means you lose the same amount of cash on selling the shares as you made through the premium, the trade wasn't worth doing in the first place.

The Expiration Date

There's a reason that the premiums on covered calls get higher the further out the expiration date. It's because, much like the weather forecasts we all deride daily, it gets harder and harder to predict what's going to happen to a share price the further out you go. Also bear in mind that your money is going to be tied up until the expiration date, so the premium will increase as a nod to that sacrifice. Most investors believe that a period between a month and three months works best.

The Strike Price

You might think that the strike price you set should be based on what you, as the seller, are comfortable with, but actually, it's the opposite. You're looking for a strike price that your buyer will feel comfortable with because otherwise, they aren't going to buy. That, in turn, is going to be dictated by the expiration date you set, as well as the premium you're asking for and how stable or volatile the underlying stock is. Your best bet is to put yourself in the shoes of your buyer: would you purchase that contract? How much would you stand to gain? Set your strike price accordingly and then take a look at it from your own point of view. Would this be an acceptable profit for you? If so, you've hit the nail on the head.

CHAPTER - 5

The Fundamentals of the Pricing Options and How Options Prices Are Determined

Pricing is a complex subject when it comes to options trading. Not only is the price of an option based on the value of the asset, but other external factors also have influence.

As an options trader, you want to make sure that you maximize your efforts to make a profit. Learning how to determine the prices you, should pay for options is one of the basic ways that you can ensure that your yield is as high as it can be. You do not want to be stiffed by paying higher premiums than you should.

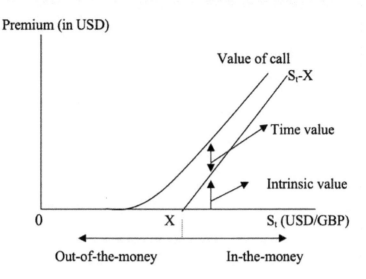

Pricing of options is determined by several factors.

The Value of the Asset

The effect this has on options prices is straightforward. If the value of this asset goes down, then exercising the option to sell becomes more valuable, while the right to buy it becomes less valuable.

On the other hand, if the value increases, the right to sell it becomes less valuable, while the right to buy it becomes more appealing due to this increase.

The Intrinsic Value

When an options trader pays a premium, this sum represents two values. The premium is made up of the intrinsic value, which is the current value of the option and the potential increase in value that this option can obtain over time. This potential increase over time is known as the time value.

The intrinsic value is how much money the option is currently worth. It represents what the buyer would receive if he or she decided to exercise the option at the current time.

Intrinsic value is calculated by determining the difference in the current price of an asset and a strike price of the option.

For an option to have an intrinsic value of zero, the option must be out of money. Therefore, the buyer would not exercise the option because this would result in a loss. The common strategy here is allowing the option to expire so that no pay off is made. As a result, the intrinsic value results in nothing to the buyer.

For a buyer to be in the money, the intrinsic value has to be greater than the premium to increase the value of the option, this places the buyer in a position to make a profit. The intrinsic value of the money for call options and put options are calculated slightly differently. The formulas are as follows:

In the money call options

Price of Asset - Strike Price = Intrinsic Value

In the money put option

Intrinsic Value Formula

$$\begin{array}{c}\text{Intrinsic}\\\text{Value}\\\text{of Business}\end{array} = \frac{FCFE_1}{(1+r)^1} + \frac{FCFE_2}{(1+r)^2} + \cdots + \frac{FCFE_n}{(1+r)^n} + \frac{\text{Terminal Value}}{(1+r)^n}$$

$$\begin{array}{c}\text{Intrinsic}\\\text{Value of Stock}\end{array} = \frac{\text{Intrinsic Value Business}}{\text{No. of Outstanding Shares}}$$

Strike Price - Price of Asset = Intrinsic Value

The Time Value

This value is the additional amount an investor is willing to contribute to the premium of an option in addition to the intrinsic value. This willingness stems from the belief that an option will increase in value before the expiration date reaches. Typically, an investor is only willing to put forth this extra amount if the option expires months away. There would be little to no change in the value of an option in a few days.

The time value is calculated by finding the difference between the intrinsic value of an option and the premium. The formula looks like this:

Option Premium - Intrinsic Value = Time Value

Therefore, the total price of an option premium follows this formula:

Intrinsic Value + Time Value = Option Premium

Both time value and intrinsic value help traders understand the value of what they are paying for if they decide to purchase an option. While the intrinsic value represents the worth of the option if the buyer were to exercise it at the current time, the time value represents the possible future value before or on the expiration date. These two values are important because they help traders understand the risk versus the reward of considering an option.

Volatility

This describes how likely a price change will occur during a period on the financial market. If a financial market is non-volatile then the prices change very slowly or remain totally unaffected over a specific amount of time. Volatile markets, on the other hand, have fast-changing prices over short periods.

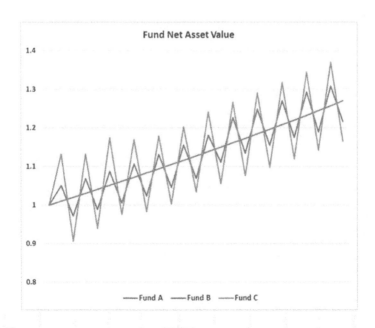

Fund Net Asset Value

Option traders can make use of a financial market's volatility to get a higher yield for their investment in the future. Options traders normally avoid slow-changing financial markets because these non-volatile markets often mean that no potential profit is available to the trader. Therefore, option traders thrive on volatility even though it increases the risk of option trading. As a result, an options trader needs to know how to read the financial market correctly to know which options are likely to yield the highest returns. This ability comes with experience, continuous learning and keeping up to date on the happenings of the financial markets.

Many factors affect the volatility of the financial market. These factors include politics, national economics, and news reports. Options traders typically use one of two options strategies to gain the best yield from volatile markets. They are called straddle strategy and the strangle strategy.

Interest Rates

Most people are familiar with the term interest rates. Interest rates apply to mortgages bank accounts and more. Interest rates, as it applies to option trading, are slightly different from the common variations.

The interest rate is defined as the percentage of a particular rate for the use of money lent over some time. This interest rate of an option has different effects on the call option and put option. The premiums for call options rise when interest rates rise and fall when interest rates fall. The effect is the opposite on puts options. The premiums for put options fall when interest rates rise and rise when interest rates fall.

Interest rates affect the time value of options no matter what category they fall in!

You will come across the term risk-free interest rate many times in your study of options trading. This is described as the return made on an investment with no loss of capital. This is a misleading term because all investments carry some level of risk, no matter how minute. This more serves as a parameter in options pricing models such as the Black-Scholes Model to determine the premium that should be paid.

Dividends

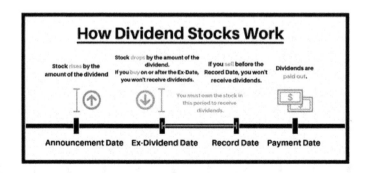

Dividends are distributions of portions of a company's profit at a specified period. This distribution must be decided and managed by the board of directors of a company. It is paid to a particular class of shareholders. Dividends can be distributed in the form of cash, shares of stock, and other types of property. Exchange-traded funds and mutual funds also payout dividends.

As it relates to options trading, options do not actually pay dividends. However, the associated assets attached to that option can have them and thus, options trader can receive those dividends if he or she exercises that option and takes ownership of those particular assets. While both call and put options can be affected by the presence of dividends of the associated asset, this effect on the types of options is widely varied. While the presence of dividends makes call options less expensive due to the anticipation of a drop in price, it makes put options more expensive because the price will be decreased by the amount of the dividend.

CHAPTER - 6

Steps of Optional Trading of a Beginner

You have learned different aspects regarding all the factors that go into making a good options trade; it's time to start putting your new knowledge into action. This is a two-part process, the first part is coming up with the right plan and the second is executing that plan in the right way.

Work Out a Plan

Before you can begin trading successfully, the first thing you are going to need to consider is creating your own personalized trading plan. This plan will include several facets that are unique to you and proceeding without taking the time to create your own plan. It is a good way to kill your options trading career before it starts.

Start by considering your skills: When it comes to ensuring you have the right options trading plan, the first thing you are going to want to do is taking a look at your overall skill level and familiarity with trading in general, if not options trading specifically. Many new options traders are tempted to overestimate their skills early on, but this will do nothing but hold you back in the long run. Be honest and accurately catalog your strengths and weaknesses.

Think about other challenges: When it comes to determining what plan or system works for you, it will be important to take into account any other potential challenges that you might need to face in order to achieve the level of success that you are hoping for. These types of challenges could be anything from a lack of resources or planning to something more complicated and personal. The point is that anything outside of the normal market inconsistencies that prevent options trading from being purely profitable should be accounted for to ensure your success rate remains as high as possible.

Consider the right amount of risk for you: When it comes to deciding how much risk is the right amount for you, the first thing you will want to do is to decide how much your total investment budget is going to be. If you have never invested anything before, then this investment budget can be seen as your portfolio. Never put more than 5% of your total into any one trade, which makes it difficult to lose anything too substantial all at once. What's more, you will want to determine if the trade is worth the effort by ensuring it will pay off at least 300% when compared with the initial investment.

Do your homework: Every day in the hours before the market opens, you need to plan on being in front of some type of screen, learning about everything that happened while you were sleeping and deciding how you think it is going to affect the markets you are interested in the most. This means checking foreign markets, the premarket forecast, and the index futures, to name a few. All in the name of deciding what the market's mood of the day is going to be after the day gets going properly and trading actually begins.

Decide on an exit strategy: No matter what plan or strategy you settle on, it is important to have a clear idea of what an acceptable level of profit or loss means to you and setting a firm exit strategy accordingly. While it can be tempting to wait on an underlying stock to rebound before exercise your option or walking away, the results are rarely going to end in your favor and it can lead to a bad habit of hanging on to sub-par trades that could possibly cost you big in the long term. The right exit strategy for you will vary based on how much risk you can accept, coupled with how many trades you are planning to make each day and what level of micromanaging you are comfortable with. Regardless, the point at which you decide to bail on a bad trade should be the same for all of your trades.

For example, if you have a pair of options totaling 200 shares of a stock that is worth $20 to start. You would set a stop loss at $19.75 to prevent yourself from losing much money. If the stock then hits your price target of $30, then the best course of action is to sell 100 shares to ensure you see some profit from your price target before holding on to the remaining shares and setting a new stop loss of $30. This way you are guaranteed to see the profits of your price target while at the same time leaving yourself open for additional profits assuming the positive trend in the underlying stock continues.

Find a point of entry: Once you know when you are going to want to get while the getting is good, you will next want to determine when you are generally going to want to jump in on a profitable option trade. Start by considering your acceptable risk, and then decide what you want to do when you find an option that falls within your risk level. The most common entry decision is to buy a single option. Depending on your level of risk, you are also going to want to consider secondary factors, as you want your entry point to be discerning enough to weed out lousy propositions but no so stringent that the good ones also fail to get through. It will get easier to find the perfect entry point; the more practice you obtaining at trading options.

Ask yourself about your goals: When it comes to creating the type of trading system that is right for you, it is important to have a clear idea of just what you hope to accomplish when it comes to long term trading so you then have a better idea of how each individual trade can help you come one small step closer to your goals. You want to keep any limiting factors in mind when it comes to determining your goals, but you also want to keep your goals realistic as well as what is known as SMART.

S: The best goals are specific in that they make it clear why you want to reach the goal in question as to which requirements stand in the way of your success. It will also make it clear when the goal is likely to be completed, where the completion will take place and who, besides yourself, you are going to need calling upon to complete it successfully. Specific goals are important because they are far more likely to be completed than general.

M: The best goals are measurable, which means they have several points that can provide distinct feedback as to the overall success or failure of the goal as a whole. If you clearly know when you have reached a new milestone, then your goal is measurable.

A: The best goals are attainable when all of your unique challenges are taken into account. No matter your intentions, a goal that is unattainable is never a good goal.

R: The best goals are realistic, which means that not only are they attainable, they can be completed based on the amount of time and effort you will be able to put forth on average.

Timely: The best goals are those who have a specific but reasonable timetable for completion. Goals that are too strict when it comes to a timetable will never come to fruition in time; meanwhile, goals that are too vague when it comes to a timetable will also never see success because it is too easy to put them off indefinitely.

Keenly track your progress: If you are new to options trading, you will likely find it useful to keep extremely precise notes when it comes to the trades you made, the mental state you were in when you made them, and the ultimate outcome of each. Keep track of the metrics throughout your day, every day, but also to avoid pouring over them at the end of each day with the goal of passing judgment on your system. A good system needs at least a few weeks to determine if it is at all worthwhile, and then another 2 weeks if its results are near 50 percent or better. Nothing is gained by looking for results where there are none that are strong enough to be accurately seen.

Place the first order

Placing your first order is not as difficult as many newbie traders seem to think. All you have to do is obtain the right information and apply yourself. Following are the steps for placing your first order (Plessis, 2012):

- Login into your brokerage account. When you sign up for the services of an online broker, you will be issued a username and password. These are the credentials that will enable you to log in to your account. You must keep them secret. In fact, you should even add more security features to keep your account fail-safe. There are many degrees of fraudulent activities on the internet, but protecting yourself against these frauds starts with securing your account."

- Find the trade or order page. It depends on the user interface of various platforms, but since you have opened a trading account, there must be an item on the page labeled "trade" or "order." Brokerages invest in a simple interface so that traders could interact with the options exchange quite easily.

- Pull up a stock or ETF quote. Stocks are the commonest underlying securities that options are based on, so you have to pull the quotes of the company shares that you're targeting.

- Search for the options quote table. Next up, you have to check the underlying and options price, which are placed conveniently on the search results.

- Choose your expiration date. Unlike shares, options have time constraints, so next, you have to select the frame of time within that you will trade, which requires you to set the expiration date of your options contract.

- Select your strike price. The strike prices for both put options and call options are clearly shown in the table, and you have to select the strike price that you want.

- Select either "call" or "put." The calls are typically listed on the left side of the page while the puts are listed on the right side. Select the option that you want and check the quotes. The order form for the option will come up.

- Enter the quantity. Now you have to enter the number of contracts that you wish to purchase. But remember that as a beginner, you have to be careful, which means you have to purchase a relatively small amount of options contracts before you dive all the way in.

- Set your desired price. Set the price at which you'll acquire the options contract. The premium is influenced by many aspects, among them, the stock price of the underlying.

- Pick out the order type. It is an advanced feature that can help you manage the risk to an extent.

- Day order or GTC order. At this point, you will decide how long the order will stay open if it's not filled. Day orders stay open during the day and automatically turn off at the close of the market. GTC orders refer to "Good Till Canceled Orders," which means they will stay open until they are either filled or canceled.

- Confirm and send. At the click of a button, your order is placed. Don't rush to do it. Take a moment to read your order to ensure that there are no errors.

CHAPTER - 7

Binary Options Trading

This is similar to traditional options in many ways except that they ultimately boil down to a basic yes or no question. Instead of worrying about what exact price an underlying stock is going to have, it only cares if it is going to be above one price at the time of its expiration. Traders then make their exchange if they think that the answer is just a yes or a no. While it may seem simple on its face, it is important that you carefully understand how binary options work, as well as the time frames and markets they work with. It is also important to understand the specific criteria that they have and what legal companies are allowed to offer binary options for trade.

If you are currently considering trading in binary options, then it is also important to be aware that outside of the US, it has a different structure. Also, when hedging or speculating, it is important to keep in mind that doing so is considered an exotic option trade, so the rules are still different. Regardless, the price of a binary option is always going to be somewhere between $0 and $100, it is also going to come with a bid price as well as an ask price, just like any other type of option.

They are also a great way for those who are interested in day-trading but do not have the serious capital required to get off the ground, to ply their trade. Traditional stock day trading limits do not apply to binary options, so you are allowed to start trading with just 1, $100 deposit. It is also important to keep in mind that binary options are a derivative created by its association with an underlying asset, which means they do not give you ownership of that asset in any way. This means you cannot exercise them to generate dividends or enact voting rights as you would with standard options.

For example, assume you are considering purchasing a binary option that states that the gold's price will be greater than $1,250 by $1:30 pm. If you have faith in the scenario that is going to come true, then you would want to buy into the option. Otherwise, you would want to sell it. Further assume that the option is trading at a bid price of $42.50 and an ask price of $44.50, 30 minutes before it is set to expire. If you opt to buy the binary option at this point, you have to pay $44.50. Otherwise, you would pay $42.50 to sell it.

If you buy in at $44.50 and then by 1:30 the gold's price is north of 1,250, then your option would expire successfully and has reached its max, which is $100. You garnered a profit of $55.50 before fees are taken into account. But, when the price ends up lower than $1,250, then the option becomes worth $0, and you lose out on your $44.50. The offer and bid prices are going to continue to oscillate until it has to expire, but you have the opportunity to close your position whenever you like, just as with other types of options.

Sooner or later, every option is either going to be worth $100 or be worth $0. The bid price and the ask price are set as the traders who are considering the trade determine the likelihood of success. The higher the bid and ask price are, the greater the overall perceived likelihood of the option coming true. If they are near 50, then the odds are average, and if they are very low, then they are not skewed in favor of the average at all.

Where to trade binary options: Binary options are now traded on the Nadex exchange, the original exchange dedicated to legally selling binary options in the US. It offers browser-based trading via its own platform, which offers real-time charts as well as market access to the latest binary options prices.

Binary options can also be traded via the Chicago Board Options Exchange (CBOE). It can be accessed with a brokerage account that is approved for options trading via their standard access routes. It is important to keep in mind, however, that not all brokers are equipped to offer options trading. As such, before you get started trading in options, you must make sure your broker offers all the trading possibilities that you may one day consider as changing horses mid-stream can be quite complicated.

Trading on the Nadex costs 90 cents when entering a trade and the same when exiting from one. The fee is capped at $9 per trade, so purchasing a lot of 15 will still only cost $9. If you hold your trade until it expires, then the fees will be taken out at that point. If the trade ends up being out of the money when it expires, you will not be charged a fee. Trading via CBOE is handled through specific options brokers who charge a variety of different commission fees.

Choosing a binary market: You are free to trade in multiple classes of assets with binary options, Nadex allows for trading in all of the major indices including the Dow 30, Russell 2000, the Nasdaq 100 and the S&P 500, global indices including those from Japan, Germany, and the UK are also available. Trades are also available for a variety of forex pairs, including AUD/JPY, EUR/GBP, USD/CHF, GBP/JPY, USD/CAD, AUD/USD, EUR/JPY, USD/JPY, GBP/UDS AND EUR/USD.

Additionally, Nadex also offers trading in commodity binary options, including soybeans, corn, copper, silver, gold, natural gas, and crude oil. You are also provided with the option of trading based on specific news events. You can buy options based on whether the Federal Reserve is going to decrease or increase the rates of things like joblessness claims or whether or not the number of nonfarm payrolls is going to beat its estimates or not.

The BVOE offers a smaller variance of binary options to choose from that is not currently available anywhere else. There you can buy binary options based on their own interpretation of the current state of the S&P 500 and a volatility option index based on its own volatility index.

Risk and reward: Binary option risk is capped at the cost of the initial trade as the worst thing that will ever happen is that your option expires at 0. The risk is also capped, though it can still offer up significant returns depending on the amount of the initial investment. For example, if you purchase a binary option for $20, which ends up paying out, then you will still make $100 off of it ($80 profit) which means you have a 4:1 reward ratio which is more than you could find if you invested in the related stock directly.

This only works out in your favor to a point, however, as your gains will always top out at $100, no matter how much movement the underlying stock actually experienced. This downside can be mitigated to some extent simply by purchasing multiple options contracts up front.

Binary Option Strategies

Pinocchio strategy: This is the perfect strategy to put into play if you come across a candle bar with an extremely long wick and a very small body during your technical analysis. This type of bar is known as a pin bar, but it was given its more descriptive name because the longer the wick grows, the more likely it is to be giving you false information.

If you come across this scenario and the wick is already quite long, then you can generally assume that the price of the underlying stock will have moved about as far as it can in the current direction and that it will likely be reversing quite soon. As such, when you see this bar, then you will know that your best bet is to start trading against the majority as the trend is likely going to turn and benefit your new position. After the wick begins shrinking, you will then want to generate a prediction on a call, and if it begins to increase again, then you will want to change your prediction to a put.

Binary option reversal strategy: The effectiveness of this strategy is because the market naturally seeks balance, which means that any price is bound to turn around eventually when confronted with extreme highs or lows. As such, when it comes to binary options, you can get a jump on the movement by predicting what is likely going to happen next.

For this strategy to work out effectively, you are going to predict the need for a put or a call based on the situation as it stands with help from information from external sources. You will find this to be a very useful strategy during periods of rapid asset movement because the speed at which it moves one way will be the same amount of speed with which it will eventually move back the other way. Because asset movement is bound to repeat itself eventually, once you understand its patterns, you will be able to naturally tell when a given underlying asset is at its peak, making any relevant binary options a very clear-cut decision.

Martingale strategy: In scenarios where you are more or less unconfident in the current state of the market but still want to keep an eye on a given investment, the martingale strategy can be quite useful. This strategy is also different than most other strategies as it involves heavily doubling down due to binary options' unique characteristics. As an example, if you start with a $20 binary option that does not payout, then your next binary option should be worth $30 on the opposite side and so on until you make a profit. If your amounts get to the point where a $100 profit would not square you, then you would want to purchase multiple contracts at once.

This strategy is going to appeal to those who are naturally inclined to take risky investments that have a higher overall promise of return as well. With that being said, much of the risk can be minimized if you are familiar with the asset you are purchasing contracts on as you will already know the scope of the market and will not have to rely on the strategy to help you learn the ins and outs through unsuccessful contracts. This strategy is somewhat unique in that its odds of being successful are based almost entirely on your personal level of familiarity with the underlying asset.

Trade the news: Buying into binary options contracts for a variety of assets based on the news is an effective means of working with binary options that is more multifaceted than it may first appear. At its most basic, it involves purchasing contracts when good news is forthcoming and selling them when bad news is on the horizon. Unlike other types of analysis, it is much less of a science that goes in line with the more generalized nature of binary options in general. The most important thing you will need to learn to this type of analysis is how much of an effect a given piece of news is going to have on a specific underlying asset.

CHAPTER - 8

Stock Options Trading

Stock options come with an expiration date. The way to think of the expiration date is the way you would think about it if you could buy and sell insurance policies. In fact, many people use options contracts as a type of insurance to protect their investments in stock. Taking a step back for a moment, imagine you could buy an insurance policy to cover six months of auto insurance. If you bought the contract six months before it expired, it would be worth a given amount of money, perhaps, equal to any six months of premiums would cost.

But if you were to buy the contract at three months until expiration, it would not be worth as much because it would only give you three months of insurance coverage. With a month left before it expired, it would still be worth something, but it would be worth quite a bit less because you'd only get one month of coverage. So, if it was worth $600 at the beginning, you might only pay $100 for it when there were five or six weeks left on the contract.

This analogy gives us an insight into an important characteristic of options. Every option contract on the stock market has an expiration date. The closer any option contract gets to its expiration date, the less value it has. This is actually more complicated than the situation involving an insurance contract because many different things can determine the value of an option at any given moment. For example, the value of the share price of the underlying stock is an important factor that needs to be considered when determining options pricing. However, be aware that the time left to the expiration date of the option impacts the options price, and all things being equal, each passing day means that the price of the option loses value because of the approaching expiration date.

An options contract on underlying stocks covers the sale of 100 shares of stock, options contracts on stocks work like any type of options contract; let's look at the basic characteristics.

An options contract covers an underlying financial asset. In the case of options on a stock, it will cover 100 shares of a specific stock. So, you can buy an option on 100 shares of IBM stock, or an option on 100 shares of Apple stock. There are options available for every publicly traded stock on all the stock exchanges. However, due to different levels of demand, there will be a wide variation in the number of available contracts.

The second characteristic of an options contract is an agreed-upon price for the asset in question. In the case of stock options, the contract will include a price that the two parties to the contract agree to use for trading the shares. This price is called the strike price. The strike price is not the same as the share price in most circumstances. However, at the time you buy an options contract, you might actually buy an option that does have a strike price equal to the share price. You would do this because you either believe the share price is going to go higher or lower than the price of the strike before the option expires.

What are the Options?

Options are those contracts that allow the bearer to be involved in the purchase or sales of a stipulated amount of asset at a fixed price. The bearer has the choice to buy or not, as long as the contract hasn't expired.

Options are bought like a lot of asset classes by making use of brokerage investment accounts.

Options are strong to the extent that they can improve the portfolio of an individual. They can get this done by leverage and added income protection.

Based on the scenarios at hand, different option situations can suit the goals of an investor.

Let's say a stock market is declining; options can be used as an effective hedge to clamp down on downside losses. One can use options to get recurring income. They can also be utilized for speculative purposes like wagering on where the stock price would go.

The way that free lunch doesn't exist in bonds and stocks is the same way that there is no free lunch with options.

There are some risks that one may face when an option trading is concerned. You have to understand these risks before you jump into options trading.

This is one reason that when you have decided to trade options with a brokerage company, you are shown a disclaimer that is similar to this:

Options are members of a bigger league of securities, which are called derivatives. The price of a derivative is linked to the price of another thing. Let's make things more transparent. The derivative of a tomato is ketchup. The derivative of grapes is wine. The derivative of a stock is a stock option.

Options can be said to be derivatives of financial securities, meaning that their worth is dependent on another asset's price.

Some examples of derivatives are puts, calls, forwards, futures, and so on.

Call and Put Options

When we say that options are derivative securities, we mean that their price is related to the pricing of another thing. This means that the other thing is what controls the price of the options.

If you purchase the options contract, you are given the right to buy or sell an asset at a stimulate price before the deal expires. You aren't under compulsion to do this.

When a person has a call option, he is given the right to purchase a stock. On the other hand, when a person is given a put option, he has the right to sell the stock.

You can see the call option as a form of down-payment for something that can be gotten in the future.

Let's use a more explicit example. A person sees a new building going up. He may want to have the right to buy it later but says he won't buy it until it has gotten to some stage, or some other condition has been met, this is an example of an option. He can decide to use the option or not. He isn't under compulsion.

Let's say the developer agrees to give the person the right to purchase the house for about a million dollars at any time within the next three years. Before the developer can agree with this, the prospective buyer has to pay a down payment, which can't be refundable. In that period, the developer isn't allowed to sell the house to anyone else until after the term expires.

CHAPTER - 9

Forex Options Trading

Instead of trading currencies directly to avoid high potential risks, you can also trade them via options. A Forex option is a derivative of Forex/ currency trading. It is also important to know that forex options trading is simply a combination of traditional options and currency, all the terms and principles of options trading apply; the only that changes is the financial instrument.

What Is an FX Option?

An FX option acts the same way as any other options contract, except you are trading currencies. Here, you (buyer) have the right to purchase an underlying currency and hold on to it for a period at a price determined with the seller (the strike price). Again, the strike price is set when the contract is drawn. It is also important to note that the owner of the FX option has the right to exercise or not to exercise the option at maturity, while the seller is bound to sell the underlying currency to the FX trader. The amount of money paid to buy the option is also called the premium.

There are a lot of factors that come into play when trying to calculate the premium price of an FX option. But, most often, experts use a statistical or probability assumption approach to help figure it out. In the FX option, a premium means two main things for both parties involved in the trade: an opportunity risk for the selling party if the other party exercises the right and buys the underlying security.

At the other end, it represents the opportunity to own the underlying currency at the contract's predetermined strike price. Upon maturity, where it was profitable, the holder of the FX option enjoys the privilege of garnering from the trade an intrinsic value for the currency. This value depends on the correlation between the currency's price and the option's strike price, and the time value can be measured by the difference between the premium and the said intrinsic value.

Why FX Options?

There is time value for any options purchased by the buyer at a premium price. The risks associated with forex trading stem from volatility, expiration time, the price of the underlying currency, and the interest rate differentials. The premium paid for the option is sometimes very high. The option contracts cannot be resold or re-traded.

The benefits of FX options cannot be underestimated. They help reduce the potential risk of buying a currency pair; traders can trade in currencies through the options contract without necessarily gaining ownership of hundreds of the currency pairs.

FX Options are also used to hedge trading positions in the forex trading market. This prevents losing the value of the underlying currency when the value goes up. Unlike the cash or futures market, it does not involve the immediate settlement of transactions. An FX option is also used as a form of hedge to prevent losing the value of a currency pair when the market is generally falling in value.

Types of Options

Basically, there are two types of FX options trading available in the market. To do well in the current market, it is essential to understand and know how these forex options trading works.

Traditional FX Options

This is known as the vanilla FX options type, involving both call and put options. As usual, this right goes without any obligation.

For example, A EUR/USD option would provide the buyer with the right to sell €1500 and buy $ 1000 on January 2. The strike price for the option is EUR/USD 1.50. The holder of the currency pair will incur revenue in this trade if its exchange rate is not more than 1. 50.

The underlying contract will expire in the money and generate profit. Let's say that the EUR/USD has fallen to 1.00. The profit derived from the FX option will be as follows: (1.50 - 1.00) x 1,000 = 500. In this case, the holder is benefitting from the fall in the currency rate.

The buyer of the option will have to tell how many options contracts they want to buy, pay the premium for the contract, and hold onto the contract until it gets in the money before exercising the due rights to buy or sell the underlying currency. The only loss here is the premium paid for the option when the option expires without any of these options exercised.

Sing Payment Options Trading (SPOT)

Single payment options Trading (SPOT) operate just like a binary option, offering the buyer an all or nothing type of offer for placing and making associated deals. Traders receive payouts based on the probability of a prediction about current prices in the future being right or wrong.

When you expect the market to rise up, you place a call option. When your prediction comes through, then you will win the agreed profit set forth for the option.

Losses are made when the prediction for the FX options are wrong. Premium payments for SPOT are often higher than the traditional options trading for currencies. Traders should understand the risks and rewards associated with this type of options trading before engaging in it.

Where to Trade Forex Options

If you are looking to trade in forex options, you have to research many retail forex brokerage firms to check whether they provide that service. Due to the recent losses that many traders have been having when trading forex options, many brokers have decided to ensure that only traders with capital protection are allowed to cap the risks of enormous losses, especially with SPOT.

Some brokerage firms provide access to the option and future exchanges, while others simply provide you with an OTC contract. Before signing on any broker platform, ensure you examine the fees and deposit requirements for trading. Check out the CBOE to learn more about the market before placing a trade on the platform.

CHAPTER - 10

Basic Options Strategies Going Long

While it can be easy to feel as though there is too much information out there regarding options trading to ever hope to keep it straight, there are several key strategies you will regularly use that you can focus on at the start to make the entire process far more manageable. As long as you take the time to utilize them correctly, you will find that each of the strategies outlined below will dramatically improve your success rate while decreasing your overall risk at the same time.

Keep in mind that the strategies that you use aren't nearly as important as the fact that you choose strategies that suit your trading style and compliments the trading plan you are focused on using for the time being. Keep in mind just because a strategy seems useful, doesn't mean it is going to be useful in your hands.

Play name: Married put

Details: A married put is a great strategy if you have reason to take a bullish attitude towards the price of a given underlying asset while at the same time aiming to shore up any potential losses you might come across. To use this strategy properly, the first thing you will need to do is to purchase any amount of the underlying asset in question while at the same time purchasing a put that covers the same amount. This will act as the price floor that will help you to prevent serious, unexpected losses in the case of a sudden price drop.

While the married put will not be the best choice in any situation, if used in the right way, and with plenty of caution, it can be a reliable way to improve your successful trading percentage successfully. To ensure this always works out in your favor, you will never want to begin a new transaction without having a clear understanding of the risk you are working with beforehand. You will then be able to factor in additional costs more easily and compare the total cost to the amount of risk you are going to mitigate as a result.

After that, all that's left is going to be doing the math and choosing the option that makes the most fiscal sense at the moment. What's more, married puts also help to reduce the potential for risk when it comes to early options to exercise as it ensures you always have available shares waiting in the wings.

Play name: Bull call spread

Details: To utilize the bull call spread successfully, you will want to start with a call option that is purchased at a strike price that is worth returning to in the future. You will also need to sell an equal number of calls at a strike price that is above the initial strike price yet still within a reasonable distance. Both of these calls will also need to include the same timeframe as well as the same underlying asset. This is an excellent strategy to use if you feel bullish on the strength of the asset in question or you have research that shows the price is likely to increase during your chosen timeframe.

This strategy also goes by the name vertical credit spread thanks to its mismatched legs. Those that sell close to the money result in a credit spread that includes a positive time value and a net credit. Debit spreads are created if a short option ends further away from the money than the point it started from. Regardless, you can consider this strategy a net buy.

Play name: Bear put spread

Details: Similar in practice to the bull call spread, the bear put spread is useful under opposite circumstances. To use it effectively, you will need to purchase a pair of put options that have different strike prices, own lower and one higher. You will then need to purchase an equal number with the same timeframe and the same underlying asset. This can be an especially useful strategy if you have a bearish opinion of the underlying asset in question as it will help to limit your losses if you judge the market incorrectly. It is still important to be cautious; however, as the profits that it will bring, you are always going to be limited to the difference between the two puts you initially purchased, minus any relevant fees.

The most profitable time to utilize this strategy is if you are already planning on short selling a specific underlying asset and a traditional put option won't provide you with the protection you need. You will likely find them especially useful if you plan on speculating and also feel that prices are going to decrease. This will allow you to avoid employing additional capital while only waiting for the worst to happen. As such, you will be able to hope for the best and plan for the worst at the same time.

Details: The protective collar strategy can be executed by buying into a put option that is already out of the money. From there, you will then want to write a secondary call option that is based on the same underlying asset and is also out of the money. After that, you will then be able to create one already. Thus, this strategy is useful if you are already committed to a long position on an underlying asset that has a history of strong gains. Using a protective collar properly then allows you to ensure that you can anticipate a steady level of profit while also retaining control of the underlying asset if the positive trend does continue.

Play name: Straddle

Details: The straddle can be used to either go long or short. The long straddle can be extremely effective if you feel as though the price of a given underlying asset is going to move significantly in one direction, you just don't know what direction that will ultimately be. To utilize this strategy, you will need to purchase a put and a call, both using the same underlying asset, strike price, and timeframe, after the long straddle has been created successfully you will be guaranteed to generate a profit if the price in question moves in either direction before it expires.

Play name: Strangle

Details: Functionally, strangle is similar to a straddle except that it is often cheaper to execute on as you are buying into options that are already out of the money. As such, you can typically pay as much as 50 percent the cost of a straddle for strangle which makes it even easier to play both sides of the fence. Typically, a long strangle is more useful than a short straddle because it offers up twice the premium for the same amount of risk.

To use the long strangle correctly, you will want to purchase a call along with a put that is both based on the same underlying asset with the same timeframe and different strike prices. The strike price for the call will need to be above the strike price for the put and both should be out of the money. This strategy can be especially useful if you plan on the underlying asset moving a great deal without having a clear idea as to the direction. When used properly, this will virtually ensure you turn a profit once you have taken any fees out of the equation.

Play name: Butterfly spread

Details: A butterfly spread is a combination of a bear spread and a traditional bull strategy that uses a total of three strike points. To begin with, you will need to purchase a call option at the lowest point you can manage before selling a pair of calls at a higher price and then a third call that has an ever-higher price. Your end goal with these purchases is to make sure that you have a range of prices you can profit from when everything is said and done.

This strategy can prove particularly effective when you have a completely neutral opinion on the current market. What's more, you should also expect the underlying asset to move in the direction you favor, even if you don't have all the details locked down just yet. This then means that you will want to strive to keep the market volatility as low as possible. The greater the overall level of volatility, the greater the cost of this strategy will be. Furthermore, it is extremely important to keep in mind that if you choose incorrectly when it comes to the direction the underlying asset is going to move, then the amount you stand to lose can be significant.

Play name: Iron Condor

Details: To utilize the iron condor strategy, you will need to begin by taking a short position as well as a long position via a pair of strangles that is situated so they will take full advantage of a market that is staunchly low volatility. The pair of strangles should include both a long and a short, with both sets to the outer strike price. You can accomplish the same general effect with a pair of credit spreads if you are so inclined. In this scenario, the call spread would be placed above the market price and the put would be placed beneath the current market price.

Play name: Iron Butterfly

Details: The iron butterfly strategy can be anchored by either a short straddle or a long straddle, depending on your needs. Regardless, you will want to then orchestrate strangle based on the straddle you needed to use. The iron butterfly utilizes a mixture of puts and calls to limit the potential for loss (but also profits) around the strike price you formerly determined. This strategy is best used with options that are out of the money as they allow you to minimize both risk and cost.

ROI or Return on Investment

The Term ROI stands for Return on Investment. ROI is a measure of performance and is used by both investors and traders to measure the effectiveness and efficiency of an investment. This includes your trading capital. ROI deliberately endeavors to measure directly the total return derived from a particular investment.

One of the most important aspects of your investment portfolio is its profitability. You need to regularly monitor your investments, which are best achieved using the ROI or return on investment. It is advisable to work out what each dollar invested has generated. There is a formula for working out this figure.

R.O.I = (Profits - Costs) / Costs

Even then, investors need to understand that the ROI depends on numerous other factors such as the kind of investment security preferred and so on. Also, note that a high ROI implies a higher risk, while a lower figure means reduced risk. For this reason, appropriate risk management must be undertaken.

A Brief Introduction to Technical Analysis

What is technical analysis? It is simply a method used by traders, investors, and other market players to examine and predict price movements in the markets. Technical analysis makes use of market statistics as well as historic chart prices. The idea behind this type of analysis is that identifying past market performance can help to accurately predict future performance.

As a trader, you want to be able to identify the shares to trade, the best entry points, volumes, price, and the best exit points. The best way to find out information about all these is through technical analysis.

Two Different Approaches

According to finance experts, there are two basic approaches to technical analysis. These are the top-down approach and the bottom-up approach. In most cases, short-term traders will opt for the top-down approach, while long-term investors prefer the bottom-up approach.

CHAPTER - 11

All about Buying Covered Calls

We'll investigate a trading strategy that is a good way to get started selling options for beginners. This strategy is called covered calls. By covered, we mean that you've got an asset that you own that covers the potential sale of the underlying stocks. In other words, you already own the shares of stocks. Now, why would you want to write a call option on stocks you already own? The basis of this strategy is that you don't expect the stock price to move very much during the lifetime of the options contract, but you want to generate money over the short term in the form of premiums that you can collect. This can help you generate a short-term income stream; you must structure your calls carefully.

Setting up covered calls is relatively low risk and will help you get familiar with many of the aspects of options trading. While it's probably not going to make you rich overnight, it's a good way to learn the tools of the trade.

Covered Calls Involve a Long Position

To create a covered call, you need to own at least 100 shares of stock an underlying equity. When you create a call, you're going to be offering potential buyers a chance to buy these shares from you. Of course, the strategy is that you're only going to sell high, but your real goal is to get the income stream from the premium.

The premium is a one-time non-refundable fee. If a buyer purchases your call option and pays you the premium, that money is yours. No matter what happens after that, you've got that cash to keep. If the stock doesn't reach the strike price, the contract will expire, and you can create a new call option on the same underlying shares. Of course, if the stock price does pass the strike price, the buyer of the contract will probably exercise their right to buy the shares. You will still earn money on the trade, but the risk is you're giving up the potential to earn as much money that could have been earned on the trade.

You write a covered call option that has a strike price of $67. Suppose that for some unforeseen reason, the shares skyrocket to $90 a share. The buyer of your call option will be able to purchase the shares from you at $67. So, you've gained $2 a share. However, you've missed out on the chance to sell the shares at a profit of $35 a share. Instead, the investor who purchased the call option from you will turn around and sell the shares on the markets for the actual spot price and they will reap the benefits.

However, you really haven't lost anything. You have earned the premium plus sold your shares of stock for a modest profit.

That risk–that the stocks will rise to a price that is much higher than the strike price always exists, but if you do your homework, you're going to be offering stocks that you don't expect to change much in price over the lifetime of your call. So, suppose instead that the price only rose to $68. The price exceeded the strike price, so the buyer may exercise their option. In that case, you are still missing out on some profit that you could have had otherwise, but it's a small amount and we're not taking into account the premium.

If the stock price doesn't exceed the strike price over the length of the contract, then you get to keep the premium and you get to keep the shares. The premium is yours to keep no matter what.

In reality, in most situations, a covered call is going to be a win-win situation for you.

Covered Calls Are a Neutral Strategy

A covered call is known as a "neutral" strategy. Investors create covered calls for stocks in their portfolio, where they only expect small moves over the lifetime of the contract. Moreover, investors will use covered calls on stocks that they expect to hold for the long term. It's a way to earn money on the stocks during a period in which the investor expects that the stock won't move much at price and so have no earning potential from selling.

An Example of Buying a Covered Call

Let's say that you own 100 shares of Acme Communications. It's currently trading at $40 a share. Over the next several months, nobody is expecting the stock to move very much, but as an investor, you feel Acme Communications has solid long-term growth potential. To make a little bit of money, you sell a call option on Acme Communications with a strike price of $43. Suppose that the premium is $0.78 and that the call option lasts 3 months.

For 100 shares, you'll earn a total premium payment of $0.78 x 100 = $78. No matter what happens, you pocket the $78.

Now let's say that over the next three months, the stock drops a bit in price so that it never comes close to the strike price, and at the end of the three-month period, it's trading at $39 a share.

The options contract will expire, and it's worthless. The buyer of the options contract ends up empty-handed. You have a win-win situation. You've earned the extra $78 per 100 shares, and you still own your shares at the end of the contract.

Now let's say that the stock does increase a bit in value. Over time, it jumps up to $42, and then to $42.75, but then drops down to $41.80 by the time the options contract expires. In this scenario, you're finding yourself in a much better position. In this case, the strike price of $43 was never reached, so the buyer of the call option is again left out in the cold. You, on the other hand, keep the premium of $78, and you still get to keep the shares of stock. This time since the shares have increased in value, you're a lot better off than you were before, so it's really a win-win situation for YOU, even though it's a losing situation for the poor soul who purchased your call.

Sadly, there is another possibility that the stock price exceeds the strike price before the contract expires. In that case, you're required to sell the stock. You still end up in a position that isn't all that bad, however. You didn't lose any actual money, but you lost a potential profit. You still get the premium of $78, plus the earnings from the sale of the 100 shares at the strike price of $43.

A covered call is almost a zero-risk situation because you never actually lose money even though if the stock price soars, you obviously missed out on an opportunity. You can minimize that risk by choosing stocks you use for a covered call option carefully. For example, if you hold shares in a pharmaceutical company that is rumored to be announcing a cure for cancer in two months, you probably don't want to use those shares for a covered call. A company that has more long-term prospects but probably isn't going anywhere in the next few months is a better bet.

How to Go About Creating a Covered Call

To create a covered call, you'll need to own 100 shares of stock. While you don't want to risk a stock that is likely to take off soon, you don't want to pick a total dud either. There is always someone willing to buy something–at the right price. But you want to go with a decent stock so that you can earn a decent premium.

You start by getting online at your brokerage and looking up the stock online. When you look up stocks online, you'll be able to look at their "option chain" which will give you information from a table on premiums that are available for calls on this stock. You can see these listed under bid price. The bid price is given on a per-share basis, but a call contract has 100 shares. If your bid price is $1.75, then the actual premium you're going to get is $1.75 x 100 = $175.

An important note is that the further out the expiration date, the higher the premium. A good rule of thumb is to pick an expiry that is between two and three months from the present date. Remember that the longer you go, the higher the risk because that increases the odds that the stock price will exceed the strike price and you'll end up having to sell the shares.

You have an option (no pun intended) with the premium you want to charge. Theoretically, you can set any price you want. Of course, that requires a buyer willing to pay that price for you to actually make money. A more reasonable strategy is to look at prices people are currently requesting for call options on this stock. You can do this by checking the asking price for the call options on the stock. You can also see prices that buyers are currently offering by looking at the bid prices. For an instant sale, you can simply set your price to a bid price that is already out there. If you want to go a little bit higher, you can submit the order and then wait until someone comes along to buy your call option at the bid price.

To sell a covered call, you select "sell to open."

Benefits of Covered Calls

- A covered call is a relatively low-risk option. The worst-case scenario is that you'll be out of your shares but earn a small profit, a smaller profit than you could have made if you had not created the call contract and simply sold your shares. However, you also get the premium.

- A covered call allows you to generate income from your portfolio in the form of premiums.

- If you don't expect any price moves on the stock in the near term and you plan on holding it long term, it's a reasonable strategy to generate income without taking much risk.

Risks of Covered Calls

- Covered calls can be a risk if you're bullish on the stock, and your expectations are realized, and there is a price spike. In that case, you've traded the small amount of income of the premium with a voluntary cap of the strike price for the potential upside you could have had if you had simply held the stock and sold it at the high price.

If the stock price plummets, while you still get the premium, the stocks will be worthless unless they rebound over the long term. You shouldn't use a call option on stocks that you expect to be on the path to a major drop in the coming months. In that case, rather than writing a covered call, you should simply sell the stocks and take your losses. Alternatively, you can continue holding the stocks to see if they rebound over the long term.

CHAPTER - 12

Fundamental & Technical Analysis

Many new traders often find it challenging to choose the vast range of methods to trade the financial markets. However, we can break down these methods into either fundamental analysis or technical analysis of the financial markets. In as much as some traders today use both methods, the majority of them, however, focus on technical analysis.

This will teach you as a trader on how you can perform a technical analysis of the financial markets. We will teach you how to go about using the best technical analysis software that is found in today's marketplace.

Technical Analysis

Let's begin by understanding what technical analysis means. In financial markets, technical analysis refers to the study of the patterns of prices of particular assets. Basically, there exist many ways with which technicians use to identify patterns in the market. However, the following are the common ways;

Technical Analysis Chart Patterns

This analysis involves the use of technical drawing tools like Fibonacci levels, horizontal and trend lines for the identification of classical chart patterns. The patterns identified can include consolidation patterns and symmetrical triangle formations etc. These patterns are important in giving clarity on the strengths and weaknesses of buyers and sellers in the market.

Technical analysis of candle patterns

This method involves the use of technical analysis charts like candle charts where the price levels (such as high, low, open, close) of a given timeframe to identify the characteristics of buyers and sellers within a given period.

Technical analysis indicators

This analysis method involves the use of price action indicators to provide a detailed understanding of the market condition. For instance, indicators will provide signals when the market is overbought or oversold. Some indicators will provide signals when there is rising or falling momentum.

Forex Technical Analysis

The Forex market is very liquid. This means that it attracts all types of traders ranging from one-minute traders to daily traders. Forex technical analysis supports all these different types of traders involved in the market. All the different types of technical analysis, including chart patterns, candle patterns, and indicators are used in Forex technical analysis. As a beginner, we prefer that you download MetaTrader 4, that is the best fits the needs of a beginner because it supports multiple languages, has advanced charting capabilities, trading is automated, it can be fully customized, and you can change trading preferences based on your needs, for example, you can customize it to technical analysis, or provide you with trading news.

Does Technical Analysis Work?

In most cases, as humans, we tend to have limited time and focus; thus, when analyzing these factors, we are likely to make errors in the cause and effect. However, with technical analysis, a more reliable way that comes with the short-cut is provided to analysts. Technical analysis is also referred to as chart analysis. With chart analysis, traders are able to analyze historical price movements.

The Basics of Technical Analysis

As a trader, here are some of the basics about technical analysis that you should have in hand.

Price action discounts everything

The technical analysis derives its logical framework from Dow Theory. According to Dow

Theory, the price of an asset accurately reflects all the relevant information about the asset. This means that any factor that impacts on supply and demand by default will end up on the chart. When it comes to the case of researching or the events outside price action, Dow Theory renders them useless because these are things that cannot be quantified thus may give unreliable data.

Price moves in trends

As observed, most technicians are always seen to favor trends, including the nature of the market. This is another reflection of Dow Theory. Basically, markets can move in an uptrend (bullish market). In such a case, it means that the market will continuously create higher highs as well as higher lows, and the big picture, which is the price will be seen to be jumping up and down but mostly within an upward corridor. A bearish market has similar market behaviors as it is characterized by a downtrend of lower lows as well as lower highs.

There is also a ranging market, which is a horizontal trend. However, this is a trend that is not desirable to trend-based traders. This is because traders are not able to know what will happen next, particularly when faced with ranging periods. In a ranging market, the bulls and the bears somehow have equal powers; thus, there is no side strong enough to dominate the other for a long period. It is also important to note that Forex statistical analysis does not give major concerns on why things happen. This means that it will not look into why certain trends occur. Therefore, as a technical reader, you must be able to understand this. Most technicians do not know how to quantify answers because they often feel that trends are empirically proven facts.

The Pros of Technical Analysis

- Traders using forex technical analysis only need to have a few basic tools. In most cases, these tools are usually free.

- Traders using forex technical analysis are sometimes offered with high probability directional views as well as the entry and exit points from the market.

- With the advancement in technology today, traders can choose technical analysis tools and indicators they wish to use in helping them identify the available trading setups.

Disadvantages of Technical Analysis

- Technical analysis is widespread and widely used. Therefore, Forex technical analysis can sometimes trigger abrupt market movements, particularly when many traders come up with the same conclusions.

- There are complex markets that technical analysis fails to cover some aspects, thus calls for the combination of technical analysis and fundamental analysis.

Fundamental Analysis

In this era of globalization, our financial markets continue to be impacted and influenced by a large number of factors. For instance, today, the central banks of each country must administer its monetary policies, governments must also deliver their fiscal policies, and on the lowest level, companies and consumers also determine the internal economic factors. All these are factors that must be studied in order to understand how they impact on different assets and markets. Therefore, it is always very hard to know the factors with significant impacts. This can be solved using fundamental analysis.

The Pros of Fundamental Analysis

- Fundamental analysis is a perfect tool for understanding market trends (i.e., why a market is going down or up).

- Fundamental analysis, when combined with technical analysis, can enable traders to know the long term market trends.

Disadvantages of Fundamental Analysis

- It is easy to have cases of conflicts. This is because there are many fundamental analysis tools, and some of these tools may show bad data, thus giving the wrong indicators.

- Its time consuming because it involves keeping track of all the different news announcements.

- It is not a guarantee that the market will respond to the things said by fundamental analysis. For instance, if data on the Japanese economy suggests that it is weak, it is not a guarantee that the Japanese Yen will go down.

- It requires traders to master the outcomes associated with different economic data like inflation reports. To learn these outcomes takes a longer time.

Here are the benefits that come with both analysis methods

- Using the analysis, traders can make sound judgments relating to trade based on the information on the chart.

- The analysis information can enable traders to look for a potential trade setup

- Traders are also able to identify where they can find potential trade setups

Through the analysis, traders are able to learn how they can manage the identified trade setups.

A Comparison of Technical Analysis and Fundamental Analysis of the Financial Markets

Before proceeding into finer details, technical analysis focuses on studying price charts and price patterns while fundamental analysis, on the other hand, focuses on studying data on the economic aspects of company aspects. The economic or company data that fundamental analysis focuses on includes figures from retail sales, the reports on inflation, country's employment patterns, earnings announcements, and news from companies. Fundamental analysis uses this data to identify market trends as well as the possible changes or turning points that a particular market needs. Fundamental analysis is mostly used in stock markets and not fit for the forex market. Due to this, technical analysis has become a popular option for most traders. The reason why most traders prefer to use technical analysis is that technical analysis aids in decision making about trade. However, some traders prefer to combine these two analysis methods as they present a high profitability trading opportunity.

CHAPTER - 13

The Strategies and Tricks That Can Be Applied With Technical Analysis

Several investors in the finical market are known for analyzing options they own based on the fundamentals they possess. This includes looking at an option's valuation and revenue. However, fundamentals have low odds when it narrows down to portraying the current market prices of options as the underlying financial assets. It is where technical analysis comes to save an options trader in the financial markets. It is because it is it helps an individual to maneuver through the gap that is created between market prices and the intrinsic value of options. The action is made to be simple because of fundamental analysis has a way of leveraging behavioral economics and statistical analysis. This has seen the rise of numbers in traders and investors using technical analysis.

There are major approaches that are used by participants of options trading when it comes to technical analysis. These major approaches are two and they include a top-down approach and bottom-up technical forms. The top-down approach has several traders who prefer it. Most of the traders that are characterized by using the top-down approach in the options market are the short term traders. The long-term trader and investors are prone to using the bottom-up approach because it favors them.

- Top-Down Approach; it involves an options trader or investor screening for particular options. The intended options are supposed to be able to fit certain forms of stocks that fit the intended criteria. A good depiction can be sourced from a trader looking from options that have their moving averages at fifty days.

- Bottom-Up Approach; this entails an options trader analyzing options that have a fundamentally interesting appearance. These stocks tend to give an individual an added advantage in knowing the exit and entry points in the trade of options. An easy illustration can be used for those options that have a downtrend. With the use of technical analysis, a trader in the options trading can be able to identify entry and exit points. These points are critical in moments, the options are swaying in the market.

The current world has millions of options traders who prefer to use different forms of technical analysis. Options traders who perform day trading tend to prefer simple volume and trade indicators in moments they make trading decisions. On the other hand, swing traders tend to have a preferential of using the chart patterns and other technical indicators. The trade of options has seen several technological advancements in it. It has to lead to several traders developing highly automated algorithms. They tend to anchor their analysis on volume and technical indicators to base their decisions in the options markets.

Steps to the Strategies Used in Analyzing Options

Five steps are core in realizing the strategies used to analyzing options using technical analysis. These steps include;

Identification of a Technical Analysis Strategy

This is the first step and it can also be referred to as the development of a trading system. We can use a situation of a beginner in this case who is participating in the options market. He or she is supposed to follow the strategy that involves the usage of moving averages. The option trader is supposed to track two moving averages in a specific option market. The two moving averages can be those of fifty or two hundred days. The fifty-day moving average can be used for the basis of supporting the short term trading options. On the other hand, options traders aiming for the long term trading of options can use the two hundred moving averages. A buying signal is always portrayed when the trends in a price move upward while the signal of a trader to sell his or her options is realized in moments the prices of options have a downward trend.

Identification of Tradable Options That Fit with the Technical Strategy

The common knowledge in option trading is that not all kinds of options have similar strategies that are applied to them. Most of the techniques stated above tend to favor options that are highly gyrating in nature than those that are not volatile. This case might favor the usage of moving averages that are characterized by fifty days. However, an individual can use the two hundred days if the option he or she is trading is not volatile in the options market.

Finding of a Brokerage Account for Existing Trades

An options trader is supposed to be in apposition that he or she has found the right brokerage account to be able to conduct his or her trade. The account is supposed to have a certain minimum requirement for its success. An account used by a trader in options trading is supposed to be an able function to the utmost best in being able to track and monitor the technical tools used in technical analysis. A good account is supposed to do this function with the reduction of costs involved in accessing this data. One will be on a very good side of options trading if his or her account can be able to incorporate candlesticks.

Selection of a Good Interface to Track and Monitor Trade

Options traders can differ on the level of functionality which is dependent on the functionality of the strategy he or she is using. A good depiction can be made of a trader who requires a margin account that provides information about the market. On the other hand, several people prefer basic accounts because they have low-cost options for them.

Identification of Other Applications That Can be implemented on the Settled Strategy

There might be other options that might need extra happening for a trader to realize maximum gains from them. Some options traders have gone to the extent of receiving mobile notifications about any changes that can be experienced in the options markets. Some other options traders have automated their accounts to an extent they perform automated functions for them.

CHAPTER - 14

Rolling Out Options

Arollout is a strategy that is used to extend the lifetime of an option that hasn't quite worked out. This is going to be a strategy used by options sellers. So a rollout might be something you would consider doing when you've sold a naked call, and the share price is closing in on your strike price, creating a risk that the option will be exercised. By doing a rollout, you can keep the trade going longer, and possibly make some changes to give the trade better odds of being profitable. Typically, you will choose to do a rollout when it is close to the expiration date.

Definition of Rollout Strategy

A rollout strategy works in the following way. You will close your current option contract by buying it back, and simultaneously open a new contract of the same type, with changes. One way to change is by altering the strike price. Another more common method is to move out of the expiration date. A common practice is to open the new contract with an expiration date that is further out in the future. So, for example, you could close a naked put option that is expiring in two days by buying it back and opening a new contract by selling a new naked put option. You would use the same stock and the same strike price, but with an expiration date that is three weeks into the future.

This is a standard strategy where we say that the option contract was rolled out.

You can also follow the same strategy choosing either a higher strike price or a lower strike price. For example, if we have an Apple naked put with a strike price of $205, we could roll up the option by closing this position and selling a new naked put on Apple with a strike price of $206. Alternatively, you could choose a lower strike price. Using the same example, instead of going with a $206 strike price, we could go with a $203 strike price. Maybe, in that case, the Apple share prices are dropping and it got a little too close for comfort. When you select a lower strike price, they say that you have rolled down the trade.

It's also possible to roll out and roll up or down. In other words, you can close your current contract and open a new one that has a further expiration date, but you also change the strike price.

Types of Options Where Rolling Strategies are used

You can use a rollout, roll up, or roll down strategy on any type of option, including options that you buy to open (long calls and puts). However, the vast majority of options contracts that are rolled are short (buy to open) options. You can use rolling techniques on any of the major strategies covered in this book, such as put credit spreads, strangles, or iron condors.

Why Roll an Options Contract

The main reason that options traders roll an option contract is that they are in the money and there is an assignment risk. By rolling it out, you can keep the trade going but avoid assignment. Sometimes just moving the expiration date is good enough to accomplish this. An option can be assigned at any time, but in most cases, it has to reach expiration in order to be assigned. So, by using a rollout, the trader can avoid this situation.

Of course, rolling up or rolling down can also help avoid assignment, since changing the strike price might allow you to move from an in the money situation to an out of the money situation.

Other reasons are sometimes used to justify rolling an option. For example, when you are selling for income, you can roll the trade to keep generating more money. Changing market conditions might also be a reason to roll a trade.

When rolling a spread, strangle, or iron condor, there are many possibilities for altering the trade. Suppose you have a put credit spread with strikes of $207 and $204. We could change one or both of the strike prices, and we could also change the expiration date. Maybe we want to tighten or widen the spread, so we could roll out and also roll down the lower strike price, and have a new spread with strike prices of $207 and $202, for example.

A rollout is a Single Trade

It's important to note that a rollout is one trade, and not two. So you are simultaneously closing one option (possibly with multiple legs) and opening a new contract in its place.

CHAPTER - 15

Top Trader Mistakes to Avoid In Options Trading

As a new options trader, it is very common to easily feel overwhelmed or overzealous in your pursuit of this business. Even though the risks of such a business are relatively low, making mistakes can be very costly. This is dedicated to increasing the awareness of common mistakes that are made by beginners (and sometimes by advanced traders) so that you can avoid them with practical approaches.

Mistake #1 - Not Having a Trading Plan to Fall Back On

Unfortunately, many people enter the arena of options trading out of desperation or greed with no plan as to how they will make this a successful venture. They are looking to make a quick buck and do not think things through because they are not thinking rationally. This leads to them trading with their emotions rather than with logic.

There is no place for emotions and feelings in options trading. While gut instinct has a time and a place in options trading, being led by anger, sadness and other emotions can lead to heavy financial losses.

Developing this plan relies on asking several questions, which include but are not limited to:

- What are your goals?

- How much time will you commit to options trading?

- Which financial markets do you want to trade-in?

- What strategies will you use to find opportunities in the financial market?

- How much capital do you have available to dedicate to options trading?

- How much are you willing to risk for every trade?

- What determines this risk?

- What are your risk management rules?

- When will you enter the trading market?

- What strategies will you implement to minimize your losses?

- What is your exit plan?

- How will you maintain a record-keeping system?

To answer these questions effectively, you need to take your emotions out of it and use your logical brain. Developing this plan is the only thing that will keep you moving forward and facilitate improvement as an options trader. With your plan finalized, you will realize that there is predictability and repeatability in options trading. Realizing these trends can help you maximize your profit by taking advantage of these features.

Mistake #2 - Choosing the Wrong Expiration Date for Options

Having expiration dates that are too short or too long can be costly. While you develop your trading plan, you will definitely come across the factor of how you will select expiration dates for your options. Each option is unique and this requires setting up a system whereby you can select proper expiration dates so that profits are maximized every time.

When developing your options for choosing an expiration date, relying on a simple checklist system can help. Here are a few questions that you can add to this checklist so that you choose the best expiration date for that particular transaction:

- How long is this trade likely to play out?

- Does this timeline align with my own goals?

- Do I have adequate liquidity in the timeline to support my trade for the duration of the contract?

- What is the historical and implied volatility of the financial market?

- Have I factored in the Greeks like delta and theta?

- How will my particular strategy relate to time decay and profitability?

Mistake #3 - Not Factoring In the Volatility of the Financial Market

Even the most stable financial markets can have days where they take off in an unexpected direction. This affects the value of the associated asset and so the options trader needs to be aware of this. Some traders only look at the reactivity of the financial markets during one time period and not others and so do not rely on historical data or focus on forecasting the future. These are costly mistakes.

Ensure that the factoring of market and stock volatility are always a consideration, even after the option has been finalized. Volatility in the market is inevitable. Look at the stock market and you will see how quickly it moves up and down over the short term. You mustn´t get carried away with short-term fluctuations. Know your strategy before you invest so that you are not distracted by short-term fluctuations.

Mistake #4 - Not Having a Sound Exit Plan

This is a trading strategy that many novice options skip in their eagerness to get started. While they may have a strategy in place for entering options trading, they forget or are ignorant of the fact that an exit strategy is just as important.

One of the biggest reasons for developing an exit strategy is to prevent emotions from clouding your judgment during that time when tough decisions need to be made. As a result, make the plan before things hit the fan to take out that emotional aspect.

Two factors need to be considered when creating an exit plan for an option. They are:

• What is the absolute point you will get out of the trade if things are not working out in your favor?

• How will you take profits if things are working in your favor?

Many experienced options traders place a percentage cap on the trade to know at which point they will back out of the trade if things are not working out profitably for them. While it is normal for the value of the transaction to fluctuate between 10% and 20%, most experienced traders will cut their losses if their fluctuation goes between 30% and 50%.

This fluctuation needs to be also considered if things are working out in your favor. If the transaction has increased in value between 30% and 50%, you need to be thinking about how you can protect your profits or how to ensure that you do not lose any money through that option.

Your exit strategy can also be time-based. You may decide that pursuing a certain option is only worthwhile for you for a certain time and not beyond.

Mistake #5 - Not Being Flexible

Never say never with options trading. Many traders get stuck in their ways when it comes to options trading and refuse to try out new strategies. Remember that having a growth mindset is necessary for success in any part of life and this philosophy also applies to trading options.

You have to be willing to keep in the know when it comes to options and also be willing to learn and try new strategies. That does not mean try any strategy you come across. It simply means that when you do come across new strategies, assess them carefully to see if they have the potential to fit into your trading plan to help you accomplish your goals.

Liquidity describes how quickly an asset can be converted to cash without a significant price shift. The more readily the asset can be traded, the more liquid it is. Having a liquid market means there are ready and willing active buyers and sellers.

Highly liquid options have certain characteristics. Being high in volume is one such characteristic. The higher the volume of options, the easier they are to enter and exit. Having the ability to move in and out of a contract is a huge advantage to an options trader. Being easily adjustable is another characteristic. Seeking out option with these characteristics makes the job of an options trader that much easier

Examples of highly liquid assets attached to options include stock and ETFs.

On the other hand, there are illiquid options and establishing such a contract is a mistake that many novice options traders make. There are not easily moved or converted into cash. They drive up the cost of doing business because of this characteristic. This makes the trading cost of that option higher and thus, these cuts on the trader's profits.

To avoid this, trade options that are higher in liquidity. For example, stocks that trade less than 1 million shares per day are liquid. Pursue such options at the beginning of your career as an options trader. Also, seek options with a greater volume and that are easily adjustable.

Mistake #7 - Not Factoring In Upcoming Events

Of course, the financial market is volatile and unpredictable. Some things cannot be foreseen. However, there are others that can be foreseen and it is the job of the options trader to keep these things in his or her foresight.

There are two major common events that an options trader needs to know in advance and these things are the earnings (the measure of how much a company's profits is allocated to each share of stock) on the associated assets as well as the dividend payout dates in these assets if they apply. Not knowing these future events can mean losing out on extra payout like these because no action was made to ensure that the trader had a right to them.

In the case of dividends, payment on the associated assets could have been collected by the trader if only he or she had the foresight to purchase that asset before those payments were processed.

To ensure you get such extra earning, you need to be on the ball of the date of such events. Do not sell options that have pending dividends and avoid trading in the earning season to avoid the common high volatility associated with that time.

Mistake #8 - Waiting Too Long To Buy Back Short Strategies

You need to always be ready to buy back short strategies early in the game. Never assume that profits will continue to come in just because you are having a good period. The market can change any time and so your profits can be lost easily if you fail to react properly.

There are many reasons why some options traders wait to do this and they include not wanting to pay commissions, trying to gain more profits out of the contract and thinking that the contract will be worthless upon expiration. Thinking in such a manner is a mental trap that can lead to financial losses.

To avoid this, consider buying back your short strategies as long as you can keep at least 80% of your initial gain from the sale of that option. If you enter an out of money positions, reduce the risk by buying back.

Mistake #9 - Getting Legged Out Of Position

Legging out means that one leg of the option closes out and essentially becomes worthless to the trader. The leg gains an unfavorable price that does not benefit the trader. This does not automatically spell the death of the option made up of several legs, but it can expose the trader to loss.

Legging can be performed in several types of options, including straddles, strangles and spreads. These types of options can be enhanced by multiple legs and gain the options trader a leg up. However, the complexity of using the legging technique can elude even experienced options traders. The timing and order of executing legs make this a delicate process that needs a fine eye for the market. Therefore, this is a technique that must be attempt only after a trader is confident in his or her experience, knowledge and success rate.

Mistake #10 - Trading Options on Complicated Assets without First Doing Proper Research

In their overexcitement, many new traders like to go for complex assets because they believe that this where the big bucks are. Even if this is true in some cases, if the trader does not have a good grasp of how the asset works in its market, then he or she will fail to implement the right strategies to gain profits. Never just jump into an option. Do your research first. Also, as a newbie options trader, it might be best to get your feet wet with more common options rather than jumping into the deep end of the pool.

CHAPTER - 16

Risks That You Need To Avoid

Understanding Options Risks

Options trading process does carry some risks with it. Understanding these risks and taking mitigating steps will make you not just a better trader but a more profitable one as well. A lot of traders love options trading because of the immense leverage that this kind of trading affords them. Should an investment work out as desired, then the profits are often quite high. With stocks, you can expect returns of between 10%, 15%, or even 20%. However, when it comes to options, profit margins over 1,000% are very possible.

Basically, these kinds of trades are very possible due to the nature and leverage offered by options. A savvy trader realizes that he or she can control an almost equivalent number of shares as a traditional stock investor but at a fraction of the cost. Therefore, when you invest in options, you can spend a tiny amount of money to control a large number of shares. This kind of leverage limits your risks and exposure compared to a stock investor.

As an investor or trader, you should never spend more than 3% to 5% of your funds in any single trade. For instance, if you have $10,000 to invest, you should not spend more than $300 to $500 on any one trade.

Also, as a trader, you are not just mitigating against potential risks, but are also looking to take advantage of the leverage. This is also known as gaining a professional trader's edge. While it is crucial to reduce the risk through careful analysis and selection of trades, you should also aim to make huge profits and enjoy big returns on your trades. There will always be some losses, and as a trader, you should get to appreciate this. However, your major goal as a trader should be to ensure that your wins are much, much larger than any losses that you may suffer.

All types of investment opportunities carry a certain level of risk. However, options trading carry a much higher risk of loss. Therefore, ensure that you have a thorough understanding of the risks and always be on the lookout. Also, these kinds of trades are very possible due to the nature and leverage offered by options. A savvy trader realizes that he or she can control an almost equivalent number of shares as a traditional stock investor but at a fraction of the cost. Therefore, when you invest in options, you can spend a tiny amount of money to control a large number of shares. This kind of leverage limits your risks and exposure compared to a stock investor.

Risk #1: Time Is Not on Your Side

You need to keep in mind that all options have an expiration date and that they do expire in time. When you invest in stocks, time is on your side most of the time. However, things are different when it comes to options. Basically, the closer that an option gets to its expiration, the quicker it loses its value and earning potential.

Options deterioration is usually rather rapid, and it accelerates in the last days until expiration. Basically, as an investor, ensure that you only invest dollar amounts that you can afford to lose. The good news though, is that there are a couple of actions that you can take in order to get things on your side.

- Trade mostly in options with expiration dates that are within the investment opportunity

- Buy options at or very near the money

- Sell options any time you think volatility is highly-priced

- Buy options when you are of the opinion that volatility is underpriced

Risk #2: Prices Can Move Pretty Fast

Options are highly leveraged financial instruments. Because of this, prices tend to move pretty fast. Basically, options prices can move huge amounts within minutes and sometimes even seconds. This is unlike other stock market instruments like stocks that move-in hours and days.

Small movements in the price of a stock can have huge implications on the value of the underlying stock. You need to be vigilant and monitor price movements often. However, you can generate profits without monitoring activity on the markets twenty-four hours a day.

As an investor or trader, you should seek out opportunities where chances of earning a significant profit are immense. The opportunity should be sufficiently robust so that pricing by seconds will be of little concern. In short, search for opportunities that will lead to large profits even when you are not accurate when selling.

When structuring your options, you should ensure that you use the correct strike prices as well as expiration months in order to cut out most of the risk. You should also consider closing out your trades well before the expiration of options. This way, time value will not dramatically deteriorate.

Risk #3: Naked Short Positions Can Result in Substantial Losses

Anytime that your naked short option presents a high likelihood of substantial and sometimes even unlimited losses, shorting put naked means selling stock options with no hedging of your position.

When selling a naked short, it simply implies that you are actually selling a call option, or even a put option but without securing it using an option position, a stock or cash. It is advisable to sell a put or a call in combination with other options or with stocks. Remember that whenever you short sell a stock, you are, in essence, selling borrowed stock. Sooner or later, you will have to return the stock.

Fortunately, with options, there is no borrowing of stock or any other security.

CHAPTER - 17

The Option Trader Mindset

When it comes to trading successfully every single day, if you let your emotions dictate your actions, you will never find the success you seek. Instead, you will need to develop the type of emotionless mindset that makes the best options traders so successful. Following the suggestions outlined below will allow you to focus on long term success regardless of what distractions are currently taking place around you. Studies show that as little as 10 percent of options traders have the right mindset to cultivate success in the long term, changing your mindset is the first step to ensuring you are one of them.

Manage Expectations

The first thing that is required if you hope to develop the mindset of a successful options trader is to understand just what to expect when it comes to the results of your early day trading experiences. Only by tempering your expectations of major successes in a short period will you be able to prevent the types of negative emotions that can lead to negative trades in the long term. It is important to understand what types of emotions you are going to feel regularly, so that you can more adequately control your responses.

When you first start out, it may be helpful to keep a journal of your individual trades as well as the resulting emotions you felt, both on the good trades and the bad. It is important to know what you expect as you go through your standard trading process, so that you can be prepared to rationally counter any emotions that you might expect to encounter. Only by completely keeping your emotions in check will you be able to put the plan you will ultimately create into action and not vary from it no matter what.

The biggest cause for emotional concern comes from the fact that many new options traders view trading as if it should always produce the desired results when a plan is followed correctly. This is, in fact, not the case and even when you do come up with a winning plan, it will not be 100 percent successful. Understanding that losses are a very real part of the daily trading game is the first step to keeping your emotions regarding every loss in check. To mitigate these feelings, it is important to understand that a good trade is not one that made money but rather one that followed your system to the letter.

Find a System

Once you find a system that works for you, either by creating one uniquely from scratch or finding the published work of a master trader and putting it work for you, it will be important to stick with it until you reach the recommended number of trades before tweaking a single variable and then repeating the process.

While it may be difficult to jump ship immediately if the results of a specific system don't work out, in reality, it is much more beneficial in the long term to instead determine just why the system in question worked for someone else but did not work for you. A major moment in your evolution as an options trader will be the moments you can see why the trader who struck it rich after a few random trades is actually less successful than a trader with a few different plans that are always executed properly no matter what. In the long term, a reliable strategy is one that is infinitely more profitable than any single trade, no matter how lucrative.

Viewing options trading as a marathon, not a sprint, is crucial to your long term growth as a trader and has the added benefit of making every losing trade a valuable learning experience instead of one that is an abject failure. This will help you keep your spirits up, and your resolution to your system in check, throughout all the natural ups and downs the market is likely going to bestow upon you. Keeping this unilaterally positive mindset will also give you an edge over the competition who will, statistically speaking, likely let their emotions alter their system in real-time, which will ultimately cost them greatly, if not in the short term, then definitely in the long term.

Understand When Not To Exercise or Trade Out

If you plan on trading successfully in the long term, then you need to develop a mindset that encourages inaction as a probable road to success. Just because you have gone ahead and created either a call or a pull, doesn't mean you have to do anything with it, as long as you are not the writer. While this should seem explicit to anyone in the calm light of a hypothetical situation, it is actually something that many new traders commonly forget once the stress of actually having money in the mix is added into the equation.

Every single successful trader has determined exactly when they should go through with a trade and when they should exercise their option to not exercise an option. The answer should be clear by now, successful traders listen to their systems and don't let the fact that they have an actual profit (or loss) on the line deter them from making the correct choice every single time. It can be difficult to keep a cool head, especially amid numerous losses in a short time; conversely, this is also the time you need to keep a true option trader mindset as doing otherwise is akin to giving in to the temptation to go off plan and pay for it even more heavily.

You Cannot Overvalue Patience

You cannot be a successful options trader unless you have the patience to wait for the right moment to execute every trade. This means personally reinforcing the notion that the market doesn't move immediately and even the most volatile options will require time to build up steam. Likewise, it is important to never let your focus be exclusively on a single trade as doing so will only artificially inflate the importance of that trade in your mind, which will make it easier for emotions to take over at a critical moment.

Those who are serious about becoming regular options traders need to focus on the fact that every individual trade is only a small part of the overall goal of being a successful trader and treat it with the relevant amount of care. A major part of being a patient trader is, likewise, knowing that some days are simply not worth the risk or effort of trading and that overtrading is just as hazardous as not taking advantage of positive trade conditions when they do materialize.

This is why it is important to only set weekly or monthly expectations and to never try and reach a goal amount at the end of every trading day. Even if you do end up making the target amount of trades each day to hit your goal, likely, at least some of these trades will not have stood up to the strict level of scrutiny that a good plan requires. Stick with making only the right types of trades and your weekly or monthly average will take care of itself, if not, then you can think about changing your plan.

Be Ready To Adapt

The successful options trades know when to follow their plans, but they also know that no plan will be the right choice, even if early indicators say otherwise. There is a difference between making a point of sticking to a plan and following it blindly and knowing which is which one of the more important indicators of the separation is between options trading success and abject failure. This means it is important to be aware of when and where experimentation and new ideas are appropriate and when it is best to toe the line and gather more data in order to make a well-reasoned decision.

Likewise, an adaptive options trader knows that market conditions can change unexpectedly and is prepared to respond accordingly. This means understanding when the time is right to go in a new direction, regardless of the potential risks that doing so might entail. Sometimes a good trader has to make a leap of faith, and a trader who is successful in the long term knows what signs to look for that indicate this type of scenario is occurring in real-time. Unfortunately, this type of foresight cannot be taught, and instead must be found with experience.

Prioritize Consistency

If you ever hope to develop the type of mindset that allows professional options traders to be successful, you will need to understand how important it is to be consistent in your trades, not just in theory, but in practice. To reach this point, however, you will likely need to deal with both subpar gains as well as financial setbacks. To alter the rate at which either of these occurs, you need to not just experience gains but understand why those trades proceeded in the way that they did. Being inquisitive when it comes to your gains is just as important as analyzing your errors when it comes to your long term success.

While more volatile traders are interested in scenarios that offer great rewards and ever greater risks, options traders that tend to be successful across the long term understand that the most reliable way too long term success is to focus on trades will medium or small returns that turn around reliably time and time again. An occasional outstanding return is nice, but it is no way to build a steady trade record. What's more, a system that works on mediocre trades is also more likely to work on more substantial variations as well, test your system thoroughly before putting it to work on a major trade.

Know Yourself

A good options trader understands their own strengths and weaknesses when it comes to trading and looks for systems that maximize their strengths and minimizes their weaknesses. There is no one perfect system that is right for everybody in any given situation, no matter how much easier it would make things if there were. This is another reason it is so important to keep a journal during your early days of trading so you can look for certain repeating tendencies that you may want to factor into your system choosing process.

Likewise, this will help you to understand when you are becoming emotional or approaching a trade in the wrong way. While at first, it will be helpful to have an outline of what types of emotions to expect in given situations, with enough practice you will find you can tell when you are becoming emotional, even without the cheat sheet. If you find yourself having difficulty with this part of the mindset building exercise, you may find it helpful to simply take a break and come back later. Focusing too thoroughly on a problem can lead to just as many problems as it may potentially solve. Focus on keeping a clear mind and you will find that not only is it easier to focus on sticking to your system, but that you are more easily able to determine the specific causes for the success or failure found in every trade. Practice keeping this mindset during every trade and you will see a greater percentage of successful trades sooner than you may expect.

CHAPTER - 18

The Best Strategies to Invest With Call and Put Options Trading

Selling Call Options

Now we are going to shift gears and consider selling options for income rather than buying options hoping to profit by trading. Many traders prefer selling options. Although there are risks, selling options is actually a more reliable approach for earning money than trying to speculate with trading. There is still a level of speculating when you are selling options, but the speculation is one-sided, making it less risky. We will see how this works in a minute.

Covered Call

The simplest way to sell options for income is by using covered calls. To sell a covered call, you must own 100 shares of stock for each option that you want to sell. So, if you have been investing in some of your favorite stocks over the years and you have built up some shares, you can start earning money off the shares by selling call options against them.

The strategy involves selling the options with a strike price that is out of the money. If you sell in the money options, while you are going to be able to get a nice payment, your options will be "called away" if they expire in the money, and there is even a risk a buyer might exercise the option before expiration. So, beginning traders are better off selling out of the money options, even though you earn less money.

The money you are paid for selling an option is called the premium. This is analogous to an insurance premium, and many people trading stocks invest in options for insurance. This is especially true to get protection against falling stock prices, buying a put option can give you insurance by giving you the out of being able to sell the stock at the strike price of the put if prices drop significantly.

With a covered call, you find the option that you want to sell in the options chain, and then just use the interface of your broker to sell to open the option. You will be credited with the amount that the option is trading at the time. If the option expires, and the share price did not put your option in the money, then you will actually be able to take that out as cash.

Breakeven Price

Breakeven price is important to note when selling options. If the share price has not gone above the breakeven price, nobody is going to exercise the option. To take a simple example, if the share price is $100 and it costs $2 to buy the option (per-share), then the breakeven price for a call option is $102. So, the stock price has to rise above $102 to make it worth it to a buyer to exercise the option.

For a put option, subtract the price paid for the option to get the breakeven price. For our $100 stock, if a put option costs $2, then the breakeven price is $100- $2 = $98.

Buying an Option Back

One strategy used by traders who sell options is to reduce the risk of having the option exercised, they will buy the option back before it expires. This will reduce your overall profit, but eliminate the risk that a sudden price movement will put the option in the money (past breakeven) and it will be exercised. Remember that if a call option is exercised, you will be required to sell 100 shares of stock at the strike price. If a put option is exercised, you will be required to buy 100 shares of stock at the strike price. The key to this strategy is time decay. So, if you sell an option for $2 a share or $200, if it is out of the money as it nears expiration, it will be worth pennies on the dollar. So, you can buy it back without losing too much income. In the event, an option goes in the money and it looks like it is not going to move again in your favor, you can always take a slight loss and buy it back to avoid having to sell the shares.

Protected Puts

Another strategy is to sell put options, and if you are only a level 1 or level 2 traders, you can sell a protected put. However, this requires tying up a large amount of capital. To sell a protected put, you must have enough money in your account in the form of cash to buy 100 shares of the stock in the event the option is exercised. While this could be a way to earn a regular income, it requires a lot of money in proportion to small earnings, and there are better ways to earn money.

Debit Spreads

Now let's consider one of the most popular ways to earn money from selling options that don't involve having to own the shares of stock or putting up large amounts of cash. This is done using so-called bull and bears spreads or put and calls spreads. We will use the latter terminology.

A spread involves buying and selling two options at the same time. With a credit spread, it is a form of earning income. With a debit spread, you are essentially trading options but reducing the risk. So, let's look at that first.

Consider a call debit spread. With a call debit spread, you will buy an option at a lower strike price, and then sell an option at a higher strike price. The reason that traders do this is that you lower your risk by selling an option at a higher strike price. So, if the lower strike price option expires out of the money and proves to be a losing trade, you still have the premium you received by selling the option with the higher strike price. So, you will lose a lower amount of money than you would have only buying a single call option. This type of trade is entered simultaneously, that is you buy and sell the 2 call options in a single trade, called a call debit spread. A trader can buy a call option that is in the money, to earn higher profits, and then sell a cheap out of the money call option to mitigate the risk.

This strategy is used when you expect the stock price to rise.

You can also invest in a put debit spread. In this case, you buy an in the money put option with a higher strike price, and then mitigate your risk by selling an out of the money put option with a lower strike price. You use this strategy when you expect the stock price to drop.

Note that to trade spreads, you must be a level 3 options trader.

Selling Naked Put Options

A simpler trading method is to simply sell one option without buying another one to mitigate risk. Professional traders prefer this method, but you have to open a margin account to do it. This will require a cash deposit of $2,500. You will also have to deposit some collateral cash, and the requirements are higher than what is required for a credit spread. However, it is far less than what is required for a protected put, a small fraction of the money in fact.

Professional traders consider selling naked put options to be a low-risk strategy. Financial advisors are going to tell you differently, but the reality is they don't know what they are talking about. If you sell out of the money put options– while carefully studying the stocks and macroeconomic situation–it is actually a simple matter to earn profits most of the time. Remember that financial advisors are motivated to get you to invest in mutual funds and other products, so they don't like the competition. Second, the buyback strategy is used by professional options traders when selling naked put options. That means you have to be paying close attention to your trades, and then be ready to buy back any options that go in the money. When you buy back an option that you have sold, your obligations are removed.

Each broker will have a formula that determines the amount of cash you must put up as collateral. Check with your specific broker to learn the details. So, the process of selling naked put options involves depositing enough cash to cover the collateral requirements, then finding the option with the strike price that you want to sell. Brokers will tell you the probability of profit for each strike price. Professional options traders recommend selling put options with a probability of profit of 70% or higher. So, think about the number—over two years if you sell 100 put options, that means 70 of them will earn profits, and 30 of them would not. That doesn't necessarily mean you would lose money, if you are on top of things, you would be buying back the 30 options that were losing trades, not waiting to the last minute.

To sell naked options, you must be a level 4 trader.

You can also sell naked call options. The principles are the same, but when you sell naked put options, you are going to be doing so, expecting the stock price to stay above the strike price of your option. So, you are going to sell naked put options when you are neutral or bullish on the stock. For naked call options, you will sell a naked call option when you expect the stock price to be neutral or drop, so it will remain below the strike price. Then, you sell naked call options when you are bearish.

It is possible to make a high income, on the order of $500,000 to $1 million or more a year, selling naked options. But it is not without risk, so be sure to get some trading experience and do a lot of studies before you embark on a career selling options. But again, remember that most professional traders sell either naked put options or iron condors.

CHAPTER - 19

Other Options Strategies

We are now going to leave the world of selling options and go back to the one that most people are interested in, which is the world of trading options. Here, we are going to have a look at strategies that can be used to increase the odds of profits when trading options. In reality, some of these strategies involve buying and selling options at the same time. Keep in mind that these techniques will require a higher-level designation from your broker. So, it might not be something you can use right away if you are a beginner.

Selling Covered Calls against LEAPS and Other LEAPS Strategies

A LEAP is a long-term option, which is an option that expires at a date that is two years in the future. They are regular options otherwise, but you can do some interesting things with LEAPS. Because the expiration date is so far away, they cost a lot more. Looking at Apple, call options with a $195 strike price that expires in two years are selling for $28.28 (for a total price of $2,828). While that seems expensive, consider that 100 shares of Apple would cost $19,422 at the time of writing.

If you buy in the money LEAPS, then you can use them to sell covered calls. This is an interesting strategy that lets you earn premium income without having actually to buy the shares of stock.

LEAPS can also be used for other investing strategies. If at some point during those two-years, the share price rose to $200, we could exercise the option and buy the shares at $190, saving $10 a share. Also, at the same time, we could have been selling covered calls against the LEAPS.

Buying Put Options as Insurance

A put option gives you the right to sell shares of stock at a certain price. Suppose that you wanted to ensure your investment in Apple stock, and you had purchased 100 shares at $191 a share, for a total investment of $19,000. You are worried that the share price is going to drop and so you could buy a put option as a kind of insurance. Looking ahead, you see a put option with a $190 strike price for $4.10. So, you spend $410 and buy the put option.

Should the price of Apple shares suddenly tumble, you could exercise your right under the put option to dispose of your shares by selling at the strike price to minimize your losses. Suppose you wake up one morning and the share price has dropped to $170 for some reason. Had you not bought the option, you could have tried to get rid of your shares now and take a loss of $21 a share. But, since you bought the put option, you can sell your shares for $190 a share. That is a $1 loss since you purchased the shares at $191. So, your total loss would be $5.10 a share, but that is still less than the loss of $21 a share that you would have suffered selling the shares on the market at the $170 price. When investors buy stock and a put at the same time, it is called a married put.

Spreads

Spreads involve buying and selling options simultaneously. This is a more complicated options strategy that is only used by advanced traders. You will have to get a high-level designation with your brokerage in order to use this type of strategy. We won't go into details because these methods are beyond the scope of junior options traders, but we will briefly mention some of the more popular methods so that you can have some awareness.

One of the interesting things about spreads is they can be used by level 3 traders to earn a regular income from options. If you think the price of a stock is going to stay the same or rise, you sell a put credit spread. You sell a higher-priced option and buy a lower-priced option at the same time. The difference in option prices is your profit. There is a chance of loss if the price drops to the strike price of the puts (and you could get assigned if it goes below the strike price of the put option you sold). You can buy back the spread, in that case, to avoid getting assigned.

If you think that the price of a stock is going to drop, you can sell to open a credit spread, the difference in price is your profit, and losses are capped.

We can also consider more complicated spreads.

For example, you can use a diagonal spread with calls. This is done in such a way that you earn more from selling the call than you spend on buying the call for a considerable strike amount, and so you get a net credit to your account.

Spreads can become quite complicated, and there are many different types of spreads. If a trader thinks that the price of a stock will only go up a small amount, they can do a bull call spread. Profit and loss are capped in this case. The two options would have the same expiration date.

You seek to profit if the underlying stock drops in price. This can also be done by using two put options.

Spreads can be combined in more complicated ways. An iron butterfly combines a bear call spread with a bear put spread. The purpose of doing this is to generate steady income while minimizing the risk of loss.

An iron condor uses a put spread, and a call spread together. It involves selling both sides (calls and puts).

Iron Butterfly

An iron butterfly is another strategy to use if you think the stock price will stay within a certain range.

The strategy is to get as close to the money as possible. We will call the strike priced used the central strike. Then you set a differential price we will call x.

Like an iron condor, the profit from an iron butterfly is fixed at the net credit when you sell to open. This is given by the sum of the premiums earned from selling the money call and put, minus the prices paid for the out of the money options.

The maximum loss is the strike price of the purchased call–strike price of the sold put–total premium.

CHAPTER - 20

Avoiding Common Pitfalls in Options Trading

All successful options traders go through a learning curve before they start profiting consistently. Some of them put in an all-out effort to learn by spending countless hours reading on the topic or by watching video tutorials. Others learn at a more leisurely pace and once they get a grip of the basics, they lean more towards learning from their own experience. Irrespective of the type of learner you are, one way to cut short that learning curve is by learning from the mistakes of others.

This lists out six of the most common mistakes made by inexperienced traders that can be easily avoided.

1. Buying Naked Options without Hedging

This is one of the most fundamental mistakes made by amateur options traders and is also one of the costliest ones that could make them go broke in no time.

Buying naked options means buying options without any protective trades to cover your investment if the underlying security moves against your expectations and hurts your trade.

Here is a typical example:

A trader strongly feels a particular stock will go up in the short term and assumes he can make a huge profit by buying a few call options and therefore goes ahead with the purchase. The trader knows if the underlying stock's price were to rise as expected, the potential upside on the profits would be unlimited, whereas, if it were to go down, the maximum loss would be curtailed to just the amount invested for purchasing the call options.

In theory, the trader's assumption is right and it may so happen that this one particular trade may pay off. However, in reality, it is equally possible the stock would not move as per expectations, or may even fall. If the latter happens, the call options' prices would start falling rapidly and may never recover, thereby causing major losses to that trader.

It is almost impossible to predict the short-term movement of a stock accurately every time and the trader who consistently keeps buying naked options hoping to get lucky is far more likely to lose much more than what he/she gains in the long term.

For a person to make a profit after buying a naked option, the following things should fall in place:

1. The trader should predict the direction of the underlying stock's movement correctly.

2. The directional movement of the stock price should be quick enough so that the position can be closed before its gains get overrun by time-decay.

3. The rise in the option's premium price should also compensate for any potential drop in implied volatility from the time the option was purchased.

4. The trader should exit the trade at the right time before a reversal of the stock movement happens.

Needless to say, it is impractical to expect everything to fall in place simultaneously always and that is why naked-options traders often end up losing money even when they correctly guess the direction of the underlying stock's movement.

Having said all this, many such traders often think they would fare better the next time after a botched trade and rinse and repeat their actions till they reach a point where they would have lost most of their capital and are forced to quit trading altogether.

My advice to you – never buy naked options (unless it is part of a larger strategy to hedge some position) because it's simply not worth the risk.

Note: While buying naked-options has only finite risk limited to the price of the premium paid, selling of naked-options has unlimited risk and has to be avoided too, unless hedged properly.

2. Underestimating Time-Decay

A second major mistake of inexperienced traders is underestimating time-decay.

Time-decay is your worst enemy if you are an option buyer and you don't get a chance to exit your trade quickly enough.

If you are a call options buyer, you will notice that sometimes even when your underlying stock's price is increasing every day, your call option's price still doesn't rise or even falls. Alternately, if you are a put options buyer, you sometimes notice that your put option's price doesn't increase despite a fall in the price of the underlying stock. Both these situations can be confusing to somebody new to options trading.

The above problems occur when the rate of increase/ decrease in the underlying stock's price is just not enough to outstrip the rate at which the option's time-value is eroding every day.

Therefore, any trading strategy deployed by an options trader should ideally have a method of countering/ minimizing the effect of time-decay, or should make time-decay work in its favor, to ensure a profitable trade.

The spread based strategies do exactly that.

3. Buying Options with High Implied Volatility

Buying options in times of high volatility is yet another common mistake.

During times of high volatility, option premiums can get ridiculously overpriced and at such times, if an options trader buys options, even if the stock moves sharply in line with the trader's expectation, a large drop in the implied volatility would result in the option prices falling by a fair amount, resulting in losses to the buyer.

A particular situation I remember happened the day the results of the 'Brexit' referendum came through in 2016. The Nifty index reacting to the result (like most other global indices such as the Nasdaq 100) fell very sharply and the volatility index (VIX) jumped up by over 30%. The options premium for all Nifty options had become ludicrously high that day. However, this rise in volatility was only because of the market's knee-jerk reaction to an unexpected result and just a couple of days later, the market stabilized and started rising again; the VIX fell sharply and also brought down option premium prices accordingly.

Option traders who bought options at the time VIX was high would have realized their mistake a day or two later when the option prices came down, causing them substantial losses because the volatility started to get back to normal figures.

4. Not Cutting Losses on Time

There is apparently a famous saying among the folks on Wall Street - "Cut your losses short and let your winners run."

Even the most experienced options traders will make a bad trade once in a while. However, what differentiates them from a novice is that they know when to concede defeat and cut their losses. Amateurs hold on to losing trades in the hope they'll bounce back and eventually end up losing a larger chunk of their capital. The experienced traders, who know when to concede defeat, pull out early and reinvest the capital elsewhere.

Cutting losses in time is crucial, especially when you trade a directional strategy and make a wrong call. The practical thing to do is to exit a losing position if it moves against expectation and erodes more than 2-3% of your total capital.

If you are a trader who strictly uses spread-based strategies, your losses will always be far more limited whenever you make a wrong call. Nevertheless, irrespective of the strategy used, when it becomes evident that the probability of profiting from a trade is too less for whatsoever reason, it is prudent to cut losses and reinvest in a different position that has a greater chance of success rather than simply crossing your fingers or appealing to a higher power.

5. Keeping too many eggs in the same Basket

The experienced hands always know that once in a while, they will lose a trade. They also know that they should never bet too much on a single trade, which could considerably erode their capital were it to go wrong.

Professionals spread their risk across different trades and keep a maximum exposure of not more than 4-5% of their total available capital in a single trade for this very reason.

Therefore, if you have a total capital of $10,000, do not enter any single trade that has a risk of losing more than $500 in the worst-case scenario. Following such a practice will ensure the occasional loss is something you can absorb without seriously eroding your cash reserve. Fail to follow this rule and you may have the misfortune of seeing many months of profits wiped out by one losing trade.

6. Using Brokers who charge High Brokerages

A penny saved is a penny earned!

When I first entered the stock market many years ago, I didn't pay much attention to the brokerage I was paying. After all, the trading services I received were from one of the largest and most reputed banks in the country, and the brokerage charged by my provider wasn't very different from that of other banks that provided similar services.

Over the years, many discount brokerage firms started flourishing that charge considerably less, but I had not bothered changing my broker since I was used to the old one.

It was only when I quantified the differences that I realized having a low-cost broker made a huge difference.

If you are somebody who trades in the Indian Stock markets, check the table below for a quantified break-up of how brokerage charges can eat into your earnings over a year if you choose the wrong broker. The regular broker in the table below is the bank whose trading services I had been using and the discount broker is the one I use now. For the record, the former is also India's third-largest bank in the private sector and the latter is the most respected discount broker house in the country.

	Regular Broker	Discount Broker
Brokerage charged per options trade	₹ 300	₹ 20
Cost of entering any directional spread and exiting the position before expiry	₹ 1,200	₹ 80
Cost of entering an Iron Condor and taking it to expiry	₹ 1,200	₹ 80
Percentage of profits surrendered as brokerage for a typical Iron-Condor on Nifty index (Considering profit of ₹ 3300 for a trade with 70% winning probability)	36.36%	2.42%

Comparison of brokerages : Regular Broker versus Discount Broker

It is obvious from the table above that using a low-cost broker makes a huge difference especially when trading a strategy such as the Iron Condor (a relatively low-yield but high-probability strategy).

Also, it is not just the brokerage that burns a hole in your pocket; the annual maintenance fee is also higher for a regular broker and all these costs will make a huge difference in the long run.

Irrespective of which part of the world you trade from, always opt for a broker that provides the lowest possible brokerage because this will make a difference in the long term. Do a quantitative comparison using a table (something similar to the one I used above) and that would make it easier to decide who you should go with.

Note for India-based Traders: If you are a trader based in India or if you trade in the Indian Stock markets, I would strongly suggest using Zerodha, which has been consistently rated the best discount broker in the country. I have been using their services for the past couple of years and have found them to be particularly good. Their brokerage rates are among the best in the country, and on top of that, they provide excellent support when needed, and also maintain an exhaustive knowledge-base of articles. Lastly, their trading portal is very user friendly and therefore, placing an order is quick and hassle-free.

CHAPTER - 21

Choosing a Broker

Brokers and Trading Platforms

The use of shares, whether it is to collect dividends or to speculate on their listing, is an increasingly widespread and interesting practice. The risk of loss is always present, but depending on the way you buy and sell your shares, this risk can be reduced. If you are wondering how to buy and sell the shares of large listed companies online, here are some explanations that may interest you.

Buy shares to become shareholders

A large part of private individuals and institutions that buy stocks do so in order to become shareholders.

It is the simplest use of actions and their main purpose.

In fact, when a company issues its shares, it is possible to buy them directly online.

However, for the already listed shares to do so, it is necessary to go through an intermediary, which can be an online broker or an online bank.

Buy and sell shares with online banks

The easiest way to buy and sell shares is to go through one of the placement products offered by banks and, in particular, by online banks. Thanks to 100% online operation of these banks, you can easily pass your purchase and sale orders directly via the internet without moving.

The advantages of this system are numerous because it is your bank that will take care of executing your orders and then buying and selling your shares. To take advantage of stock market shares through these systems, you must underwrite an Investment Plan in Shares, a securities account or life insurance, which are the main banking products on the stock market. The only drawback of this method concerns the expenses that may be higher than those that you would have to pay if you bought and sold the shares yourself.

However, bank commissions rarely exceed 4%.

One of the main advantages of bank placement products is that market intermediaries supervise your purchases and sales of shares and you can benefit from advice.

Buy and sell shares with online brokers

Another method is to contact an online mediator. Their operation is almost identical to that of online banks, with the difference that you do not enjoy assistance and advice, but at the same time, the costs are lower because you decide for yourself what actions to buy or sell.

These online brokers, also allow trading through stock

market shares, without actually having to buy them. To do this, you just need to speculate on the evolution of their value. The tools that allow you to proceed in this way are CFDs.

Ultimately there are several methods to buy and sell shares on the internet. Before deciding on one or other of these solutions, take care to correctly evaluate the commissions involved as well as your level of knowledge on the stock exchange. Depending on these criteria, each of these two methods has different advantages. It is also good to understand the quotation system of an action to be able to speculate on this type of asset.

Choosing and using a financially sound and responsive brokerage should be a high priority for every trader. And that brokerage should provide access to every trading venue: equities, options, futures, or forex. Many brokerages are running slick TV ads that do not qualify. When you examine the list of financial products served by brokerages, you may be disappointed. Some well-known brokerages support stocks and options. But they do not offer futures or foreign exchange. So walk away and keep looking.

Many who are new to trading select a brokerage because they know someone who has an account with that particular brokerage. But this is not how you should choose your brokerage, particularly if you are an entry-level trader. Conduct some research before you make a final decision. You want to choose a brokerage that fits your investment and trading style. This may not be the same as your friend's.

Fortunately, you can use the Internet to evaluate brokerages. A website provided by the Financial Industry Regulatory Authority (FINRA) provides a substantial amount of information about the conduct of both individuals and firms. Of course, it essentially lists regulatory citations, and never makes recommendations or posts complimentary comments. The listed regulatory citations are mostly for failures in oversight or careless trading practices. Corresponding fines are also listed. You can read these to find FINRA citations similar to the following:

This permits you to see a list of former employers, the time a counselor has been working with financial securities, and any past FINRA citations that may exist.

Charts like these never tell the entire story. And like so much Internet content, they are often misleading. It is obvious that the range of securities supported in addition to the sophistication of the trading platforms were ignored. The Kiplinger rankings are far from accurate when you consider the breadth of services, platform technologies, number of branch offices, availability and quality of customer support, and more.

In the author's opinion, TD Ameritrade's thinkorswim® platform would rank #1 for trading options and stocks. It has the most extensive feature set. And TradeStation, which is superior to many of those listed, wasn't even included. Furthermore, a trade that costs $0.0050/share looks good at first glance. But a 4,000-share trade costs

$20 in commissions. Most experienced investors know brokerages will likely reduce their commissions and exchange fees to meet competition. This is especially true for high net worth clients and/or high-volume active traders.

Full-Service and Discount Brokers

Full-service brokers typically provide financial investment counselors. The counselors may suggest financial securities products, managed funds, or recommend investment management companies with which they maintain business relationships. These full-service brokerages also provide research and education to their clients. The fees charged by full-service brokers are usually higher than those charged by discount brokers. Required minimum account deposits may also be higher than those required at discount brokerages. Besides, the maintenance of a minimum account balance may be required.

Discount brokerages also require a minimum account deposit and the maintenance of a minimum account balance. This can range from $500 to $1,000. And experienced active traders who manage their own trading activity have little interest in receiving trading advice from an investment counselor, who may not have as much trading experience or knowledge as their clients.

Many old-timers have clear recollections of their dealings with the traditional brick and mortar brokerage houses and the so-called "stockbrokers" in their employ. They'd look at the lists of stocks in the daily news or the Wall Street Journal. When they spotted a trade opportunity, they'd phone their broker to put on a trade, and pay a $70 commission. They also remember receiving phone calls from their broker who had been advised by the "boys in New York" to solicit their clients to buy shares of stock that were part of an issue that their brokerage house was promoting. Some clients wised up and referred to these stocks as the "stock de jour."

This was an unscrupulous "pump and dump" practice used by brokerages to increase the sales of an underlying stock held within the brokerage's own portfolio. Once the solicitations drove the price up as a result of the sudden influx of buy orders, the brokerage dumped the stock for a profit, leaving their clients "holding the bag." Obviously, they couldn't do this every day, and it didn't take long for regulatory agencies and clients alike to catch on. But according to many, this actually happened. Today, the regulatory agencies watch for these kinds of practices and levy heavy fines when detected.

But stories like these often drive traders to the discount brokerages. All an experienced trader wants, or needs for that matter is access to the market through a full-featured, reliable trading platform, reasonable commissions and exchange fees, and fast execution times.

Develop a checklist that evaluates prospective brokerages. Look for the following, arranged in no particular order:

- Account types (Brokerage, IRA Rollovers, checking, bill pay, savings, money market, etc.)

- Minimum balance requirement.

- Transaction fees.

- Margin interest rate.

- Supported trading venues (equities, options, futures, and/or forex)

- Execution speed.

- Access to different trading venues.

- Trading platforms (online for PCs and/or Macintosh Computers)

- Trade scanning engine(s).

- Market research (either web-based or trading platform-based)

- Account access via brokerage website.

- Trading via brokerage website.

- Earnings and dividend releases.

- Mobile trading apps (iPhone, Android, iPad, Android Tablets, Windows Mobile)

- Paper (simulated) trading for practice.

- Back trades (testing strategies with historical pricing data)

- Support (online chat, telephone, e-mail, and text messaging)

- Training (live and/or online)

- Complete financial reporting (monthly, year-to-date, prior years, 1099s, IRA minimum required distribution calculations, commissions paid, margin fees, etc.)

- Nearby branch offices.

Financial Security and Stability

When opening an account, you may want to know who is underwriting the security of your account in addition to the maximum amount protected. Congressional action in 1970 requires all brokerages to register with the Securities Investor Protection Corporation (SIPC). The SIPC is to brokerages what the FDIC is to banks. The SIPC protects the brokerage accounts of each customer. If the brokerage firm is closed due to bankruptcy or fraud, the SIPC protects customer assets up to $500,000 in securities and $100,000 in cash. If your accounts exceed these insured values, you may want to consider distributing your funds across more than one brokerage, although very few investors actually do this.

Although the SIPC protects against bankruptcy and fraud, it doesn't protect against market losses caused by a decline in security values. If a brokerage firm does fail, the SIPC works to merge the failed brokerage into a successful one. Failing this, the SIPC will transfer a client's securities to another firm. If stocks or bonds are missing from an investor's portfolio, the SIPC will rebuild portfolios by replacing every missing share of stock or bond, penny for penny, up to the insured limits.

Many investors never consider what can happen to their account holdings in the event of a run on the financial markets or an institution. What effect can this have on the stability of your broker, also called broker-dealer?

It's somewhat reassuring to know that during such condition's insurance is extended and liquidity facilities are created to back depositor accounts. The Securities and Exchange Commission (SEC) has instituted several reforms on liquidity. These liquidity reforms ensure that each broker-dealer maintains a suitable reserve to cope with inordinate levels of client withdrawals.

Despite these regulations, short-term unstable funding can prevent broker-dealers from order fulfillment. This can be due to a short-term lack of funds required to carry temporary imbalances in the volume of buy and sell orders. This impairs the ability of traders to buy and sell a wide variety of stocks and bonds. It can also have the effect of bringing trading to an abrupt halt.

Many investor-traders remember the failures of broker-dealers Lehman Brothers and Bear-Sterns during the housing mortgage fiasco of 2008. As a result of the lessons learned then, many broker-dealers have increased their capital holdings, increased liquidity, and reduced their holdings in risky assets. All of these policies are attempts to protect themselves against the reoccurrence of events like those that brought down these huge brokerage houses.

As the holder of a brokerage account, you should know that the potential for broker-dealer failures still exists. Both broker-dealers and banks have been encouraged to form either asset-rich bank holding companies or intermediate holding companies to help spread capital risk.

Broker-dealers typically find short-term security by negotiating repurchase agreements with underwriters, such as money market funds. This provides the financing needed by broker-dealers to fund their transactions. In exchange, the underwriters receive reasonably low financing fees. The money market funds, among a few others, avoid long-term, risky securities. They happily settle for shorter-term, low-risk securities with less vulnerability to a potential market run.

CHAPTER - 22

How to Start

Determine whether you will proceed as a company or an individual

Both these alternatives are a lot different when actual options trading comes into practice. The legal obligations of both vary significantly. Besides, check whether you can trade with an offshore company and/or an offshore bank account. This could be advantageous in some tax-related situations. Non-resident citizen offshore companies and bank accounts are quite beneficial.

Open a trading account

Setting up an online trading account is the foremost thing to do when starting trading in options. Step by step instructions is provided by companies, which makes it extremely easy to manage the account. But this process does take some time, so start early. A lot of factors are taken into consideration while deciding on your trading account. The amount of money you are planning to invest in is the first thing that defines the type of account, which will be opened.

Another choice one may get if they want to open a margin account or not. A Margin account has its own benefits.

After selling a stock or option, you get the money immediately, which in turn enables you to buy again. Some time is required in a regular account to clear the proceeds from a sale. A Margin Account enables you to borrow money to trade while using your own capital at the same time. One can say that it is like an overdraft facility, which allows you to get extra funds.

There is a catch though. A margin account requires a lot of time to be approved. You can start with a regular account and apply for a margin account you must use your own money in a regular account and setting it up is less time-consuming.

Create a plan

The fact of the matter is that there is simply no way you can expect to be successful in the long term when it comes to options trading if you don't have a plan that has been personalized based on your very own strengths and weaknesses. While skipping this and finding a generalized trading plan online, may be the fastest way to start trading options as soon as possible, it is far from the most efficient.

Determine your current level of skill

To ensure that you create a plan with a realistic chance for success, the first thing that you are going to want to do is determine what your current competencies are when it comes to trading in general and the underlying asset you are hoping to focus on specifically. The more experience you have, the more elaborate and ambitious your plan can be, but it is important to determine your level of experience honestly as overestimating your experience is only going to make it more difficult for you to start turning a profit in the first place.

Consider other obstacles

While you will likely have a few personal issues that may need to be worked through to achieve options trading success, it is important to also consider any other obstacles that might be standing in your way so that you can approach them properly. These obstacles can be anything from the limited amount of time that you are ultimately going to have to work with to simply not having the level of capital you would prefer to get started in the most effective way possible. It does not matter what the barrier is, it only matters how you are going to circumvent it. Having a clear idea of what may get in the way of your future success will allow you to prepare for it ahead of time and mitigate its long-term impact as much as possible. Taking the time to work through this step properly will help improve not only your overall success rate, but your bankable profits as well.

Decide how much risk is right for you

When it comes to determining how much risk is the right amount, the final solution is going to be different for each trader. This is because there is no singular amount of risk that is perfect for everyone; risk is more individualized than that. To get started figuring out the perfect amount of the risk for you, the first thing that you will want to do is to determine how much capital you are going to allot solely to trading, as well as what that amount means to you. If you have saved a few thousand dollars in a month or so to give something new a try, then your overall risk is going to be low. If you saved that same amount over nearly a year of dedicated saving, then that same amount might represent a much higher risk. Regardless, it is important to never put more into a single trade than you can ever afford to lose.

Prepare yourself

In addition to the daily preparations that will be required of you, you will also need to be aware of various important due dates, both for your underlying asset of choice as a whole, as well as any holdings you might have specifically. Earnings reports of all types are sure to have a noticeable effect on the market and if you are caught unaware, you have no choice but to take a loss that, in many cases, can be quite serious. You will also need to be aware of when any dividend payments are coming due for any options that are related to stocks that you might own. Owning an option does not entitle you to a dividend so, you must know when to exercise your options if you always hope to maximize your profits.

Find the right place to start

Once you know when you are going to get out of any trade that you place, the succeeding thing that you will need to consider is the right time to capitalize on the trend of a specific option. The best way to go about doing this is to consider the amount of risk that you deem acceptable before considering what type of purchase you want to make when you come across an option that meets your criteria for purchase based on your earnings goals and your risk assessment.

Set clear goals

You are going to want to ensure that the goals you set are specific, which means setting goals with clear instances of success and failure for three months, six months and a year down the line. Having a strict timeline will make it easier for you to follow through on your goals, as you know exactly when you will have failed if you do not get to work. This means you will want to carefully consider all the logistics related to meeting your goals, as well as anything that may be standing between you and completing the goal successfully. Remember, the more specific you are when it comes to setting your goals, the more likely you are to achieve them. Remember, there is nothing more important than having a timeline set up from the get-go as if your goals do not have timeframes, then it will be much easier to put them off overall.

Keep track of your progress

When you are first making your way into the world of options trading, you must track your progress to ensure that you do not start on the wrong foot. This means you will want to track all the details of each trade that you make for closer analysis. Depending on how useful you find this process early on, you may even want to continue it on into the foreseeable future. This means that you are going to want to track the time and date of each trade, the relevant financial specifics, why you choose the option in question, your emotional state, how long you held the option for, and the end result of the trade.

The first trade

Once you have a firm trading plan in mind, there is nothing else to do except to put your plan to the test and see how things shake out in the real world. While there are plenty of opportunities out there for you to practice trading before you get started doing the real thing, the fact of the matter is that if real money isn't on the line, then you are going to inherently be in a different mental space about the entire thing which, by and large, will make the entire exercise moot. As such, it is recommended that you instead simply start by making trades that are at one percent or less of your total trading amount so that you aren't hobbled by high stakes while still not being in any real danger should things not go according to plan.

Making a trade

When it comes time to make your first trade will want to select Trading Options from inside your trading account after you have already logged in. This will take you to a page that will allow you to search for various stock market options based on the ticker symbol of various underlying stocks. A search of a specific company will provide you with the current stock price as well as all the options related to the stock in question that are currently available.

Taking a Closer Look at Your Results

While it is perfectly natural to be curious as to the results of your personalized trading plan, it is important to keep in mind that if you check in on your results too early, the available data is unlikely to be telling the whole story; to put it another way, you need to give you plan time to breathe before looking for hard and firm results.

What's more, if these early risky moves do work out, then you have negative trading habits to contend with that are sure to hamper your overall earnings potential further down the line. Instead of setting this type of largely irrelevant and frequently damaging goals, you are going to want to simply keep track of all the details without interacting with them until the time is right.

When it comes to tracking your trades properly, the strongest metric for success is going to vary noticeably depending on what types of trades you tend to prefer. If you find yourself constantly making risky trades that may pay off significantly, then you will be most interested in the pure amount you have made overall while day trading. However, if you are a trader that prefers to take things at a more cautious pace, then you will be interested more in the number of trades you have completed that ended successfully versus the number that ended in a loss as a pure number might not tell the whole story in that case. Do not forget to consider which metrics are right for you, as basing your analysis on the wrong data could easily send you spiraling in a counterproductive situation when you were already on the right track to begin with.

Measure your performance

After you have amassed the appropriate amount of information, the succeeding thing you will want to do is to chart out your current overall performance. Doing so will provide you with an unbiased look at how all the rules you are using to properly determine your trades are doing without any of the daily, in-the-moment clutter getting in the way. Ideally, this data will include the results of each trade that you have made since you started options trading. Looking at all the data splayed out in this way will make it much easier to see the forest instead of the individual trees.

CHAPTER - 23

Habits

We will talk about some of the most amazing habits you can follow, which will help you to start trading and making money. The truth is, taking care of your time and health is very important when trading. Trading for a living or even part-time can get stressful, which is why it is in our best interest to get the most out of our day and have appropriate habits and routines. We will give you some fantastic techniques and habits to follow, as this will allow you to make a better living.

Amazing Start to Your Day

Once you start waking up early and start doing productive things, you will have a sense of accomplishment, which will have a snowball effect throughout the day. See the whole point of waking up early is to do what you "don't have time for," I will come back to my example. When I started my business, I couldn't get it to grow because I wasn't putting enough time and effort into it. Once I began to wake up early and got to work on it every morning things started to change, and in six months, my business was up and running, which gave me the life that I want now. So, for you to have an amazing and a productive day you need to wake up early in the morning and then, do something that makes you feel accomplished, could be anything from doing your laundry, working out or working on your business basically do anything you say you " don't have time for" in the morning.

Productivity

It is amazing how productive you become once you start to wake up early in the morning. I think we can all agree when I say this, for you to get your goals or to get to your goals faster, you need to be productive. To be more productive, you need a fresh mind with no distractions, and those circumstances tend to happen earlier in the morning. Make sure you wake up in the morning to have more time to do things that will benefit you.

Your Time

Waking up early will give you some time to be by yourself, which can be peaceful if it is hard for you to find time for yourself, for example, if you have kids you would probably have a tougher time finding some time to yourself. So, make sure you get up early and have some time to yourself, it will only help you be more productive and less stressed.

As you can there are a lot of benefits to waking up early, as listed above you will be more productive, have a fantastic start to your day, and you will have more "You time." Remember how I spoke about waking up without an alarm clock, well the whole point of this is to show you the importance of waking up and the importance of waking up without an alarm clock. That being said, let me show you three techniques in which you can train your body to wake up early in the morning without any alarm clock.

Don't Make Drastic Changes

So, it is pretty common to sleep in over the weekend and then shock your body back into waking up early. Let me tell you that it is not the way you should be going about such things. For you to wake up early consistently without an alarm clock, you need to slowly start waking up 15 minutes early every week always, so for example, if you wake up at 9 am with the help of your alarm usually. Wake up at 8:45 am with the help of your alarm until you start waking up at your desired time using the alarm clock as a tool. Every week lower the time by 15 minutes. Once you start waking up at your desired time consistently, you will begin to notice that you wake up before the alarm goes off. Once you get to that point, try and waking up without an alarm clock for a week, and you will be waking up without the help of an alarm clock by setting your natural internal alarm clock. One more thing before we move on to the next point, your ideal time for waking up depends on how much time you need to work on things "you don't have time for" so if you need two hours, wake up two hours earlier before your day starts.

Get to Bed Earlier

Well, this is pretty self-explanatory, getting to bed earlier will only help you wake up early without feeling so tired in the am. Making sure you go to bed at least 9 hours before you have to wake up is crucial if you don't want to be a walking zombie in the morning, I know for most of you going to bed early can be you just lying in bed and waiting for sleepiness to kick in. So here are some things you can do to go to bed early 1. Get yourself into a hot tub 2. Read a book 3. Take natural sleeping aids like GABA. By no means am I a doctor, so take sleepy supplements at your own risk. So, get to bed earlier!

Don't Overthink

This is the most common thing people do when waking up. Once your eyes open, you wake up. Don't procrastinate on waking up thinking, "I can sleep fifteen minutes longer" because you will oversleep if you do so. Once your eyes open get up out of bed and start moving around you will be good to go in five minutes, one more thing if you are going to be using the alarm clock until you set your internal alarm clock then don't use the snooze button as it will only set you back.

Improves Your Mood

This is one of the most significant differences you will notice once you start working on your health is that your spirit will stay elevated throughout the day! This is a great thing to have as you will be able to get more things done and be more successful. See, when you work out you release a chemical called dopamine, which is a feel-good hormone, and of course, working out will help you become less stressed.

Improves Physical Health

Yes, this is one of the most obvious points to bring up, but let's discuss it anyway. Once you start to implement healthy habits to your day, you will become more physically fit you, which will not only give you more energy thought the day it would also help you keep up with things like your daily chores and not get tired so quickly. You will see a difference in the quality of your life and your work ethic once you start to implement daily health habits and become more physically healthy.

Helps Boost Your Immune System

These ties into improved physical health, but working out will boost your immune system and lower your risk of diseases like diabetes, hypertension, etc. Once you have a boost in your immune system, you will become less likely to m get even the common flu. I know of someone who hasn't gotten flu in fifteen years simply because he started to live a healthy life, now I am not saying that you will see the same results but staying healthy will definitely help you with boosting your immune system which will help you not get sick so often and enjoy some quality time with your family and Get more stuff done.

Start Easy

Now, if you have never worked out in your life, you need to realize that you won't be going hard at the gym, as Arnold Schwarzenegger did in his hay days. So, don't push yourself too much in the gym because you are not ready for it, and you might lose motivation. So, if you are starting off getting in shape, perhaps light jogs, some resistance training a couple of times a week to get the blood moving. But make sure you get up to the point where you are working out at least three hours a week to see some health benefits. Start once a week then twice and so on.

Nutrition

Well, this needs to be talked about, staying in shape, and living a healthier life requires you to eat healthy foods. So, make sure you start to implement that are dense in micronutrients like vegetables, fruits, etc. Making sure that on your plate is essential, as you might have heard you are what you eat. So, figure out what your ideal healthy eating schedule looks like and plan your day and meals according to that, again I can't stress this enough how important this part is so making sure you eat healthily.

Meditation

The best thing you can do for your mental health is to meditate. Meditation has shown to reduce stress and anxiety, which is excellent for some of our days to day hectic life we live. Now staying healthy requires you to be mentally fit as well as physically healthy, so make sure you do your meditation every day for five to thirty minutes. Why the big time ranges you ask, well some of you won't be able to meditate for thirty minutes to start with so start with five minutes and slowly build up to that thirty-minute mark. Make sure you do this often as meditation is the best thing you can do for your mental health.

Try and Positively Take Things

I know this sounds super cliché, but it is quite right, if you take things or incidents in your life in a positively, then you will become more at peace within yourself which will help you have a more balanced outlook towards your life. So, for example, let's say you injure your elbow doing something instead of being mad at what happened to be grateful that you didn't lose your whole arm, instead of looking at the bad look at the good and just be happy the worst didn't happen, plus for you to get mad at things that have already happened and you can't fix like you're trying to uncook an egg, IMPOSSIBLE so stop getting angry or upset at things that can't and won't be fixed and just move on.

Have Some Fun

Seriously, you cannot " go go go" for the rest of your life every day, for you to be more successful and to live a happy life you need to make sure you are having some fun and not just slaving away every day. This is really a simple point, but people tend to take it for granted what I mean when I say "have some fun" is to go do stuff that you really want to do but are too shy or too scared to do so, go sky diving or go-carting in the middle of the day I'm serious have some fun!!! Enjoy yourself sometimes don't get hung up on things day in and day out... Have a balanced life!

With that being said, the whole point of life is to find your purpose what you want to do and become, etc... Balanced life won't be your balanced life and vice versa. The whole point is to find what you want you to want to be or do in your life prioritize accordingly. And once you have managed to find mental peace, you are now living a well-balanced life.

CHAPTER - 24

Differences among Forex, Stocks and Options

There are different reasons some traders love to use forex instead of the stock market. One of them is the forex leverage.

Leverage

When it comes to forex trading, the entire system is totally different. Before you can trade using leverage, you need to have opened the forex trading account. That's the only requirement that is out there, nothing else. When you open a forex account, you can easily use the leverage feature.

If you are trading in the United States of America, you will be restricted to a leveraging of 50:1 leveraging. Countries outside of the US are restricted to leverage of about 200:1. It is better when you are outside the US, than in the US.

Liquidity differences

When you decide to trade stocks, you end up purchasing the companies' shares that have a cost from a bit of dollars down to even hundreds of dollars. Usually, the price in the market tends to share with demand and supply.

Paired trades

When you trade with forex, you are facing another world, unseen in the stock market. Though the currency of a country tends to change, there will always be a great supply of currency that you can trade. What this means is that the main currencies in the world tend to be very liquid.

When you are in forex trading, you will see that the currencies are normally quoted in pairs. They are not quoted alone. This means that you should be interested in the country's economic health that you have decided to trade-in. The economic health of the country tends to affect the worth of the currency.

The basic considerations change from one forex market to the next. If you decide to purchase the Intel shares, the main aim is to see if the stock's value will improve. You aren't interested in how the prices of other stocks are.

On the other hand, if you have decided to sell or buy forex, you need to analyze the economies of those countries that are involved in the pairs.

You should find out if the country has better jobs, GDP, as well as political prospects.

To do a successful trade in the Forex market, you will be expected to analyze not only one financial entity but two.

The forex market tends to show a higher level of sensitivity in upcoming economic and political scenarios in many countries.

You should note that the U.S. stock market, unlike many other stock markets, is not so sensitive to a lot of foreign matters.

Price sensitivity to trade activities

When we look at both markets, we have no choice but to notice that there is varying price sensitivity when it comes to trade activities done.

If a small company that has fewer shares has about ten thousand shares bought from it, it could go a long way to impact the price of the stock. For a big company such as Apple, such n number of shares when bought from it won't affect the stock price.

When you look at forex trades, you will realize that trades of a few hundreds of millions of dollars won't affect the major currency at all. If it affects, it would be minute.

Market accessibility

It is easy to access the currency market, unlike its counterpart, the stock market. Though you may be able to trade stocks every second of the day, five days weekly in the twenty-first century, it is not easy.

A lot of retail investors end up trading via a United States brokerage that makes use of a single major trading period every day, which spans from 9:30 AM to 4:00 PM. They go-ahead to have a minute trading hour past that time, and this period has price and volatility issues, which end up dissuading a lot of retail traders from making use of such time.

Forex trading is different. One can carry out such trading every second of the day because there are a lot of forex exchanges in the world, and they are constantly trading in one-time zone or the other.

Forex Trading vs. Options

A trader may believe the United States Dollar will become better when compared to the Euro, and if the results pan out, the person earns.

The strategy, if it works, can help in affecting the trade when the research pans out.

When you get involved in Options Trading, you tend to get involved in the purchase and sales of options on great amounts of futures, stocks and so on, that will move either up or below at a price during the phase.

It is similar to Forex Trading since you can easily leverage the buying power to have a controlling power on futures or stocks.

There are several disparities between Options trading and Forex trading. They are:

24 Hour Trading:

When you get involved in Forex instead of Options trading, you have the capability of trading every second of the day, five days weekly. When you look at the Forex market, you will realize that it lives longer than any financial market in the world.

If you have decided to get double-digit gains in the market, it is important to possess a generous amount of time every week to carry out these trades. If a large event occurs anywhere in the world, you may end up being amongst the first to benefit from the situation in the Foreign Exchange market.

You don't expect to spend time waiting and hoping that the market opens in the market, like in the case of trading options.

With Forex, you can easily trade anytime you want, at all times of the night and day. Whenever you wish, you can trade it.

Rapid Trade Execution:

When you immediately make use of the Forex market; you tend to get instantaneous trade executions. You don't have to be delayed like in the case of Options or some other markets too.

When you place the order, it ends up being filled using the best potential price in the market, instead of wondering what price ends up being ordered.

You won't have to have the urge to slip like the case of options. When you are involved in Foreign Exchange Trading, there is a great chance of liquidity, unlike in the case of Options trading.

No Commissions:

Forex market is one that doesn't need commission because it acts as an inter-bank market, where buyers are matched with sellers instantly.

There aren't cases of brokerage fees, like in the stock market and other markets.

You will see a spread that exists between the ask price and the bid, which is the way a lot of Forex trading firms earn their money.

What this means is that when you trade Forex, you stand to save the brokerage fees unlike in the case of options trading, where you are expected to pay communion since you have no choice but to use a brokerage firm.

Forex Trading Risks

Like every financial market out there, there are risks that one may have to face. The interbank market is known to have different degrees of regulations. Apart from that, forex instruments aren't as standardized as other financial market instruments out there. Do you know that in some parts of the globe, there are no regulations on the forex market?

The interbank market consists of different banks all over the world, trading with one another.

The banks have no choice but to determine an asset to credit risk and sovereign risks. They have come up with different internal processes, in a bid to ensure that they remain quite safe. These types of regulations are imposed in the industry to ensure that every participating bank is protected.

The market pricing comes from the forces of demand and supply because the market is made up of different banks giving bids and offers.

The fact that there is a great amount of trade flows in the market means that rogue investors can't influence the worth of a currency. This ensures that there is transparency in the foreign exchange market for those traders that are privy to interbank dealing.

A lot of countries have regulations concerning the forex, but not all do.

Pros and Cons of Forex

First Pro

When it comes to a daily trading volume in every market out there, the forex is the largest, meaning that it possesses the largest amount of liquidity.

This is one reason that one can easily enter or exit a position whenever he wants, for a small spread in a lot of market conditions.

First Con

Brokers, banks and dealers are known to give a great level of leverage, meaning that investors can easily control huge positions using a tiny amount of money.

Though you don't see it every time, a high ratio of leverage of 100:1 is possible to see in the foreign exchange market.

A trader must know how to use leverage, as well as the risks that using leverage brings to an account. Using a large amount of leverage has forced a lot of dealers to become bankrupt unexpectedly.

Second Pro

You can trade in the foreign exchange market every second of the day, six days in a week. It usually begins daily in Australia and ends in New York.

The main centers for forex are Singapore, Hong Kong, Sydney, Tokyo, New York, London and Paris.

Second Con

Before you can trade currencies in a profitable manner, you have to understand economic indicators and basics. A currency investor has to possess a great understanding of how a lot of economies function, as well as how connected they are. You need to understand these fundamentals that are able to alter the values of currencies.

CHAPTER - 25

Tips for Better Options Trading

At its heart, a trading scheme of options is a mechanism for the creation and selling of signals using a validated stock analysis tool.

The program can be based on some kind of alternative approach and includes both basic and technical evaluations. Options trading systems may concentrate on changes in the underlying stock price, interest, decay time, unusual purchasing/selling behavior or a mix.

Essentially, it is a checklist of conditions that must be met before entering the trade. When all conditions are fulfilled, a signal is produced to buy or sell. The criteria for each type of option trading strategy are different.

Whether its long calls, covered calls, bear spreads, or naked index options, each one has its own type of a trading system. An optional salt trading program can help you get out false signals and create trust in entries and exits.

How relevant is a trading network for options?

The demand for options is very complex. Trading without a framework is like building a house without a plan. Movements of price, time, and stock will all impact your earnings. You must be mindful of each of these variables.

Emotion can easily be swayed as the market shifts.

With a program, the response to these natural and usual emotions can be controlled. How much did you sit and watch a trade losing money when your order was filled?

Or, have you ever seen a stock price spike when you think of buying it? It is important to have a clear strategy in place to make rational and reasonable trade decisions. You can boost your trade executions by designing and following a good program, as emotionless and automatic as a machine.

Advantages of Trading Scheme Leverage Options – Selling options have the stock market leverage. You can control hundreds or thousands of shares with options at a fraction of the stock price itself.

A change in stock values from five to ten percent may be equivalent to an increase of one hundred percent or more. Seek to focus on percentage gains against dollar losses in your exchange. It needs a radical shift in traditional thinking, but it is necessary for the effective management of the trading system.

Objectivity – A successful trading scheme of options is focused on observable parameters that allow signals to be bought and sold. It takes subjectivity and second-guessing out of your business so that you can focus on predetermined variables that trigger explosive trade.

Flexibility – Almost all options traders can tell you that options give your trading flexibility. The demand for options makes it remarkably easy to take advantage of short-term positions.

You may build strategies for overnight gains with clearly specified risk with earnings events and weekly options. There are many ways to benefit from the trend to the range of any kind of market situation.

Security – The options trading program will serve as a hedge against certain investments, depending on an acceptable strategy in prevailing market conditions. This is a way of using defensive puts.

Risk – The trading structure of good options reduces risk in two essential ways. Cost is the first method. The option prices are very small relative to the same quantity of inventory. The second way issues end. A successful system will easily reduce losses and keep them low.

The more tools in your toolbox, the more able you are to adjust business conditions. Unless the markets were to act in the same way every day, trading would become a play for children. To start designing your options trading, you have to build a trading strategy or strategy to lead you in the right direction.

Start with the basic framework and tweak it to identify and enhance your trading criteria. It takes time and experience to develop a productive options trading program that can return 100 percent or more in consistently profitable businesses. If you are pleased with your machine parameters, you can look at the automatic trading of your own program.

Five Steps to Get Started With an Options Trading System

Pick a strategy – You can select any strategy to start developing a program. The best way to get going is to buy calls and puts. You will add new approaches to your trade to boost your method by researching and understanding more about how prices move.

Adding long-term equity protected calls and protections is a sensible next step, so that you can debit your account by generating a monthly or weekly cash flow.

Trade – It is time to trade once you have established the fundamentals of your strategy. Start small contracts, one or two contracts, and keep detailed transaction records. Be sure to include the underlying inventory price at the time you purchased or sold your right.

Notes will allow you to evaluate how and where you can change. When you add new trading requirements to your system, your statistics should be strengthened. If not, it is time to re-evaluate your given criteria.

Measure-Assess the successes and shortcomings

The duration of the research depends on the amount you traded. If you trade actively, it is important to have a weekly or monthly summary. Compare your winnings to your losses. Zero on the main factors that make up a good trade and seek to change your parameters to boost your results.

Analyze your mistakes as frustrating as it can be. Tune the requirements to avoid the same errors again. Analyzing your errors is as critical, if not more, to research your productive businesses.

Change – If there is a losing streak or spot in your option trading scheme, change it. Adjust it. It's no shame to be wrong. This is part of the trading industry. The irony is that you are blind to and repeat your mistakes. You are likely to fail in trade by feeding your ego and justifying your failure with excuses.

You will keep the device in line with changing business patterns and conditions by identifying the blind spots and making modifications. It sounds so basic, but perseverance and discipline are important.

Know – A method of trading is not static. Keep your mind engaged by learning always. The more you research the stock market and the trading system of options, the more you learn and the better. If a trading system for options were like a tic-tac-toe, we would all be rich.

Thankfully, options' trading is not as dull as a kid's game. Learn something new every day and integrate it into your trading program of options.

CHAPTER - 26

Volatility

The majority of types of trading get affected by a very important aspect, and that is volatility. Volatility is common in the trading of options as well. Anything tends to have a drastic change or fluctuate. In the investment terms, it is linked to the price rate of any kind of trading instrument that tends to move up and down. A financial instrument that comes along with a not so stable price rate is termed to have low volatility. On the contrary, a financial instrument that makes sharp movements in the price rate in any fixed direction is termed to have high volatility. You can measure the volatility of the markets of financing as well. When it is very tough to properly predict the condition of a market and the concerned prices tend to have rapid change daily, the market is called to be volatile in nature.

In the world of options trading, volatility plays a very important role as it comes with the power of imparting some effects on the price of the option. The majority of beginner traders cannot understand the related signs to volatility properly. This ultimately results in the development of huge problems. You won't be able to be a successful options trader without having proper knowledge about the volatility of the market.

Understanding Volatility

Volatility is the rate of the speed and amount related to changes. In the world of financing, it is the rate of the price movement of any financial instrument. Before starting with trade of any kind, it is important to gain proper knowledge about the price of the related instrument. You are also required to know the rate by which the price is most likely to change. It is a very useful tool, as with the help of volatility, you can determine the price of any trading instrument in the future. While talking about options trading, two main types of volatility are taken to be important. The first one is the historical volatility which determines the volatility of the past. In short, it helps in determining the changes in price that happened in the past over a certain period. The second one is the implied volatility, which projects the price changes in the future.

Historical Volatility

It is also known as statistical volatility. It helps in determining the price changes of the underlying security. It finds out the speed at which the price of the underlying security has moved. So, the higher the value of statistical volatility, the more has been the price movement for the underlying assets. The price movement is determined for a particular period. Theoretically, when the value of SV is higher, it indicates that the underlying asset's price has high chances to have some significant movement in the upcoming days. However, it only indicates a price movement of the future and does not guarantee anything.

One thing that you should always keep in mind regarding statistical volatility is that it is incapable of providing an insight into which particular direction the price will move. When the SV is high, it indicates that the security price has been rapidly moving up and down over a certain time. But, it also indicates that the current price might not have gone too far than the actual price. Similarly, when the value of SV is low, it indicates that there hasn't been much movement in the price of the security. But, it might be making a steady move in one direction at a particular speed.

The investors use SV for having a clear idea about the price change of the underlying asset, which relies on the changing speed of the past. There is no need to find out the present trend.

Implied Volatility

It is also known as projected volatility. Implied volatility is called IV in short. It is the volatility estimate of the future days for any underlying security. It is the projection of the speed along with the price of any underlying security that is most likely to move. The majority of traders are concerned about the total profit in addition to the time that is left until the expiry date as the prime factors for determining the option price. However, IV also acts as a very important factor in determining the option price. IV is calculated by considering various factors: the price of the underlying security, option's strike price, time left till the expiry date, statistical volatility, along with the current interest rate.

Since IV helps to indicate the price movement of an underlying asset, the price will be higher when the value of implied volatility is also higher. The main reason behind this is that for generating some potential profit, the underlying asset's price needs to show some drastic movement in price.

CHAPTER - 27

Financial Leverage

By definition, Options trading is a speculative stock market trading practice where traders try to profit from any future specific stock price movements. It entails predicting the chances of a particular stock price going up in a set period and staking on its resulting future profit. Its concept is almost akin to gambling, but on unknowable stock price fluctuations within a strict time frame. An option trading is contractual and is bound by stipulations within a fixed period.

We are now going to look at four primary areas of interest concerning options trading, as explained below:

What is Financial Leverage in Options Trading?

When you engage in options trading, you participate in what is called financial leverage. Financial leverage refers to the concept that instead of buying the stock outright and paying the full share price amount, you can put up an initial less capital. Besides, based on the type of your options trade, you can enhance the return on your equity within or after the set time frame. Often, the amount of capital you leverage is lower than the actual share price of the stock. This apparent less capital is what gives options trading its appeal.

Advantages of Financial Leverage in Options Trading

You have rights. There are two types of options, both of which have rights: call option and put option. Call options allow you to buy shares at a given strike cost before the expiry of that contract's duration. On the other hand, put options will enable you to sell a specific amount of your stock at an agreed price any time within the stipulated period of the trade contract.

You will own a given number of shares as stipulated in the options contract. We call it the option contract multiplier (most options have a multiplier of x100) which means you get to own 100 shares of stock per option. Any return on your prospect is factored into this multiplier, giving you an accurate figure on your overall investment return. This multiplier is the number of shares that your option contract can be converted into if you exercised that option. You can use your right to sell your trade contract at any time within the stipulated time frame as long as it is before the expiry date.

Your profit margins are highly magnified when compared to directly buying stocks and selling them at a profit later. In an options trading scenario, you leverage your investment at a given strike price against a future rise in the share price of that same stock price. Now, if the stock price rises as per your speculation, the return on your investment will be much higher than direct stock trading. Your profit margin ratio is much higher, as shown by this example:

Let us assume a current stock price of $20. A broker predicts the stock price to rise to $30 in a month. The trader issues a call option to buy the 20call for $5 strike price, which expires in 1 month.

Given an option contract multiplier of 100, you can see below the marked difference in profit margin between direct stock trade of 100 shares and options trade at the specified strike price.

If the final stock price is $30 in a month:

- Direct stock trade gives you a profit of $1000, which is 50% of the original investment.

- Options trade gives you a profit of $500, which is 100% of the original investment.

If the final stock price is $35 in a month:

- Direct stock trade gives you a profit of $1500, which is 75% of the original investment.

- Options trade gives you a profit of $1000, which is 200% of the original investment.

Your initial cost is low. Buying options are less expensive than buying stock since it depends on the strike price at which you purchased the option. Buying stock depends on the stock price, which is usually markedly higher than the strike price. It, therefore, becomes favorable for you to buy a stake in the stock at a discounted rate.

Your call option value goes up whenever the share price rises above the stipulated initial cost.

Your put option value goes up as the share price falls below the stipulated initial cost.

You have an extra revenue stream. Profits from options trading are a source of income for your business. Given the potential for much higher returns than conventional profit revenues, it gives you the ability to engage in much more ambitious business endeavors.

Financial leverage in options trading allows you to settle debts incurred in the course of business. Your business may have a margin account used to accrue debt and leverage the debt in an options contract in anticipation of receiving markedly higher returns. Once you have taken care of liabilities, options trading gives you room to invest in other business opportunities.

Disadvantages of Financial Leverage in Options Trading

You have obligations when you sell, depending on your options. When you are selling a call option, you are obligated to sell a specified amount of shares for the determined amount whenever any call buyers trigger their contract. As a put option seller, you must buy a given number of stocks for a listed amount whenever any put buyers use their commitment. Your obligations force you into buying and selling at strike prices with much higher loss margins than if you had traded at the final stock prices.

Your get magnified losses. In as much as your returns may have a higher profit margin, the same margin also applies to stock prices which move in the opposite direction to the ones initially speculated. These losses have a significant higher-margin compared to losses incurred in cases of direct stocks trading. You end up with disproportionate losses, which can leave you in financial ruin.

You are exposed to higher risks. Losing on your leverage does not depend on an unfavorable final stock price per se. In case your final stock price remains the same as the initial strike price by the end of the options period, you lose the whole of your initial investment. Using the earlier example, you can see this situation:

Let us assume a current stock price of $20. A broker predicts the stock price to rise to $30 in a month. The trader issues a call option to buy the 20call for $5 strike price, which expires in 1 month.

Given an option contract multiplier of 100, you can see the difference between the direct stock trade returns from 100 shares and the effect on options trade when the stock price remains the same.

If the final stock price is $20 in a month:

- Direct stock trade gives you neither profit nor loss since the original investment remains unchanged.

- Options trade makes you lose your original investment of $500 since the call option becomes worthless at an unchanged final stock price.

It costs more to return to your original capital baseline. In cases where you incur losses, it will paradoxically cost you more to regain your initial investment. Look at the following example:

- If you had $1000 capital and lost 25%, you remain at $7500. Now, to regain your original money, you need to make a profit of $2500 from your existing $7500 (which means a return of 33% on $7500). As you can see, you will need a much higher yield of 33% to cover an initial loss of 25%.

- Your put option loses value if the final share price rises above your specified initial value. Also, the closer you get to the option's expiration, the less valuable it becomes.

The value of your call option depreciates when the final share price goes below the initial cost amount.

Fear of the unknown. You depend on a chance or probability situation to go your way, and market forces have a nature of unpredictability. When leveraging high-risk accounts such as margin accounts your debt liability increases significantly. You become overleveraged and possibly may lead you into bankruptcy.

You are contract-bound. The contract specifies the conditions and duration relating to the option. Terms become void once the expiration period has lapsed. When the market trend on stock prices is not going your way, you do not have the option of opting out as a means to avoid further loss. You will have to wait it out and incur the full loss at the end of the specified period.

You may become addicted. Any situation in life, which promises the chance of a higher return from little or no input, is prone to be abused. When it comes to money, people's greed knows no bounds. You may end up in a vicious loop of perpetual leveraging to gain higher and higher returns despite of losses. A loss leads to a tendency to try to recover what was lost. The cycle becomes self-propagating.

Options trading in valued stock are expensive. Stocks with lower strike prices will cost you more because they are valuable to traders. Whenever you engage in financial leveraging within options trading, you will prefer to buy options at a much lower stock price, which has the potential to increase in value. However, options that involve these highly volatile stocks are valuable and tend to cost you more.

You have a deadline. Every option trade has a specified time frame within which the financial leverage is of value. Beyond the expiration date, your options can no longer trade. There is a limited window for your stock to gain profit.

Risk Management in Options Trading

You should only leverage what you can afford to lose. Risk in options trading is significantly higher than typical stock trading. Therefore, Options trading is discouraged unless you have the financial capacity to cushion against significant losses. For instance, if your business has vast capital reserves or multiple steady revenue streams.

Avoid debt at all costs. You should avoid financing your strike capital using debt. The more overleveraged you become, the more likely you are to end in bankruptcy or collapse your business. Remember, the more debt you accrue, the more difficult it becomes to settle it.

You need to exercise financial responsibility. You have to know that addictive behavior may arise if you are not vigilant. Initial profitable returns have a habit of clouding your judgment from the high risks involved. Always be aware that you are leveraging your money on the chance of an outcome that is not guaranteed. Do not get into a routine because those initial profits encourage habit-formation. Given the high margin that potential losses are magnified into, you may end up losing more than you bargained for leading to your bankruptcy.

You should equip yourself with fundamental skills on options trading. You need to know the stock trading options that are in the market. You have to understand all the potential risks associated with each one and make an informed choice as to which option suits you. In as much as you look forward to accruing the benefits of a given trade, you should appreciate their disadvantages and potential downsides as well.

Seek expert assistance in options trading. Options trading are hard for the individual trader who may not have a grasp on the various market forces, which influence stock prices. You need to seek help from industry experts such as brokers. Stockbrokers and brokerage firms, which specialize in options trading, have a vast array of resources to make informed predictions. Such brokers have the experience to identify the profitability potential of any options and will advise you accordingly. In addition to trading via brokerages, your fiscal responsibility remains intact since it falls on the brokers to minimize risk.

CHAPTER - 28

The Most Common Questions about Trading

1. Can you live on trading?

Yes, just as you can live from medicine, from being a teacher, from being an architect, engineer, or lawyer. You require the same weapons: education, training, practice, guidance, discipline, perseverance, and a lot of determination to be a great professional in your field. Trading is no different. Perhaps many people have been wrong to think that when opening an account in a broker, funding their accounts, and starting trading means having the results to live from trading in less than what a rooster sings and being millionaires. Very wrong!!! It's like pretending to be a surgeon overnight. If you can live from trading, the question is, do you have what it takes to do it and achieve it?

2. What do I do to start trading?

The first and most important thing is to educate yourself about what trading is and how to do it effectively. Start by knowing the nature of trading, what it is about, how you win, who participates, how is the market that has been chosen, etc., are some of the things you should keep in mind. Don't get to war empty-handed. Go prepared. How? Find someone to inspire you, to teach these things, to guide you, invest money and time in your education. There are many online trading schools, and you can be overwhelmed at first by searching, but choose the one that has a simple system, that its philosophy resonates with you, and that has your feet set on the ground. Avoid those that promote phrases like "fast millionaire trading in the Stock Exchange," "trading is straightforward," etc. You have to be realistic, and a school that tells you from the beginning what is trading, how it works, how it is earned, how it is lost and that it is not as easy as many want to make it believe in profiting, is a school that is worth considering.

3. When will I start seeing results?

When you have firmly rooted in a simple trading system, faithfully and disciplined, fulfilling your trading plan and adequately managing the risk-benefit, paradoxically, you will also begin to see the results when you detach yourself from the results and focus on the process. The process of trading involves the observation and reflection of our performance, the emotions experienced, the most frequent mistakes and annihilation, the analysis of the logbook, and the correction of the things that you can change and improve. You will begin to see results when, in addition to all these things, you continue working on your mind without giving up.

4. How much money can I start trading, and what broker should I use?

It depends on each broker and the instrument you use. If you want to trade stock options in Thinkorswim, for example, you will need at least $ 2,000 to access the options. If you're going to trade with stocks, you will need $ 25,000. With the other brokers, it will be different. On the website of the brokers are the most frequent questions and customer service that can take you from all doubts regarding minimum money to start, documents such as funds and how to remove, etc. Find the broker that is regulated, that has a good reputation that other people are using and tell you about their experience.

5. How much money per month can I generate by trading?

The one that allows you the size of your account and the amount you are going to invest per operation, as long as you have the capabilities required to make money consistently. This brings us to question # 1. It's that easy.

6. How to achieve consistency?

Consistency is achieved by having consistent behaviors and actions. That is if I have planned trading that tells me what it looks like an opportunity, where to go, where to place the stop, how to manage and how to manage risk, and do it over and over again which tells me that plan consistently then I'll have consistent results. But, if you change the policy, each has a stop, or every time you have a losing streak, then you will go into an endless loop in which as emotional and impatient trader will modify, or change it again and again, the plan and the results will be different. This is what happens to 95% who lose money doing trading; there is no clear, defined, and precise plan to follow consistently, disciplined, and with a lot of confidence.

7. What is the best strategy or trading system?

The one that is simple to understand, that you can even explain it to a child and the child understands it. Stay away from those systems that require more than five different indicators, that your attention away from price action scribbles filling your screen and does not have proper management of risk-benefit. The best strategy or system is simple, clear, proven (functional), and above all, fits your personality and type of trader. The method of a trader may not be the system that suits you; for that reason, you must define what type of trader you are if you are scalper, intraday or swing, and of course, your risk tolerance (conservative or risky). These are just a few things to consider when choosing a trading system.

8. I have lost much of my capital; what do I do?

If you have lost a large part of your capital, it is because you do not have a clear, defined and proven trading plan, there are no consistent behaviors that lead to consistent results; emotions dominate you, and there is also no proper risk-benefit management. In that sentence is the answer to this question. What you should do is simple: make a clear trading plan with a clear and straightforward strategy, try it in a demo, manage risk-benefit properly, trust 100% in your plan, work on your emotions being aware of them before, during and after of operations, record, and evaluate to be able to learn from your failures.

If the results are positive, return to real account and repeat the process focusing your attention on the emotions you experience and your reactions.

9. What actions do you recommend operating to start?

I recommend trading stocks that do not have a widespread, that are not very volatile and offer economic contracts near ITM. These are terms that you may not understand if you are starting. Once you know what the ideal requirements are, go to the Finviz map of actions and look for the best-known actions in each sector, write them down, go to your platform and look at their contract and spread grid, so you are choosing and removing from the list until having your ideal portfolio of at least 6 shares.

10. I have no time to trading regularly, what are my options?

You can choose to do swing trading. The swing will allow you to open an operation today and close it several days later. Some brokers have mobile applications that allow you to monitor operations from your cell phone. If the situation is that you cannot trade in the morning, you can choose to make a trading plan for the afternoon hours, and it will work the same.

CONCLUSION

Thank you for making it to the end. Bearing in mind that an option is all about the right to buy a stock, it might seem strange that most traders are not looking to do that. Instead, they are looking to immediately pass the stock on as a sell, making the profit by taking the premium along with the increased price on the stock from what they paid for it.

That's what you should be basing your strategy around: the idea of gaining stocks to instantly sell back onto the options market, making your profit in the process. In 99 out of 100 cases, that's what you will be aiming to do.

Nevertheless, there are still going to be times when you want to exercise your right to purchase the underlying stock itself. Usually, this is when you genuinely want to add a particular stock to your portfolio. It's up to you to decide when those times arrive.

First things first: be very aware that you will automatically exercise your right at the expiration date if the option is in the money unless you tell your broker not to take that action. That won't happen if it's out of the money, but it's still imperative that you keep a calendar of your trades so that you aren't surprised by the sudden arrival of stocks in your portfolio you'd completely forgotten about.

If and when you decide to exercise your right, you should almost always do it at the expiration date and not before, because you'll lose the time value if you exercise early. When you alert your broker to this decision, it's also important to know that you cannot then change your mind–the decision is permanent.

Buying puts can be a winning strategy if done right. The stock market wouldn't be the stock market if it only moved in one direction; by buying puts as well as calls, you're making the most of the market by profiting no matter which direction it is heading. Puts, during a bear market, are your ally.

Buying a put means that you are going to make a profit through the stock declining in price. Just as you're looking for the stock to skyrocket in a call, you're looking for it to plunge in a put. The strategy is therefore very similar; it's just that you're looking in the opposite direction.

Most traders buy puts either because they are speculating on a stock or think they can make a profit in a short term as that stock plummets, or because they can function as insurance for your overall portfolio. If you actually own the stock in question, you can buy puts on it if you believe it's at risk of heading downwards.

For instance, let's say you own stocks in a company and you think the business environment is going to see the share price drop. You aren't sure, but you can make an educated guess, simply leaving that stock sitting in your portfolio means potentially watching as its value bleeds away.

On the other hand, you could buy a put and give yourself the option to offload that stock if it does drop to a certain value. As the buyer, you are not obligated to sell your stock when the deadline arrives–you're just giving yourself the option to do so. Of course, as always, you'll lose the premium.

The biggest difference between buying calls and puts is that the stock market has a habit of falling much faster than it rises. A stock can drop through the floor in just a single day, whereas it can take weeks or months to climb to magical figures.

To buy puts for the sake of speculation, you'll need to master the art of spotting weaker stocks–the ones that are likely to fall. This is easiest during a bear market and when the overall economic outlook is poor.

Even the most successful companies have downtimes, after all, and if you own a put contract when that happens, you stand to make money.

When buying a put, you'll need to think in reverse. The lower the strike price, the cheaper the option will be (in other words, the opposite of buying a call). You should also factor in the speed of the market when looking at expiration dates. If you think the stock is going to drop hard and fast, you probably want a shorter deadline. If you think it will take a while for the full effects of the drop to realize, then you will want a longer one.

The most successful put strategies, at least at first, will probably be slightly in the money, because you can profit from a smaller change in the underlying value. Conversely, you'll make more money on a smaller premium with an out of the money put, but you have less chance of actually making that money.

Selling puts can be a gamble. The idea behind it is that, by selling your promise to buy stocks, you are earning a steady premium, but you're choosing contracts that you believe will never hit the strike price. That way, you walk away having been paid for the contract without having to actually own the underlying stock.

It's also a way to increase your stock portfolio and get paid for doing so. This can be useful if you think a stock's dropping price is temporary and you want to snap up a few of them before they start to rise again when you can sell them on.

Be aware, of course, that when selling a put you are obligating yourself to buy that stock if it does reach the strike price, so it's a bad gamble if you lack the funds to do that when the deadline comes. I hope you have learned something!

OPTIONS TRADING

STRATEGIES

OPTIONS TRADING ADVANCED
STRATEGIES AND TECHNIQUES IN
THE MARKET ENVIRONMENT

MATTHEW MORRIS

TABLE OF CONTENTS

INTRODUCTION

If you are considering investing in the stock market, one of the best places to start is options trading. Once you understand the fundamentals of the game, the technicalities involve the market conditions and have acquired the right mindset; you are ready to start your options trading business.

When it comes to investing, the very first thing to do before considering venturing into any market is to acquire knowledge. You may have enough cash in your bank or savings account for which you are considering investing or trading in the market. But to minimize the risk, you have to first of all invest in your education.

With little or no money, anyone can start a successful options trading in the market and do very well, as well as the fundamentals of the game are learned. As Christopher Smith, a successful options trader said, you need to ensure that you spend a considerable amount of time learning how successful options traders play the game.

Many people are making it big in options trading and you are no exception. You can start small, build on your experience through practice and then become a successful options trader, making huge sums of money all from the comfort of your home. Even though options trading has become popular in recent times due to digital technology and many other factors, this line of trading in the financial market has been there since mid-century BBC.

Options trading has been known to have originated from the Greeks. While the trading and market size has grown in volume as a result of the number of people playing the game, the underlying principles involve options trading has always been with us. The very first account of options trading can be traced to a book written by the Greek Philosopher, Aristotle in the fourth-century B.B.C entitled, "Politics." In this book, a man named Thales of Miletus, who was an autonomist and mathematician, studied the stars and realized that there's going to be a huge demand for olive presses.

Being convicted of his prediction, he set out to profit from it. At the time of his prediction, he didn't have enough funds available to buy all the olive presses. Therefore, Thales resolved to buy the rights to the olive presses prior to their harvest. Lo and behold, everything went as he predicted, during harvest time, he resold his rights to the olive presses to dealers who needed them the most and made a huge amount of profit.

In the case of Thales, it will be said that he bought a call option, and was successfully exercised at the time of the contract, amounting in a sizeable amount of profit. During those times, it was, however, not called options trading. But, in the same way, Thales understand and leverage the principles of options trading, you can also do so as long as you learn the fundamentals of options trading.

Another incidence of options trading was recalled during the Tulip Mania of 1636. It was the first mass options trading in history. Due to the soaring price of tulip bulbs during those times, options trading was created to help producers earn a substantial gain from the market volatility. Tulips were in high demand during those days leading to a large amount of Dutch growers getting into the business of tulip production. To ensure they secure a definite buying price, they created put options and started trading options. This enabled many of them to profit immensely as tulip bulbs became a hot commodity.

Options have been referred to as a derivative. This is because options don't stand on their own like other securities such as stocks and bonds. They are rather a derivative of another security. They find their relevance from the value of another asset. Due to the demands of the market at the time regarding a particular asset class, a derivative can be created for the benefit of either the buyer or the seller.

The juice is a derivative of an orange, and wine is a derivative of grape. Without the orange, the juice will not exist in the face place. For the orange juice to exit, then the orange must already be in existence and be active. Also, the value of the juice is determined by the local and international market conditions regarding the orange.

Options are a type of derivative. They are called derivatives of financial securities, thereby obtaining their performance, value, relevance and market status from the underlying investment product associated with it. Options can be created from securities such as stocks, bonds, mutual funds, real estate properties, and many others. However, options trading is usually used in connotation with stock trading in the stock market through brokerage investment firms.

Basically, there are two main types of options: call options and put options. Each has its own benefits and advantages. Again, you have to make a well-calculated risk before using any type of option.

Call & Put Options

Call Options

This is the oldest form of the option used. It is a standardized contract agreement that gives the associated investor the right to buy underlying security or asset at a specified price within a specified certain period of time.

Usually, when an investor realizes that a particular stock will move up within a period of time, he buys a call option to enable him "make a profit" from the volatility of that stock in the financial market.

On the other hand, a stockholder may hold a particular stock for a period of time and then notices that the stock is likely to go down. To hedge himself against the risk, the investor will decide to sell call options at a pre-determined price to mitigate the risk of downward movement of the stock.

What you need to know is that in a call option, there are two parties involved. One person is selling a call while the other person is buying a call. One financial expert has made it known that stocks are finite these days unless the shareholding companies decide to divide the stocks and create more liquidity. Otherwise, options trading serve as the way of buying into the share of a particular company without bearing much risk at the time of the options contract.

Put Options

A put option is a contract that gives an investor the right to sell an underlying security or asset at a pre-determined price within a specified period of time. In this case, an investor might be assuming that an underlying stock price may drop further; therefore, he decides to take on a protection position to hedge against potential losses.

A put option can be compared to an insurance policy. Say, you just bought a nice car, but you know the risks associated with owning a car. A lot of things can happen to that car. Therefore, you decided to purchase vehicle insurance to protect you against any accidental damage to your home. Either monthly or yearly, you will be required to pay an insurance premium to activate your insurance package. In this case, the insurance has a face value and gives you protection when the car should have an accident.

Consider your stock in ABC Company as the insurance. Instead of securing your vehicle, you're rather securing your stock investment against potential losses. For example, a stock investor may fear that one of his stock portfolios will lose more than 10% of its long position in the market. To hedge against the losses, they buy a put option.

If the stock is selling at 1,500 per share, you can then buy a put option that is going to allow you to sell a share at $ 1,250 during the specified term of the put contract. Let's say within the six months, you successfully sold your put option to another options trader at $ 1,250.00 for 100 shares.

Then two months later, your stock predictions came through. In this case, you have earned $ 250 for the 100 shares that will be sold. This enables you to make $ 25,000 overall on the entire transaction. If the market value of the share doesn't drop, the only thing you will lose is the initial premium paid for the put option. This example might be overly simple, but you will get the basics of how a put option works.

Normally, the high the strike price of the put option, the greater the intrinsic value of the underlying stock. And an intrinsic value of a share is not dependent on the market value of the share. Intrinsic is usually used by investors using fundamental investing to invest in a stock for a long term to obtain dividends without worrying too much about the volatility of share value in the market value.

Long-Term Options & Short-Term Options

Options can either be long term or short term. Short term options are the type of option that expires within generally a year. Some short term options do expire weekly, monthly, bi-monthly or quarterly. It is all determined by the contract stipulation at the time of signing. For example, most index and EFT options are weekly.

They are usually used by investors in short term stock or index speculation. On the other hand, long term options have more than a year to exercise a strike. This kind of securities is known as long term equity anticipation securities (LEAP). Options trader with a long term perceptive on the stock market usually takes their approach to manage their stock portfolio.

When it comes to the financial market, one of the questions most people ask a lot is the difference between trading and investing. Well, it is very important that you understand these fundamentals as you proceed with your options trading strategies. A keep understanding of these terminologies will help you carve out your plan to make a profit in the financial markets.

Sometimes, it can be very difficult to clarify the difference between investing and trading. However, they are not difficult at all. Actually, trading is the art of making profits in the financial market over a short period of time by looking at the rising and falling of the market. A trader makes his or her profit by timing the market and analyzing the volatility of the stocks.

An investor, on the other hand, doesn't focus on the profit of the stock on a short-term basis. He focuses on the value of the stock in the long run. Therefore, he invests for the long term, five, ten, twenty, and sometimes for several years. An investor's focus is to create wealth in the financial market over an extended period of time by buying and holding a high-quality portfolio of stocks, bonds, mutual funds, and other investment vehicles.

An investor's main goal is to compound profits through reinvesting profits or dividends earned to acquire additional shares of stock. An investor can be compared to a farmer. He takes a seed, plants it into the ground and takes care of the seed, and then the seed starts producing fruits. It might take a long time for the fruits to start appearing but the investors are patient enough to wait for the fruits to come. The fruits will be harvested and sold for profit for which the farmer will derive dividends.

CHAPTER - 1

Understanding Stock Options

To get an understanding of the meaning of stock options, we first must know the meaning of the two words independently.

Stock Refers To:

The total money a company has from selling shares to individuals.

A portion of the ownership of the company that can be sold to members of the public

Option (Finance) Refers To:

Now that we know the meaning of both stocks and options, we can easily define stock options. We can define the term in the following ways:

Stock options provide an investor with the right to sell or buy a stock at a set price and date.

The stock option can also refer to an advantage in the form of an opportunity provided by a company to any employee to buy shares in a company at an agreed-upon fixed price or a discount.

Stock options have been a topic of interest in recent years. We are having more and more people engaging in options trading. The profitability of stock options has resulted in a lot of debates. Some say it has a scam; others claim that it is not a worthy investment, while others say that they are minting millions from it. All these speculations draw us to one question, what are stock options? For us to accurately answer this question, we will have to go through stock options keenly. We will be required to know all about it and what it entails. This information makes it easy to make judgments with facts as opposed to using assumptions. You will get to say something that you can back up. Having knowledge gives you an added advantage and places you in a powerful position.

As a novice trader, acquiring information will transform your trading abilities. Having the necessary skills and knowledge will make you an expert in trading within a matter of time. This will provide you with the knowledge you need before engaging in a stock option. It is a good thing that you have taken the first step in getting this. It indicates that you are ready and will learn, and that is a major move. Asides from acquiring knowledge, it is crucial that you learn to implement it. This will mean practically doing that which you have learned. Some people acquire knowledge, but they are unable to utilize it for their own benefit effectively. I hope that after you go through this, you will have the courage to trade a stock option. This mainly addresses the beginners, and it is written to make a difference in their life. I will proceed to take you through stock options and make you aware of what it entails.

Understanding Stock Options

For us to Understand Stock Options, We Consider the Following:

Styles

There are two main option styles. These are European and American options styles. If you intend to engage in options trading, it is advisable to equip yourself with knowledge of the various styles. As you analyze the styles, you will identify those that work for you and those that do not. You will also find that some styles are easier to learn and handle as opposed to others. You can decide to engage in the one that is convenient for you and avoid engaging in the style that you have difficulties understanding.

The American style option allows one to exercise a trade any period between the time of purchase and the time a contract expires. Most traders engage in this style due to its convenience. It allows one to carry out a trade any period within which a contract is valid. The European style option is not commonly used as compared to the American style. In the European option style, a trader can only exercise their options during the expiration date. If you are not an expert in options trading, I would advise you to avoid using the European style.

Expiration Date

An expiration date refers to the period in which a contract is regarded as worthless. Stocks have expiration dates. The period between when they were purchased and the expiry date, indicate the validity of an option. As a trader, you are expected to utilize the contracts to your advantage within this time frame. You can trade as much as you can and get high returns within the period of buying and the period of expiry. Learn to utilize the time provided adequately. If you are not careful, the option may expire before you get a chance to exercise it.

We may have beginners who assume this factor and end up making heavy losses. You will be required to be keen while engaging in the stock market. Forgetting to investigate the expiry date may result in your stocks being regarded as worthless without getting a chance of investing in them. In some rare cases, the stocks are exercised during the expiry date. This is common in the European option. I would not encourage a beginner to engage in this type of option. It is tricky and could lead to a loss if you are not careful while carrying out the trade.

Contacts

Contracts refer to the amount of shares an investor intends to purchase. One hundred shares of an underlying asset are equal to one contract. Contracts aid in establishing the value of s stock. Contracts tend to be valuable before the expiry date. After the expiry date, a contract can be regarded as worthless. Knowing this will help you discover the best time to exercise a contract. In a case where a trader purchases ten contracts, he or she gets to 10 $350 calls. When the stock prices go above $350, at the expiry trade, the trader gets the chance to buy or sell 1000 shares of their stock at $350. This happens regardless of the stock price at that time. In an event whereby the stock is lower than $350, the option will expire worthlessly. This will result in making a complete loss as an investor. You will lose the whole amount you used to purchase options, and there is no way of getting it back. If you intend to invest in options trading, it is good to become aware of the contracts and how you can exercise them for a profitable options trading outcome.

Premium

The premium refers to the money used to purchase options. You can obtain the premium by multiplying the call price and the number of contracts by 100. The '100' is the number of shares per contract. This is more like the investment made by the trader expecting great returns. While investing, you will expect that the investment you chose to engage in will result in a profitable outcome. No one gets in business anticipating a loss. You find that one is always hopeful that the investment they have chosen to engage in will be beneficial. You will constantly look forward to getting the best out of a trade.

The above factors tell us more about stocks. In case you were stuck and did not fully understand what stocks entail, now you have a better understanding. You will come across numerous terms when you decide to engage in stocks. Do not let the terms scare you; they are mostly things you knew, but just did not know that they go by those terms. We have many people who are quite investing in stocks just because they could not understand the various terms being used. This should not be the case. You can take some time to go through the terms and understand what they entail carefully.

Options in the Stock Market

Stock options are not as hard as people make them appear. At times people try to make them seem difficult, yet it is an easy thing that can be grasped by almost everyone. As a beginner, do not be discouraged into thinking that options trading is a difficult investment. You will be surprised how easy it is, and you will wonder why you never invested in it sooner. When engaging in stock options, there are four factors the investors will have to consider. Putting these factors into consideration will have a positive impact on their trade.

The Right, but not the Obligation

What comes in your mind when you read this statement? Well, when we talk or rights, we mean that you have the freedom to purchase a certain type of option. When we talk of obligation, we are referring to the fact that one does not have a legal authority to exercise a duty. Options do not give traders a legal authority to carry out a duty. This means that there is freedom to trade, but it is not legally mandated.

Buying or Selling

As a trader, you are given the right to purchase or trade an option. There are two types of stock that one can choose from. We have the put option and the call option. Both differ and have their pros and cons. If you intend to trade in options, it is important that you equip yourself with adequate knowledge before trading or purchasing stocks. This information will have an impact on your expected income. The stocks you choose to buy or sell will dictate if you will earn high returns or if you will end up making a loss.

Set Price

There is a certain price that has been set to exercise the option. The price will vary depending on the option type. Some stock options tend to be valued more than other options. There are several factors that will influence the price of options. As you continue reading this, you will come across those factors. Knowing them will help you know when to carry out a trade, and when not to carry out a trade, depending on the influence of the factors; a trade may generate a high income or end up resulting in a loss.

Expiry Date

The expiry date is when a contract will be considered useless. Stock options have an expiry date. The date is set to determine the value of an option. Any period before the expiration date, a contact is regarded as being valid. This means that it can be utilized to generate income at any point before the expiry date. When it gets to the expiry date, a trader has no power to exercise the option. This is as a result of the contract being regarded as worthless. As an investor, it is good to constantly ensure that your investment is within the duration of its validity.

CHAPTER - 2

The Concept of Moneyness

A Few More Basic Concepts You Need to Understand are Explained Below:

ITM, OTM and ATM Options

ITM (in-the-money), OTM (out-of-the-money), and ATM (at-the-money) are three acronyms that will be frequently referred to in options trading.

ITM options are options that have an intrinsic value. In other words, if they were to be exercised at that point, they would yield some money. Any call option with a strike price less than the market price of the underlying stock/index is an ITM option. Any put option that has a strike price greater than the market price of the underlying stock/index is an ITM option. The intrinsic value of an ITM option is the positive difference between its underlying stock's market price and the option's strike price.

Let's put it this way – when a stock's price rises and crosses the strike price of an associated call option, then that call option becomes ITM. Similarly, when a stock's price falls below the strike price of an associated put option, then that put option becomes ITM.

For example, if Stock 'X' is trading at 500, then any put option of X with a strike price greater than 500 is an ITM option and any call option of X with a strike price less than 500 is an ITM option.

OTM options are the opposite of ITM options. They do not have any intrinsic value. At the time of expiry, every single OTM option expires worthless. Any call option with its strike price greater than the market price of its underlying stock/index and any put option with its strike price less than the market price of its underlying stock/index are OTM options.

For example, if stock 'Y' is trading at 500, then all call options of Y with a strike price greater than 500 and all put options of Y with a strike price less than 500 are OTM options.

ATM options are such options for which the strike prices are currently the same as the underlying's market price. Therefore, an ATM option can easily become an OTM option or an ITM option with any change in the market price of the underlying.

Here's a Quick Reference Chart that Depicts These Three Types of Options:

The main thing you should know is that at the time of expiry, only ITM options would have any associated value, while at that time, OTM and ATM options would be worthless.

	Call Option	Put Option
ITM	SP of Option<MP of Stock	SP of Option>MP of Stock
OTM	SP of Option>MP of Stock	SP of Option<MP of Stock
ATM	SP of Option = MP of Stock	SP of Option = MP of Stock

Where SP = Strike-Price, MP = Market Price

When to Exit an Options Trade

We saw how options were exercised successfully. In the real world, however, few traders would wait until the expiry date to take home their profits.

Squaring off the options contract early when in profit, instead of waiting for a chance to exercise the option, makes a lot of sense–this is especially true for European style options in which the exercising of an option can be done only at the time of expiry.

Either way, irrespective of whether a given option follows the American or European style, it is far more prudent to square-off a trade, when in profit, rather than waiting till expiry to exercise the option and risk losing that profit (or even ending in a loss) in the event of a reversal in the direction of the underlying stock.

Note: After you enter an options trade, you exit that trade

by squaring-off your position–this means if you are a buyer, you have to sell to close your position, and if you are a seller, you have to buy to close your position. However, at the time of expiry, if you haven't closed an open position, your position gets squared-off automatically based on the price of the underlying stock/index.

We know what happened after Bob bought a call option from Jacob - the market price for a cow eventually rose to $2,500 from the original $2,000 and Bob exercised his option, claimed his cows, and sold them off at the market price, thereby closing his trade for a handsome profit.

If this particular example was an actual stock market trade and if Bob was dealing with a stock market option, then Bob would have had the ability to exercise his option before the expiry date only if his options contract followed the American style of expiry.

In the event that Bob had an options contract that could only be exercised at the time of expiry (European style), and his position was already in profits well before the expiry date, he would not have ideally waited till the expiry date to book his profit. He would have booked a profit much earlier by selling off the options contract itself.

If you remember correctly, when Bob bought the option from Jacob, he paid a premium of $50 for the option (the overall contract amount was $250 since it covered 5 cows) and Bob's contract entitled him to buy Jacob's cows at $2,000 each. At that time, the market price for a cow was also $2,000. Therefore, in options terminology, we can say the market price of the stock was equal to the strike price of the option when Bob bought his option, or in other words, that particular option was an ATM option.

The last statement also implies that Bob's option had no intrinsic value at the time of purchase. If the market price for a cow hadn't appreciated and had remained at $2,000 for the duration of the contract validity, this option's premium value of $50 would have eroded each day and the option would have eventually expired worthless. Nevertheless, the premium of that option was $50 to begin with because it had one full month remaining for expiry, therefore, time-value.

In an alternate scenario, let us assume that 10 days after Bob's contract with Jacob was in place, Bob saw that cow prices had already touched $2,300. Since he had 20 more days remaining for expiry, Bob decides he doesn't want to wait till the expiry date and he would rather book a profit immediately by selling the call option itself to a third-party.

Bob bought the option for $50 at a strike price of $2,000 when the market price of the cow was $2,000. But when the market price for a cow went up to $2,300, the value of the call option itself owned by Bob would also have accordingly risen to about $310.

A rise from $50 to $310 is a rather steep climb up, isn't it?

Did you understand why the premium for Bob's option went up from $50 to $310 when the market price of a cow went up from $2,000 to $2,300?

It's not that complicated actually.

The option premium shots up because it is now deep in-the-money (ITM) and it has an intrinsic value of $300 already (the remaining $10 is time-value) whereas at the time the option was purchased, it was an ATM option and had no intrinsic value, but only a time-value of $50.

Previously when the market price of the cow was only $2,000, if Bob had exercised his contract; he would not have made any profit - he'd practically have to buy a cow at $2,000 (strike price) and sell it at $2,000 (market-price) were he to exercise his option immediately. However, when the market price of the cow went up to $2,300, Bob's contract entitled him to purchase Jacob's cows at the old price of $2,000 and therefore that contract's intrinsic value became $300 – in other words, exercising that option at that point in time would yield a profit of $300 (Market price of $2,300 minus the Strike price of $2,000).

With 20 days left before the expiry of the contract, there would also be some associated time premium (approximated to $10 in this case) and therefore, the value of one single call option contract would have jumped to $310 or so from the original $50.

Therefore, Bob just needed to sell that options contract to another trader at the current value of $310 to bag a profit of $260 on each cow which is covered by the contract ($260 = the current premium value of that call option, $310, minus the premium originally paid, $50). Bob's overall profit, therefore, would then be $260 x 5 (no. of cows covered as part of that contract) = $1300.

Bob will make a neat profit and the new owner of the

options contract Bob originally purchased from Jacob will now have to wait till the time of expiry to exercise that option or alternately, he/she too can sell the contract itself to a fourth person, if a suitable opportunity presents itself.

Having the discipline to sell off a contract when it becomes profitable is important, because if you hold on to it for too long, there is a possibility the tide may turn and you may end up losing a portion of your profits or may even end in a loss. Plus, if you are a buyer, then the advantage of selling an option as early as possible will ensure you retain maximum time premium, which would otherwise keep eroding everyday as the option approaches expiry.

Note 1: All options have an associated time-value and an intrinsic value - while the former is dependent on how far the option is from its expiry date and becomes zero at expiry, the latter is applicable only for ITM options and would be equal to the difference between the strike price of that option and the market price of the underlying.

Note 2: While the example above had mentioned that the premium of the option went from $50 to $310 when the price of a cow went up, the premium amount of $310 was an approximated amount for the sake of general understanding. In reality, the actual amount of appreciation in the premium could vary depending on the various factors that affect the options pricing at that time.

CHAPTER - 3

Simplified Examples of Options Trades

This profiles two trade examples that integrate the various topics covered in the book and summarize the comprehensive process for trading options. Each trade example is streamlined, focused only on key trade elements and is structured as follows:

SECTION	PHASE	DESCRIPTION
BACKGROUND	1	QUICK RATIONALE/SUMMARY IDENTIFICATION OF STRUCTURES PRICING, RISK/REWARD CALCULATIONS
PLAN & ENTRY	2 & 3	P&L PLAN, SETTING TARGET LEVELS ENTRY EXECUTION
MANAGE & EXIT	4 & 5	TRADE MANAGEMENT EXIT CONSIDERATIONS

As with the adjustment strategies, the trade examples represent the positive scenario, that is, the stock moves in one's favor – again, negative outcomes are assumed to trigger risk-reducing actions (primarily closing out the position, ideally at the predetermined loss target).

Trade Example #1

Background

Stock XYZ is a defense contractor whose stock is up over 20% year-to-date and now trades at $70. I expect (1) growing talk of government cutbacks (2) the stock's recent parabolic move and (3) its current elevated valuation to cause the stock to sell off from current levels and consolidate in a technical range of $65 to $70 by September. For this trade, I want to risk a maximum of $1,000.

Exhibit 6.1: XYZ Stock Chart

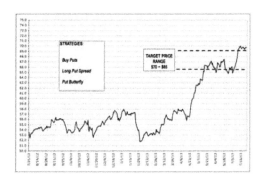

I am bearish XYZ stock and want to use only long Put strategies. I don't want to sell Calls given the recent parabolic move in the stock – I thus prefer to have my maximum risk defined at the outset. Here are the initial identified strategies to trade this situation:

Buy Puts

Buy Long Put Spread

Buy Put Butterfly Spread

Exhibit 6.2: XYZ Option Chain (Entry)

Stock: XYZ @ $69.58

Today: July 26

SERIES: SEPTEMBER

CALLS		PUTS		
BID	ASK	SERIES	BID	ASK
		SEP 62.5	0.23	0.27
		SEP 65.0	0.45	0.47
		SEP 67.5	0.91	0.96
		SEP 70.0	1.86	1.91

Based on the prices in the SEP option chain in Exhibit 6.2, the most interesting set-ups (in my opinion) are the following:

(1) Buy 10 SEP 67.5 Strike Puts @ 0.96 = $960 Debit

(2) Buy 10 SEP 70.0 Strike Puts @ 1.91 = $1,910 Debit

   Sell (10) SEP 67.5 Strike Puts @ 0.91 = $(910) Credit

   Net Initial P&L = $1,000 Debit

(3) Buy 20 SEP 70.0 Strike Puts @ 1.91 = $3,820 Debit

   Sell (40) SEP 67.5 Strike Puts @ 0.91 = $(3,640) Credit

   Buy 20 SEP 65.0 Strike Puts @ 0.47 = $940 Debit

   Net Initial P&L = $1,120 Debit

Exhibit 6.3 summarizes the Risk/Reward of these strategies:

Exhibit 6.3: Risk/Reward for Selected Strategies (XYZ)

STRATEGY	STRIKES	RISK	REWARD	RISK/REWARD
PUT BUY	67.5	$960	$1,540	1.6X
PUT SPREAD	70.0/(67.5)	$1,000	$1,500	1.5X
PUT BUTTERFLY	.70.0/(67.5)/65.0	$1,120	$3,940	3.5X

I decide to get rid of the SEP 67.5 Strike Put buy because I think the stock may not drop aggressively enough to justify the premium level. In addition, implied volatility levels have slowly ramped up; thus, I prefer to include some volatility selling in my chosen strategy. Next, I decide against the Put Butterfly because I don't want, for this example, to commit to a more complex position: I want to remain strategically flexible. I thus choose the SEP 70.0/ (67.5) Strike Put spread. I like this trade because it is at-the-money, has decent Risk/Reward and is simple enough to exit if the stock moves against me.

Plan & Entry

Now that my trade structure has been identified, I next determine my P&L Plan and prepare for entry execution. Exhibit 6.4 summarizes my Plan for this trade:

ACTION	CONTRACTS	COST PER UNIT	DEBIT/ (CREDIT)
BUY 92.5C STRIKE	10	2.35	$2,350
SELL 90.0P STRIKE	(10)	1.58	$(1,580)
NET P&L		0.77	$770
		MAXIMUM	TARGET
	PROFIT	$4,230	$3,000
	LOSS	$2,770	$1,500
	TIME	N / A	EXPIRATION

I decide my Target Profit and Loss levels are $3,000 and $1,500, respectfully–looking at the trading history of the stock; these appear to be realistic targets. The primary risk in this trade is to the downside given that I sold the Puts naked. Although I mentioned that I don't mind being assigned the shares, for risk management purposes, I decide the maximum loss I am comfortable with is $1,500– this equates to a drop in price to around the $90~$89 levels. It is difficult to say at this point the exact price level because several of the other elements in the pricing of the option premium are not known (such as time to expiration, volatility levels): the point is if I hit a loss of $1,500 on the position, I'm out. Given the huge liquidity in the options,

I'm comfortable knowing that there shouldn't be much slippage on the exit. Now that my P&L plan is complete, I next move to execute the trade. The current market is showing Bid/Ask of 2.31 / 2.35 for the 92.5 Strike Calls and 1.58 / 1.61 for the 90.0 Strike Puts for an approximate trade-in optimal mid-point (rounded up) of 0.73 or $730 (= (2.31 + 2.35)/2 − (1.58 + 1.61)/2). Executing the same trade-in process, I manage to fill the trade at 0.75 or an initial $750 Debit (92.5 Strike Calls at 2.34; 90.0 Strike Puts at 1.59).

CHAPTER - 4

The Options Greeks

Option traders use "the Greeks" to measure risk in their individual option positions and for their combined positions or portfolio. There are five Greeks employed to perform these functions: Delta, Gamma, Theta, Vega and Rho. The Greeks measure everything from how the option value will change with directional movement (i.e. up or down absolute dollar amounts) in the Underlying (Delta), how the option value will change with an increase or decrease in the volatility of the Underlying (Vega) and how the option value will change with the passing of time (Theta). Gamma is a special Greek as it measures how the value of another Greek, the Delta, will change with the directional movement in the Underlying.

Greeks are extremely important and it should be the goal of anyone wanting to trade or invest in options to gain an intuitive understanding of them; high-level math skills are not needed. An intuitive understanding of the Greeks will provide you with an understanding of the risk in your option position(s) and greatly contribute to your success as an option trader.

Delta

The Delta represents the amount the value of the option should change with a $1 move (up or down) in the

Underlying stock price. For example, if the Delta of the XYZ 5.0 Strike Call is 0.48 and XYZ stock moves down $1, then the value of the XYZ 5.0 Strike Call option should decline by $0.48. Alternatively, if XYZ stock moves up $1, then the value of the option should increase by $0.48. Delta basically means "Change." The reason I say "should" change is because many factors influence the value of an option and therefore, the amount of change could deviate substantially based on other factors such as a change in volatility, for example. Let's do some more examples–assume the following:

XYZ 21 Strike Call 0.85 Bid/1.05 Ask (mid = (0.85+1.05)/2 = 0.95)

XYZ 21 Strike Call Delta = 0.43

XYZ PRICE	CHANGE ($)	DELTA	CALL VALUE (AFTER $ CHANGE)
$21.17	+$1.00	0.43	1.38 [= {0.43 X $1.00} + 0.95]
$19.17	($1.00)	0.43	0.52 [= {0.43 X ($1.00)} +0.95]
$21.68	+$0.51	0.43	1.17 [= {0.43 X $0.51} + 0.95]
$21.00	($0.17)	0.43	0.88 [= {0.43 X ($0.17)} +0.95]

If stock XYZ sells off by $1, from $20.17 to $19.17, the XYZ 21.0 Strike Call's value should decrease by 0.43, the amount of the Delta. Therefore, after this drop, the Call option value should change from 0.95 to 0.52 (= {0.43 x ($1.00)} + 0.95). The example above relates to Calls. What about Puts? The Delta for a Put is negative (note that the Delta for a Call is positive).[16] The calculations are basically the same:

XYZ initial stock price = $20.17

XYZ 21 Strike Put 1.65 Bid / 1.95 Ask (mid- = (1.65+1.95)/2= 1.80)

XYZ 21 Strike Put Delta = (0.57)

Note: ("( )" represent a negative number)

XYZ PRICE	CHANGE ($)	DELTA	CALL VALUE (AFTER $ CHANGE)
$21.17	+$1.00	(0.57)	1.23 [= {(0.57) X $1.00} + 1.80]
$19.17	($1.00)	(0.57)	2.37 [= {(0.57) X ($1.00)} + 1.80]
$21.68	+$0.51	(0.57)	1.51 [= {(0.57) X $0.51} + 1.80]
$21.00	($0.17)	(0.57)	1.90 [= {(0.57) X ($0.17)} + 1.80]

Once again, it is important to note that Delta is only a guide to the approximate change of the value of the option with the directional change in the underlying–thus, do not view this metric as the law. Call Deltas range between 0.00 and 1.00 and Put Deltas range between (0.00) and (1.00)–that's it, Delta values cannot deviate outside of these values (i.e. there is no such thing as a Delta of, for example, 138). A Delta of 1.00 means the option's value changes exactly in-line with changes in the underlying stock (a deep-in-the-money option). Likewise, a Delta of 0.00 means the option's value doesn't change at all with the changes in the underlying stock (a deep out-of-the-money option). An option with a Delta of 0.50 (or 50) is an at-the-money option. Often you will see or hear Deltas referred to in non-decimal format and/or also excluding a negative or positive value qualifier, i.e. a Delta of 43 (for the Call) or a Delta of 57 (for the Put). This is basically the same thing as expressed in decimal format with qualifiers and is said as shorthand by traders as the actual meaning is understood.

Gamma

Gamma simply represents the change of the Delta for a given change in the underlying stock–it is basically the "Delta of the Delta." For example, if the Delta of a Call is 0.50 (and the Call is worth, for example, 1.25) and Delta's Gamma is 0.05 and the underlying stock moves up $1.00, the Delta should change from 0.50 to 0.55 (= 0.50 + 0.05) following this move in the stock. So, based on this example, the value of this Call, from this $1 increase in the underlying stock, will change by 0.50 or from 1.25 to

1.75 (= 1.25 + 0.50). At this point, the Call's Delta is now 0.55. If the stock moves again by $1, it should, therefore, change the value of the option by $0.55. Gamma basically shows the potential for your option position to "move" (in terms of value). For example, a "big Gamma" position can potentially experience explosive changes in value (and likewise the opposite for a small Gamma position). Additionally, it is important to note that Gamma can be either positive or negative.

Positive Gamma is generally good for your position and negative Gamma is generally bad for your position. For example, as the stock moves up and you are long a Call, positive Gamma will generate positive Deltas at an increasing rate. Likewise, if the stock moves down and you are long a Call, positive Gamma will generate negative Deltas at a declining rate. This is the magic of positive gamma. Confused? Let's use an example to demonstrate. Assume the following:

ABC Stock price = $30.00

Long ABC FEB 30.0 Strike Call @ 2.00

Delta = 0.45

Gamma = 0.07

Exhibit 2.3: Positive and Negative Gamma

Implied Position*

* Initial share position represents 1 Call (= 1 x 100 x 0.45).

At the $30 starting point above, the long Call has a Delta

of 0.45–this is equivalent to being long 45 shares. As the price of ABC stock increases, the Delta increases by the

PRICE	PREMIUM	DELTA	GAMMA	SHARES	OPTION
$27	0.82	0.30	0.04	45	30
$28	1.16	0.34	0.05	45	34
$29	1.55	0.39	0.06	45	39
$30	2.00	0.45	0.07	45	45
$31	2.45	0.52	0.06	45	52
$32	2.92	0.57	0.05	45	57
$33	3.49	0.61	0.04	45	61

Gamma and the implied long share position increases at an increasing rate (please refer to the "Implied Position" column). Likewise, as the price of ABC stock decreases, the Delta decreases by the Gamma and the implied long share position decreases at a decreasing rate. In both situations, positive Gamma works to benefit your position: when the stock increases, your position increases (acting as sort of a "value enhancer"); when the stock decreases, your position decreases (acting as sort of a "speed break" to value destruction). The same situation holds for long Put but in reverse (i.e. when the stock decreases, your position increases; when the stock increases, your position decreases).

Theta

Theta is very easy to understand: it measures the theoretical daily decay of the option premium, assuming no changes in the stock price and volatility. The life of an option is finite with a defined expiration and, therefore every day, it decays in value–Theta measures this decay. Exhibit 2.4 shows the simple calculation for the impact of Theta on an option premium.

Exhibit 2.4: Theta Impact on Option Premium

DAY	STOCK	OPTION	PREMIUM	THETA
MONDAY	ABC	JAN 12.0	1.25	-0.05
		PUT		
TUESDAY				1.20 (= 1.25 + -0.05)
THURSDAY	XYZ	FEB 35.0 CALL	2.50	-0.15
FRIDAY				2.35 (= 2.50 + -0.15)

Theta benefits option sellers and hurts option buyers. In the example above, the owner of the ABC JAN 12.0 Put "lost" $0.05 in premium for each option in 1 day–this $0.05 of premium went into the pocket of the individual who sold the option (the option seller). Likewise, the owner of the FEB 35.0 Call lost $0.15 in premium while the seller gained the same. As mentioned, this is the theoretical amount of decay, assuming no change in the stock price or volatility.

Exhibit 2.5: Graphical Depiction of the Impact of Theta over Time

As Exhibit 2.5 shows, Theta is initially small and therefore,

OPTION PREMIUM VALUE	TIME EXPIRATION

the impact on the option premium is small. As the option approaches expiration, however, Theta rapidly increases, which causes the value of the option premium to lose value at an increasing rate–this concept is very important to understand for both option buyers and option sellers.

Vega

Vega measures the impact of a 1.00% change in volatility on the theoretical value of an option. For example, assume the ABC JUN 35.0 Call is priced at 1.50, the volatility of ABC stock is 27% and the ABC JUN 35.0 Call has a Vega of 0.23. If volatility increases by 1.0% to 28%, the Call price should increase from 1.50 to 1.73 (= 1.53 + 0.23). Likewise, if volatility decreases by 1.0% to 26%, the Call price should decrease from 1.50 to 1.27 (= 1.50 − 0.23). It is important to monitor Vega in order to properly understand the risk in both your long and short positions.

Rho

Rho is a measure of the options pricing's sensitivity to a change in the risk-free interest rate. Since interest rates don't change by that much or that often these days, rho isn't paid much attention to. In a radically changing high-interest rate environment such as existed in the late 1970s, rho would be a more important parameter to pay attention to.

Using Delta for Target Price Probabilities

The relationship between target price estimates and Risk/ Reward calculations in determining the attractiveness of potential trades is very important. Let's say you determined your target price estimate and you calculated a solid Risk/Reward–it seems like a great trade. But is it? What is the probability of the stock actually making the move you determined in your target price? Is your target price realistic or are you deluding yourself? For option traders, it is often useful (if not essential) to put target price and Risk/Reward into the context of probability. This provides a "sanity check" on your target price and puts the trade's viability (and attractiveness as reflected in Risk/Reward) into perspective.

CHAPTER - 5

Advanced Strategies

Good strategies of any kind of options trading is the major key to any kind of success that is about to be unfolded in any activity. Strategies are normally laid in the trading plan and should be strictly implemented in every options trading move that is likely to be involved. Let us wholly venture into the best strategies so far in options trading.

1. Collars

The collar strategy is established by holding a number of shares of the underlying stock available in the market where protective puts are bought and the call options sold. In this kind of strategy, the options trader is likely to really protect his or her capital used in the trading activities rather than the idea of acquiring more money during trading. This kind is considered conservative and rather much more important in options trading.

2. Credit Spreads

It is presumed that the biggest fear of most traders is a financial breakdown. In this side of strategy, the trader gets to sell one put and then buy another one.

3. Covered Calls

Covered calls are a good kind of strategy where a particular trader sells the right for another trader to purchase his or her stock at some strike price and getting to gain a good amount of cash. However, there is a specific time that this strategy should be utilized and in a case where the buyer fails to purchase some of the stock and the expiration date dawns, the contract becomes invalid right away.

4. Cash Naked Put

Cash naked put is a kind of strategy where the options trader gets to write at the money or out of the money during a particular trading activity and aligning some particular amount of money aside for the purpose of purchasing stock.

5. Long Call Strategy

This is the most basic strategy in options trading and the one that is quite easy to comprehend. In the long call strategy for options trading, aggressive option traders who happen to be bullish are pretty much involved. This implies that bullish options traders end up buying stock during the trading activities with the hope of it rising in the near future. The reward is unlimited in the long call strategy.

6. Short Call Option Strategy

The short call strategy is the reverse of the long call one. Bearish kind of traders is so aggressive in the falling out of stock prices during trading in this kind of strategy. They decide to sell the call options available. This move is considered to be so risky by the experienced options traders believing that prices may drastically decide to rise once again. This significantly implies that large chunks of losses are likely to be incurred, leading to a real downfall of your trading structure and everything involved in it.

7. Long Put Option Strategy

First things first, you should be contented that buying a put is the opposite of buying a call. So in this kind of strategy, when you become bearish, that is the moment you may purchase a put option. Put option puts the trader in a situation where he can sell his stock at a particular period of time before the expiration date is reached. This strategy exposes the trader to a mere kind of risk in the options trading market.

8. Trading Time

It is depicted that options trading for a longer period is much value as compared to a short period dating. The longer the trading day, the more skills and knowledge the trader is likely to be engaged into as he or she is likely to get the adequate experience that is needed for good trading. Mastering good trading moves for a while gives the trader the experience and adequate skills.

9. Bull Call Spread Strategy

In this kind of strategy, the investor gets to purchase several calls at a particular strike price and then purchases the price at a much higher price. The calls always bear a similar expiration date and come from the same underlying stock. This type of strategy is mostly implemented by the bullish options traders.

10. Bear Put Strategy

This strategy involves a trader purchasing put options at a particular price amount and later selling off at a lower price amount. These options bear a similar expiration date and from the same underlying stock. This strategy is mostly utilized by traders, who are said to be bearish. The consequences are limited losses and limited gains.

11. Iron Condor

The iron condor involves the bull call spread strategy and the bear put strategy all at the same time during a particular trading period. The expiration dates of the stock are still similar and are of the same underlying stock. Most traders get to use this strategy when the market is expected to experience low volatility rates and with the expectation of gaining a little amount of premium. Iron condor works in both up and down markets are really believed to be economical during the up and down markets.

12. Married Put Strategy

On this end, the options trader purchase options at a particular amount of money and, at the same time, get to buy the same number of shares of the underlying stock. This kind of strategy is also known as the protective put. This is also a bearish kind of options trading strategy.

13. Cash Covered Put Strategy

Here, one or more contracts are sold with a 100 shares multiplied with the strike price amount for every particular contract involved in the options trading. Most traders use this strategy to acquire an extra amount of premium on a specific stock they would wish to purchase.

14. Long or Short Calendar Spread Strategy

This is a tricky type of strategy. The market stock is said to be stagnant, not moving and waiting for the right timing until the expiration of the front-month is reached.

15. Synthetic Long Arbitrage Strategy

Most traders take advantage of this strategy when they are trying to take advantage of the different market prices in different kinds of markets with just the same property.

16. Put Ratio Back Spread Strategy

This is a bearish type of options strategy where the trader gets to sell some put options and gets to purchase more options of just the same underlying stock with a similar expiration date and a lower price.

17. Call Ratio Back Spread

In this strategy, the trader uses both the long and short options positions so as to eradicate consistent losses and target achieving large loads of benefits over a particular trading period. The essence of this strategy is to generate profits in case the stock prices tend to elevate and reducing the number of risks likely to be involved. This strategy is mostly implemented by bullish kind of options traders.

18. Long Butterfly Strategy

This strategy involves three parts where one put option is purchased at particular and then selling the other two options at a price lower than the buying price and purchasing one put at an even lower price during a particular trading period.

19. Short Butterfly Strategy

In this strategy, three parts are still involved where a put option is sold at a much higher price and two puts are then purchased at a lower price than the purchase price and a put option is later on sold at a much lower strike price. In both cases, all put bear the same expiration date and the strike prices are normally equidistant as revealed in various options trading charts.

20. Long Straddle

The long straddle is also known as the buy strangle where a slight pull and a slight call are purchased during a particular period before the expiration date reaches. The importance of this strategy is that the trader bears a large chance of acquiring good amounts of profits during his or her trading time before the expiration date is achieved.

21. Short Straddle

In this kind of strategy, the trader sells both the call and putting options at a similar price and bearing the same expiration date. Traders practice this strategy with the hope of acquiring good amounts of profits and experience limited various kinds of risks.

22. Owning Positions that are Already in a Portfolio

Most traders prefer purchasing and selling various options that already hedge existing positions. This kind of strategy method is believed to incur good profits and incur losses too in other occurrences.

23. Albatross Trade Strategy

This kind of strategy aims at gaining some amounts of profits when the market is stagnant during specific options trading period or a pre-determined period of time. This kind of strategy is similar to the short gut strategy.

24. Reverse Iron Condor Strategy

This kind of strategy focuses on benefiting some profits when the underlying stock in the current market dares to make some sharp market trade moves in either direction. Eventually, a limited amount of risks are experienced and a limited amount of profits during trading.

25. Iron Butterfly Spread

Buying and holding four different options in the market at three different market prices is involved in the trading market for a particular trading period.

26. Short Bull Ratio Strategy

The short bull ratio strategy is used to benefit from the amounts of profits gained from increasing security involved in the trading market in a similar way in which we normally get to buy calls during a particular period.

27. Bull Condor Spread

This is a type of strategy that is designed to return a profit if the actual price of security decides to rise to a predicted price range during a specific trading period impacting good chunks of profits made to the options trader and a limited number of risks involved.

28. Put Ratio Spread Strategy

This strategy entails purchasing a number of put options and adding more options with various strike prices and equal kind of underlying stock during a particular options trading period.

29. Strap Straddle Strategy

Strap straddle strategy uses one put and two calls bearing a similar strike price and with an equal date of expiration and also containing the same underlying stock that is normally stagnant during a particular trading period. The trader utilizes this type of strategy for the hope of getting higher amounts of profits as compared to the regular straddle strategy over a particular period of the trading period.

30. Strap Strangle Strategy

This strategy is bullish, where more call options are purchased as compared to the put options and a bullish inclination is then depicted in various trading charts information.

31. Put Back Spread Strategy

This back spread strategy combines both the short puts and long puts so as to establish a position where the ratio of losses and profits entirely depends on the ratio of their two puts that are likely to be experienced in the market.

CHAPTER - 6

The Techniques to Control the Risk

Step by Step Instructions to Mitigate Risks In Options trading

Numerous financial specialists erroneously accept that options are constantly more hazardous speculations than stocks, since they may not completely comprehend the idea of influence. Be that as it may, whenever utilized appropriately, alternatives may convey fewer hazards than a proportional stock position. Peruse on to figure out how to compute the potential danger of options positions and how the intensity of influence can function in support of you.

Deciphering the Numbers

Think about the accompanying model. You want to put $10,000 in a $50 stock, yet are enticed to purchase $10 options contracts as an option. All things considered, putting $10,000 in a $10 option enables you to purchase 10 agreements (one agreement is worth one hundred portions of stock) and control 1,000 offers. Then, $10,000 in a $50 stock will just purchase 200 offers.

In this model, the options exchange has more hazard than the stock exchange. With the stock exchange, your whole venture can be a loss, yet just with an unlikely value development from $50 to $0. Nonetheless, you remain to lose your whole interest in the options exchange if the stock just drops to the strike cost. Along these lines, if the alternative strike cost is $40 (in-the-cash options), the stock just needs to dip under $40 by termination for the speculation to be lost, despite the fact that it's only a 20% decrease.

Obviously, there is a gigantic hazard divergence between owning a similar dollar measure of stocks and options. This hazard divergence exists in light of the fact that the best possible meaning of influence was applied erroneously. To address this misconstruing, how about we inspect two different ways to adjust hazard difference while keeping the positions similarly productive?

Elective Risk Calculation

The other option for adjusting cost and size divergence depends on hazard.

As we've gotten the hang of, purchasing $10,000 in stock isn't equivalent to purchasing $10,000 in alternatives as far as by and large hazard. Truth is told, the introduction of options conveys a lot more serious hazard because of incredibly expanded potential for misfortune. So as to even the odds, you should have a hazard identical options position in connection to the stock position.

We should begin with the stock position: purchasing 1,000

offers at $41.75 for all-out speculation of $41,750. Being a hazard cognizant speculator, you additionally enter a stop-misfortune request, a judicious procedure that is exhorted by market specialists.

You set a stop request at a value that will restrict your misfortune to 20% of the venture, which figures to $8,350. Accepting this is the sum you are happy to lose, it ought to likewise be the sum you are eager to spend on an alternatives position. As it were, you should just burn through $8,350 purchasing options for hazard equivalency. With this technique, you have a similar dollar sum in danger in the options position as you were happy to lose in the stock position.

Money Management and Risk

Accurately dealing with your capital and hazard presentation is fundamental when exchanging options. While hazard is basically unavoidable with any type of speculation, your introduction to hazard doesn't need to be an issue. The key is to deal with the hazard reserves successfully; consistently guarantee that you are OK with the degree of hazard being taken and that you aren't presenting yourself to unsustainable misfortunes.

Similar ideas can be applied when dealing with your cash as well. You ought to exchange utilizing capital that you can stand to lose; abstain from overstretching yourself. As viable hazard and cash, the board is totally essential to effective options exchanging, it's a subject that you truly need to get. On this page, we take a gander at a portion of the techniques you can and should use for dealing with your hazard presentation and controlling your financial limit.

- Utilizing Your Trading Plan

- Overseeing Risk with Options Spreads

- Overseeing Risk through Diversification

- Overseeing Risk utilizing Options Orders

- Cash Management and Position Sizing

Utilizing Your Trading Plan

It's essential to have a point by point exchanging plan that spreads out rules and parameters for your exchanging exercises. One of the viable employments of such an arrangement is to enable you to deal with your cash and your hazard presentation. Your arrangement ought to incorporate subtleties of what level of hazard you are OK with and the measure of capital you need to utilize.

By following your arrangement and just utilizing cash that you have explicitly dispensed for options exchanging, you can stay away from probably the greatest slip-up that financial specialists and merchants make: utilizing "terrified" cash.

Overseeing Risk with Options Spreads

Alternatives spreads are significant and integral assets in options exchanging. An option spread is fundamentally when you consolidate more than one situation on options agreements dependent on the equivalent basic security to adequately make one, by and large, exchanging position.

There is a huge scope of spreads that can be utilized to exploit practically any economic situation. In our segment on Options Trading Strategies, we have given a rundown of all options spreads and subtleties on how and when they can be utilized. You might need to allude to this area when you are arranging your alternative exchanges.

Overseeing Risk through Diversification

Broadening is a hazard the board system that is ordinarily utilized by financial specialists that are building an arrangement of stocks by utilizing a purchase and hold technique. The essential rule of broadening for such speculators is that spreading ventures over various organizations and divisions makes a reasonable portfolio instead of having an excessive amount of cash tied up in one specific organization or part. A differentiated portfolio is commonly viewed as less presented to chance than a portfolio that is made up to a great extent of one explicit kind of speculation.

Overseeing Risk Using Options Orders

A moderately basic approach to oversee hazard is to use the scope of various requests that you can put. Notwithstanding the four fundamental request types that you use to open and close positions, there are some extra requests that you can place, and a large number of these can assist you with hazard the board.

This will enable you to keep away from situations where you pass up benefits through clutching a situation for a really long time or cause enormous misfortunes by not finishing off in a terrible position rapidly enough. By utilizing alternatives arranges fittingly, you can restrain the hazard you are presented to on every single exchange you make.

Cash Management and Position Sizing

Dealing with your cash is inseparably connected to overseeing danger and both are similarly significant. You, at last, have a limited measure of cash to utilize, and due to this present, it's essential to keep tight control of your capital spending plan and to ensure that you don't lose everything and get yourself unfit to make further exchanges.

The absolute most ideal approach to deal with your cash is to utilize a genuinely basic idea known as position estimating. Position measuring is fundamentally choosing the amount of your capital you need to use to enter a specific position.

Decreasing Your Risk

For some speculators, options are valuable instruments of hazard to the executives. They go about as protection strategies against drop-in stock costs. For instance, if a speculator is worried that the cost of their offers in LMN Corporation is going to drop, they can buy puts that give the privilege to sell the stock at the strike value, regardless of how low the market value drops before lapse. At the expense of the options' premium, the financial specialist has protected themselves against misfortunes underneath the strike cost. This sort of options practice is otherwise called supporting.

Numerous alternatives systems are intended to limit chance by supporting existing portfolios. While options go about as security nets, they're not hazard-free. Since exchanges normally open and close for the time being, increases can be acknowledged rapidly. Misfortunes can mount as fast as additions. It's essential to comprehend dangers related to holding, composing, and exchanging alternatives before you incorporate them in your speculation portfolio.

CHAPTER - 7

Watching the Market

At this point, you've got three options for well, your option and covered call and they're important to note. The first is the stock goes down, so the call will be worthless and you have to sell it for the price of the option. If you notice that it takes a dive before the expiration date, don't freak out. While there might be some losses, you'll notice that the stock itself goes down in value, so you can buy it back for less money than you got to sell it. If the option on the stock is changed, you close the position, buy back the call contract, and go from there.

So let's say that you have an options contract that's going for $100 and the strike price is $105. If the price goes all the way down to 20, you might have to sell the stock at that price if someone bought a contract for it, but if you still have the premium, you can then buy it again for that low price. You will have to sell if the option is exercised, but again this is something that you can decide for yourself, and if someone buys a contract.

There is also the option that it stays the same or goes up, but doesn't reach too high. This isn't that bad, because the call option will expire, so you pocket the premium and you will still have the stock that you initially had. Not something that you can complain about.

Finally, you have a scenario and that is that the stock rises above what is the strike price. If this happens, then you're going to assign the call option to this stock, and that means you will be forced to share those 100 shares of stock. So, unfortunately, you still lose the stock. Most of the time though, since you're still netting a profit, there isn't as much love lost as you might think.

But, there is another issue that comes about with this. That is, if the stock skyrockets after you sell the shares, you're probably going to notice that you could've netted a huge profit from this. This is when a lot of investors tend to kick themselves for this, but the truth is, you shouldn't do that. This is actually a decision that you made when you chose to part with the stock at the strike price that you desired and you still achieved profit from this.

That is the common problem a lot of investors face when it comes to selling stocks. They think that they shouldn't have done it just because the price for it skyrocketed to a whole different height. But, that's not always the case. You shouldn't feel down about this and it can be a bit disheartening, but realize that you're not terrible for choosing the option to part with this. Sometimes, you may not even realize that the stock is going to fluctuate with time, and that is why, when you're choosing stocks for covered calls, they should be stocks that would very rarely have that much of a rise in price, and while having that volatility is good, you should also make sure that it isn't so volatile that you can't predict how it may go next.

When it comes to improving your covered calls, the best thing to do is to research and hold onto the stock. If you do have older stock that you just don't want to hold onto anymore, then I do suggest that you consider the option of writing covered calls on them. Remember, there are always times when you can buy these back too, so if you want to get the stock back and cash in on those dividends, it can be quite worth your while to do this.

Volatility

There's one final factor that affects the prices of contracts on a fundamental basis, though it's not really something we've touched on so far. The volatility of a contract is, however, an incredibly important concept to grasp for an options trader.

Volatility refers to the movement of the underlying stock. Some stocks will slowly wend their way up and down in a predictable manner–those are not very volatile. Others change on a day to day basis and change between up and down along the way.

To sum up the effect of volatility in a single sentence: the more volatile the stock, the more that an options trader is willing to pay for it. A volatile stock has a better chance of reaching the strike price and perhaps shooting far beyond it before the expiration date.

However, it's also the most dangerous of the factors that you need to bear in mind because it's arguably the most likely one to force you into a bad decision. A volatile stock, for example, can lead to a much higher premium and, therefore, a higher contract price; unless that stock shoots through the roof, you could actually end up losing money even when you should be making it.

One way to estimate the volatility of a stock is to take a look at what it has done in the recent past. This tells you how much it has moved up and down already, which some use as an indicator of how much it will move up and down in the future.

Unfortunately, it's not always true that the past repeats itself and you can't predict the future based on what's already happened. Instead, options traders use "implied volatility" to make their guesses: the value that the market believes the option is worth.

You can see this reflected in the activity on the options for that stock. Buyers will be keen to get their hands on options before a certain event takes place, such as the announcement of a new product or a release about the company's earnings. Because of this, options increase in price because there is implied volatility–the market thinks the stock is going to shoot up.

You'll see lower demand on a stock that's flat or moving gently, because there is no implied volatility and, therefore, no hurry to get in on the action. You'll also see correspondingly low prices for the option.

Volatility is obviously a good thing–as a buyer, you want the stock to be volatile because you need it to climb to the strike price and beyond. However, there is also such a thing as too much volatility. It's at that point the contracts become popular, the prices rise and you stand to pay more for a contract than you will ultimately profit. Your brokers will likely be able to provide you with a program that will help you determine implied volatility, asking you to enter certain factors and then calculating it for you. However, it's only through experience that you'll learn how to spot a stock that's just volatile enough to justify its higher price— again, practice is key. It's also worth noting that a lot of the risk in options trading comes from volatility, largely because it's impossible to be accurate in your estimates. What happens if an earthquake destroys that company's headquarters? Stocks are going to plummet, and you had absolutely no way to see it coming. That's why options traders are forced to accept that their fancy formulas are not going to be perfect predictors. They will help, but you should still be conservative in your trading and avoid the temptation to sink everything into a trade you believe could make your fortune thanks to its volatility.

Strategies for a Volatile Market

Long Straddle

This strategy is essentially an amalgamation of the long call and long put trading strategies. You will be using the money options for executing the strategy. You are required to purchase at the money calls along with at the money puts of the same amount. Execute both these transactions simultaneously and ensure that the expiry date for them stays the same. Given that the expiry date is long-term, it gives the underlying security sufficient time to show a price movement and increases your chances of earning a profit. A short-term expiration date doesn't provide much scope for any changes in the price of an asset, so the profitability is also relatively low.

Long Strangle

This is also known as the strangle strategy, and you must place simultaneous orders with your broker. You must purchase calls on relevant security and then by the same number of puts on the security. The options contracts you execute must be out of the money and must be made simultaneously. The best way to go about it is to purchase those securities that are just out of the money instead of ones that are far out of the money. Make sure that the strike prices in both these transactions are equidistant from the existing trading price of the underlying asset.

Strip Straddle

This strategy is quite similar to a long straddle – you will be purchasing at the money calls and at the money puts. The only difference is that the number of puts you purchase will be higher than the calls your purchase. The expiry date and the underlying asset for both these transactions you make will be the same. The only factor upon which your profitability lies on is the ratio of puts to calls you use. The best ratio is to purchase two puts for every call you make.

Strip Strangle

You stand to earn a profit if the underlying asset makes a big price movement in either direction is. However, your profitability increases if the price movement is downwards instead of upwards. You will be required to purchase out of the money calls and out of the money puts. Ensure that the numbers of out of the money puts you make are greater than the out of the money calls you to decide to make. So, to begin with, the ratio of 2:1 will work well for you.

Strap Straddle

This is quite similar to the long straddle strategy- you are required to purchase at the money calls along with at the money puts for the same date of expiry. You are required to purchase more calls than ports, and the basic ratio to start with is 2:1. User strategy for certain that there will be an upward movement in the price of the underlying asset instead of a downward price movement.

Strap Strangle

This is quite similar to the Long strangle strategy and uses it when you're quite confident that there will be a dramatic movement in the price of the underlying strategy. You tend to earn a profit if the price moves in either direction, but your profitability increases in the price movement are upward. There are two transactions you must execute- purchase out of the money puts and purchase out of the money calls options. However, the number of out of the money calls you to make must be greater than the out of the money puts. The ratio of out of the money puts out of the money calls must be two to one. So, you will essentially be purchasing twice as many calls as sports.

CHAPTER - 8

How to Get Started In Day Trading

Day trading is becoming a lucrative engagement in the commerce industry with recent technological advancement. Hey there, welcome to the stock market world. This end is strategically oriented and plenty of fat risks coming your way. Let's dive into some of the factors that are likely to be considered.

The Capital Needed to Start Day Trading

Capital is so necessary to set the actual day trading ball on fire. Acquiring loans from different sites has been revealed to be so common among traders. With this glue on the mind, traders tend to be so careful with the amount of capital that they actually intend to commence with. To begin, traders are ought to obtain ready capital so as to monitor any kind of slight changes that are presumed to occur during the course of the day.

Day trading requires a minimum account balance of $1000, but $8000-$10,000 is recommended by many providers and plenty of traders are not willing to risk 1% from the value. Also, the $1000 minimum amount that can be implemented can lead to your trading activities in being so not worthwhile.

Step by step kind of beginning is so vital because you get to acquire progress constantly and get to grow at a good speed with messing things out.

Choosing a Broker

Once you have set your mind on exactly what intend to trade, a broker should be following up in mind. Brokers are the navigators of several trading investment platforms. Bearing this I mind, we ought to be super perfect in choosing a broker because they reflect reliability, reputations, and expertise in your trading account.

Let us Look at Some of the Ways that are Set to be Considered:

Really Decide on What you Will be Trading.

Experts get their names by being good (perfect) in a particular field of trading. A stocks broker may be so bad in FOREX trading and vice versa, all the best in picking the best and the right one.

Sourcing for Recommendations

Sticking in mind that the actual amount of money to be used during trading is really your own money, a wake-up call is assured and a good broker who can't be dodging with your precious money is super needed.

Try to even inquire from your colleagues you may have been in the spot or who they may have heard of good brokers. Try to also have some in-depth research from varieties of social media content, online views on the investment platforms, discussion boards and also take plenty of time to examine their websites.

Commission Rate

Despite the fact that the "perfect" broker is super needed as you begin day trading, consider in mind that this is also a new project as a whole, meaning that profits too, need to be made so as this whole project can exist for a long while. Consider the rates of commissions that are likely to be spent so as to avoid any losses from being made. Pick an economic one to save yourself.

Executive Speed

Any delay of seconds can result in a massacre to a trader's profits. To prevent this, the broker should really make sure that the trading activities are at a top-notch. The broker should be able to quickly spot any rapid changes that are likely to be incurred in the trading platforms.

Charting Strategies

Getting great chatting tools and software is also fundamental. Make sure you are getting good trading strategies, reliable variable markets, and better software features to enhance good day trading

Paper Trading

It's advisable to begin day trading with paper trading, where you won't have to use your own money, though many brokers highly discourage this. Know where your heart takes you.

Technology

So, is the broker up for the new technological advancements? What kinds of accounts do they deal with? Does he/she have a real-time-data feed so that you can easily track and monitor trading activities? Which safeguard trading and Cybersecurity measures do they follow during trading? What kind of volumes of trading can they handle?

Greatly consider the kind who's so updated with the current technological happenings and pretty much informed.

Customer Service Provision

Are they willing to offer customer service services? What happens when your system during mid-trade and it costs you so much? Are they going to support you so as to get much out of trading? Which process are they going to utilize during complaint resolution? And many more. Consider these before signing the contract because it's a big deal.

Safe, Secure and Regulated

It's such a marvelous idea to inquire about the security of the broker in question. Inquire on how long they have been in business, their past work reports, what measures they have been using and their recent big measures on day trading.

Make sure they are regulated by an agency and that they strictly value and consider the rules and regulations needed to be followed by any broker engaged in day trading.

Adequate Support

Engage with brokers that are willing to provide huge support once there is a miss during your daily training activities. A few cents incremented on the broker's commission accounts is much worthwhile compared to hundreds of dollars losses that are likely to be incurred on the bad days.

How to Become a Day Trader

The Following Basic Tools are Recommended:

Computer/Monitor

Well, cheap is expensive. A slow kind of computer can cause you a great fortune. Slow working definitely implies that the day trading tracks to be unreliable and totally not trending. This is really going to cost you in that the rates of profits at the end of any activity will be way low. They can cause you to miss trades, therefore making your idea so unreliable. Remember, you have a good reputation to uphold.

With all these in mind, please bear a quite fast laptop or monitor.

Set a Target, Really Motivating

Setting a realistic trading target is going to manage and monitor your real cash big time. A certain target is put for the purpose of big motivation. Work on that. Be for it big time. Remember achieving your target is normally tough because we all have really "dream" targets. Consistent losses will be incurred too, so prepare to lose some cash. Failure is never good though and will never be, so keep up champ!

Create a Demo Account

Rehearsing has always been a good move as your head to be successful navigation. Set up a demo account that will help you master all the ropes and moves that are likely to be incurred. Reading the fluctuations, the market trends are one way of future taking master moves that are great chances for high profitability rates. Keep testing and practicing until you are sure you are ready to go. Examine the market.

Master most of the trading moves. This makes you informed and definitely enhances specialization in a particular field.

Fast Internet Connection

A constant, fast and reliable type of internet connection is highly recommended. The unreliable internet connection can cause a miss in the market trends that can hinder the trading traces in a way leading to major losses being incurred at the end. Most of the users use a cable and ADSL type of connection. Remember that day trading does not recommend any unreliable source of connection.

Type of Market

As mentioned earlier, each kind of day trading demands a different kind of day trading. Choosing the kind of market to start with is super important, choose the most preferred.

Discover the Tax Implications Likely to be Incurred

Inquire on how taxes revolve around profits. Engage with your financial adviser to let him or her explain how taxes are handled. Are they going to cause devaluation on the made profits? Are they good news? How does that happen?

Be informed so as to at the end the trader can guess on the likelihood net profits to be expected.

Choose the Right Stocks to Trade

Well, to be better in choosing the right kind of stock, doing some in-depth research on the current existing stock is way the first step. Get to know the kind of stocks that are likely to perform well. Most preferably, those that are likely to perform well on a day-to-day basis. Remember to at least try one or two different kinds of stock until you are so sure that you have picked out the right one.

Plan a Good Financial Figure

You will need to prepare yourself early enough on the amount of money that can be risked on the day trading business. It is mostly advised not to risk more than 1-2% of your account money so as to avoid future losses.

Another piece of advice to the beginners, stay away from trading on the margin until you are set with enough moves and good trading wisdom. This will save you some extra cash in time.

Venture into Several Day Trading Courses to Get Educated

Before Getting Involved in a Particular Course of Study, Kindly Consider the Following Tips:

- The Course Should be Taught by a Professional

Ignoring his/her profession, just pick out a teacher who happens to be an expert in a specific trading field. Why? So as to acquire detailed, accurate, reliable and up-to-date pieces of information, this will so motivate you in your trading journey.

- Availability of Educational Support Tools

The presence of proper educational tools will give the learner an audience to readily grasp every fundamental piece of information. The professional should also be ready to face time or live chat with any student who really needs great help.

- Based on your Particular Field

Well, we agreed on picking out a particular trading sector field and really working on it. Well, your educational source should go hand in hand in whatever field that you have selected. Make sure that the learning source is detailed so as to acquire a bigger piece of information.

- High Rated Learning the Source

A perfectly detailed piece of learning information entails that a lot has been covered. Go for that. We have to make our day trading journeys so well, and then meaning that our start-off spots should be good.

CHAPTER - 9

Finding a Suitable Market

How many times have you turned unrealized gains into losses? If this happens to you, you may need to learn how to implement your market strategy reliably. There is an old saying: "Never make a profit at a loss." This simple rule is always so crucial for successful trading.

Unless you always implement a reliable market strategy, your trading success is far from what it could or should be. Your profitability is unreliable. You increase your chances of success against yourself. This can lead to a more significant loss, dissatisfaction with the trading performance, and even distrust.

By reliably applying your market strategy to each trade, several of your trades will be profitable. Your winnings are usually more substantial. Over time, you become more successful. And for losing trades, your losses are generally smaller. Emotions will no longer pollute your decision. And you will never allow unrealized gains to become losses.

You need to have complete confidence in your market strategy because if you trust my market strategy, it is psychologically easy to implement it into every transaction automatically. You should never experience doubt, confusion, or hesitation.

Three Phases of the Transaction

Each transaction has three phases: input, knowledge, and go out. Each step has an exit strategy. Your trade will be more successful if you let the profit run, and the losses will be reduced. It means that you should always determine where your prognosis is bad before opening a position. As soon as your prediction turns out to be incorrect, close your position immediately. Leave what's left. You no longer have a reason to stay in this store.

Stop-loss determines when a trade needs to be closed. I use three-loss methods, one for each phase of my trades:

- Loss of input loss, set before opening the position;

- Loss of rear brake, set if the trade moves in my favor and

- Profit stop loss gain profit after reaching my waypoint.

Before opening my position, I always set a loss. I put it one percent below the recent strong swing on the daily stock price chart for bull trades. If the stock creates an everyday closing price during this loss of income, I will leave in the morning. My prediction was wrong: stocks are falling, not up.

If the stock rises as expected and does not stop when entering at the entry-level, I will increase the rear stop losses by one percent in the event of subsequent damages due to fluctuations. I was just rattling them. The ratchet effect reduces potential losses and blocks profits. My stops are also due to the daily closing price. The next day, each regular closing price is activated in the event of another loss of a stop.

Your Business Waypoint

You should also estimate where you reasonably expect the stock price to go. You need to decide in advance how to close your trade to maximize your profit when you reach your waypoint. Once the transaction reaches your waypoint, implement your exit strategy with strict discipline. It is not a good idea to simply end a trade when you reach your point on the route. It is better to stay in the trade as long as it continues in your favor.

However, you should leave your trading at the first sign that the market poses an unrealized risk of your unrealized profits.

When I reach my waypoints, I use much stricter termination criteria that make it easier to activate the output. After start-up, stocks are reduced rather than continued. I'll just stay in the box while stocks keep growing. Every day I move my surplus to the intraday layer. As soon as the shares are trading below yesterday's minimum, I will immediately leave as at. By definition, stocks fell. At this point, the population is more likely to continue to shrink than to keep.

Adjust Your Excessive Losses

The market provides a lot of advice that your unrealized profit is at increased risk. Profit losses cease to threaten unrealized gains. You can use one or more of the following criteria to make a profit. You can stop:

- As soon as the share price turns towards you;

- As more quickly as the trend line breaks;

- As more quickly as price support is interrupted; or,

- As more quickly as a simple moving average break.

Each of these terms warns you that your trade is likely to start. And that your unrealized gains are more likely to be at risk. If all these criteria are met: you must close the course permanently!

In addition to this standard procedure, I will be able to override other stop-loss strategies based on the pricing model, indices, options, and time. In the bear, I'm just about the process.

This way, you manage your Exits Strategy. You can make profits and reduce losses. And that should keep you from turning unrealized gains into losses.

The identification of exits falls into the category of the trading system; exits must be located in meaningful places on the market-determined by support and resistance. However, it is always essential to determine the initial output before starting a transaction. And then you have to leave the trade when the stop asks you to.

1. Order to Lose the First Stop

The goal of the first step is to get you out of the trade if the trade goes wrong at the beginning of the operation.

In general, many systems have both a first and a rear stop, but the rear stop may not be known until certain conditions are met.

The ideal first stop should also allow for a "breathing space," but not so large that the trader can take excessive risk.

Use a strategy to stop the loss based on market price, critical levels of support, or some level of retracement.

2. Break-Even Stop is Another Common Exit Strategy

Loss of clues can be shifted to the entry price when the market moves in your favor is one way to secure a winning trade before using reverse cessation strategies. This method is widely used and popular because it reduces anxiety in trading.

3. Use the Backstop to Capture Profits when the Market Moves in Favor of Traders

There are many reversal strategies to choose from. A fundamental exit strategy is two steps. The highest or lowest of the last two measures are the levels to which the trader must shift his stop loss to secure earnings. This strategy is excellent for trading within a day or when a trader expects the market to move to a consolidation sentence.

4. For Emotional Reason, do not Move the Stop

This is the rule, and I would like to add a comment on this topic with exit strategies because it is the number one rule to follow. Acting according to plan and sticking to plan excludes emotions. This rule ensures that exit strategies serve their purpose, and traders can reap the benefits.

5. Apply Timeout

Most trading systems would terminate trade before a significant economic event, such as the payment of non-agricultural farms. A time stop is used to stop trading before this reporting event to prevent market fluctuations. Market volatility risk decreases with delay.

Each time you enter trading of any kind, you must first make sure that your exit strategy is planned, regardless of whether the trade ends in a winner or a loser. Knowing how to manage your trading and the right exit strategy are the most critical aspects of trading in the market.

Options trading, like any other type of trading, require careful planning and execution. I could say that every day you have some kind of participation in the market. We are all in the business. As a trader, it is easy to enter and leave the market at the touch of a button. But once you're inside, do you mean a clear exit strategy?

Trading is like a business that requires planning with strategies that show that you want to grow your business. In trading, a solid business plan is necessary for successful trading. Blinding in the market is just a sign that you are speculating or "rushing" to see which direction you are heading. Like all plans, you need the right approach and an even better exit strategy.

What do you do when your trade goes bad? Can you find a way to save what's left, or will you just let go when you think the market can recover? Most of us can choose the first opportunity to try to keep what we can and therefore propose a strategy to save the current situation. At that point, it may be too late, because all planning must take place before starting a trade.

Depending on the trade, you should have a good exit strategy that complements your trading strategy and timing. In short time frames, such as 5-15 minutes, an exit strategy must be planned before executing a trade, because you do not have time to think about your termination. If you have 1 hour - 4 hours, you have much more time, and you can still afford to come up with your exit strategy.

In professional trading, these "professionals" always have in mind an entry and exit strategy after analyzing market conditions and only need to follow their plan. They emphasized the balanced conduct of trade and already favored entry or exit. Both are equally important to them.

So if you are like most beginners who believe that with all the exact entry points you can achieve an individual winner, then I am amazed at the result. I came across several "safe winners" based precisely on entry points, but it turned out that I was a massive loss due to the inability to leave at the right time. Think about it every time you trade with a clear exit strategy?

CHAPTER - 10

Useful Third-Party Resources

Leonardo DiCaprio stated in the famed Wolf of Wall Street movie: "Simplicity is the ultimate sophistication." A good portfolio excels in a good diversification strategy. A portfolio does not have to contain 30 items, but a correctly balanced mix that keeps risk and returns in balance. Or, as John Templeton said: "Diversify. In stocks and bonds, as in much else, there is safety in numbers." There are plenty of options: from gold, over ETFs, to real estate, currencies, index funds or shares. Create a clear portfolio where you, as an investor, know how to deal with the risk.

View the Total Financial Picture

Making a profit on an investment is quite a pleasant feeling. But investments are not alone, not on an island, or floating in a vacuum. Investments are part of your total financial life. Many asset managers give their clients wise advice: you have to manage your accounting as a business.

How Can You Monitory our Stock Portfolio?

If you decide to invest in shares, drawing up an investment plan is the first step. However, once you have compiled your equity portfolio, you are not yet ready. Monitoring your equity portfolio to monitor whether it still meets your original objectives is just as important. Some investors like to check the status of their investments every day. But for many investors, this is not desirable or necessary. In other words, monitoring your equity portfolio depends on both the type of investments in your portfolio and the type of investor that you are.

Monitor Shares

The moment you have invested not in funds, but self-selected individual shares, it is interesting to monitor these continuously. The most important goal here is to check if a share still meets your initial criteria. In almost all cases, this will depend strongly on your estimate of the future expectation for the underlying company or the estimate of the stock market. Many of these estimates are based on company income. You have to monitor the changes that affect income.

Newspapers, Press Releases, and Reports

Check the financial news and announcements about your shares daily, weekly, or monthly. This includes new products, changes in management, or news about competitors. If analysts report on your share, it is wise always to read it immediately. Since these can be of great importance for market sentiment.

Online Sources of News

Many brokers allow you to monitor your stock portfolio online. In some cases, there is even a direct link to news and analysis of the relevant share. This way, you not only see at a glance how your portfolio is doing, but you also have an overview of relevant news sources that can influence the price. Many brokers also offer the option to receive alerts by e-mail or text message when certain developments occur on the market. Does your broker not have such an option? Then online portals like finance. Yahoo allows you to enter your portfolio. After which they will provide you with a large number of relevant news sources. Both through your broker and financial websites such as Yahoo Finance, Morningstar, and Bloomberg, you will be provided with information in real-time. Since the stock market also responds to developments in real-time, this information can enable you to react promptly to developments to maximize your returns.

Follow up your Portfolio Mobile

Although many professional traders still have an old-fashioned Bloomberg terminal in the office, there is an easier way. Some many mobile sites and apps provide you with the same information, but at the same time also fit in your pocket. For example, newspapers such as De Standard, De Tijd have their apps, but you can also find everything with Bloomberg Markets +, Yahoo Finance, and Google Finance. Most major brokers also have mobile applications available, with which you cannot find information, but can also easily invest in mobile.

How Do You Choose the Top Options Trading Blogs and Virtual Trading Platforms?

One of your most important decisions as an investor has

nothing to do with shares or bonds. It is the choice for the investment platform that you will use. Because there are numerous investment sites, and the differences are often large. But how do you choose the most suitable one for you?

Via an online investment platform or online broker, it is usually easier and cheaper to submit stock market orders yourself. They are specifically made to meet the needs of siege-enthusiasts, offer more options, and also take into account that you do your part of the work in terms of costs. So you certainly don't have to be a super active investor to take advantage of such an online investment platform.

Choosing the Right Online Broker

Every investor is different. So first, determine what is really important to you. A starting investor needs more support: in contrast to a discount broker, a full-service broker offers a lot of stock market information, free interesting webinars, an extensive Academy, etc., etc. That will help you get step by step at home in the stock market.

A buy-and-hold investor who only occasionally buys a few 'good-hearted father' shares has no message for complicated investment platforms with, for example, advanced options strategies.

Powerful software offers many services, with advice, if required. You can often create a test account as an exercise. You get to know the service better, and you can monitor your portfolio in a risk-free manner. You should also be careful with well-intended advice from friends and acquaintances. They have the best of intentions but never accept advice from someone with less knowledge than you.

On Which Stock Exchanges Do I Want to Invest?

All brokers have a fairly wide range. In addition to the main European markets, they offer New York (Wall Street, Nasdaq) and Toronto stock exchanges. But there are accent differences. With KBC subsidiary Bolero, you can also invest in the stock exchanges in Prague, Budapest, and Warsaw, at the same rates as the Euronext stock exchanges. Also, for Tokyo, Singapore, Hong Kong, and Australia, you can go to Bolero and the Dutch DeGiro. Lynx is expanding its 'exotic' range to include China and Mexico.

The brokers have not only shares, bonds, and investment funds in their offer, but also a range of products for advanced users, such as trackers, options, and turbo. In funds, the supply is generally wider than at the large banks, because they distribute the funds from various asset managers.

How Much Does a Stock Market Order Cost?

Opening an account with an online broker is always free, and you do not have to pay a custody fee. If you want to compare the costs, you must, therefore, mainly look at the transaction rates. If you limit yourself as a small investor to Euronext Brussels, there are no major differences between the brokers. The transaction rates are usually between 6 and 7.50 euros per transaction up to 2,500 euros (see table). Only DeGiro plunges far below the other rates with

2.95 euros. DeGiro is a Dutch online broker. As a Belgian investor, you can open an account, but it is a Dutch account.

If you also head towards Wall Street, then you should pay attention. Keytrade Bank charges 29.95 euros per transaction. At Bolero and MeDirect, you pay 15 dollars for transactions up to 2,500 euros. At Binck Bank, you are asked for 9.75 euros and at Lynx for only 5 dollars. But the absolute prize breaker is again DeGiro. There, a Wall Street transaction costs just € 0.50 plus $ 0.004 per share traded, regardless of the amounts traded. DeGiro says it can offer low rates by limiting the number of employees and using its own IT system. DeGiro also gets a little extra in cash by lending your securities to shorter, parties speculating on a fall in prices. But that would only contribute to the low rates to a limited extent. If you buy and sell securities, you must also take into account the Belgian stock exchange tax, but this is, of course, the same for every broker.

How Much Does It Cost if I Leave?

The day you want to change your broker, you have to pay a fee to transfer your securities to your new broker. The amount depends on the number of positions you have. The total costs are calculated based on the number of lines in your securities portfolio.

MeDirect recently decided to increase the transfer costs from 35 to 150 euros per position for shares, and from 75 to 150 euros for funds. This puts the online broker at the level of a major bank such as BNP Paribas Fortis, which doubled the transfer costs to 150 euros. With the increase,

MeDirect serves the 'broker hoppers' with an answer. "We want to prevent some investors coming to us when we take a commercial action and then leave when another bank takes action," says Philippe Delva, CEO of MeDirect. The higher transfer costs will make MeDirect customers think twice before moving to another broker. But they can also scare off new customers. MeDirect is for the sake of new customers who come from another online broker. It reimburses their transfer costs up to a maximum amount of 500 euros per customer.

What Offer of News, Research, and Tools Do I Get?

News sources and analysis tools are also of great importance for small investors to make informed investment decisions. All six online brokers that we put under the microscope offer them. But one already does that more extensively than the other. MeDirect and DeGiro collect information about the different markets, but you miss the finger on the pulse because you do not have a live feed. They partly make up for that with newsletters and offline seminars and webinars. Keytrade Bank provides news from the Dow Jones Newswires news agency and sends out a morning and afternoon newsletter every day with figures and comments on the European and American markets. The newsletter with background articles and analyzes is added every month. Binck Bank has expanded its news offering in recent years. "The important messages on which the share price is moving have certainly been covered and are posted on our website quickly," says spokeswoman Marie Lammertyn. "Moreover, you can also act quickly because it contains buy/sell buttons."

At Lynx, you, as a customer, are entitled to the Reuters news feed. In addition to a monthly newsletter, you will also receive a technical analysis of five shares every week. The broker also organizes an online seminar almost every week. If you do not necessarily want to rely on your judgment, you can also 'copy' the transactions of three model portfolios at Lynx.

CHAPTER - 11

Introduction to Spreads

Positions that are composed of at least two of the same options that have limited risks, but also limited gains, are called Spread strategies. These strategies can be horizontal, vertical, diagonal and box range. Vertical ranges include purchase and sale of an equal number of the same options with the same maturity date.

Depending on whether you bind on expectations of price change of the underlying assets or the level of its volatility, the spreads can be bull, bear, and wingspreads, and each one of them can be achieved by the call and put options. Each this spread must be made "in a package."

The horizontal spread represents the investment strategy being carried out simultaneously by taking long and short positions in the same type of option on the same underlying assets at the same time of maturity but with different exercise prices. Depending on which options are used in the preparation of the horizontal range, we can see the difference between:

Bull Call Spread

Bull Put Spread

Bear Call Spread

Bear put Spread

Bull Call/Bear Put Spread

A spread is a difference between prices. Here, the spread will be on the strike prices of two sets of options. As with the straddles and strangles, this will require more than one piece. This involves buying and selling in the same trade, but we will limit the risk in the option writing with this strategy. I will give you an example here of a bull call spread, but the same applies (using the converse) for bear puts.

Winning outcome of bull spread is related to the increase in the price of the underlying assets, while the success of the bear spread is the expected substantial decrease in prices.

Bulls call spread is assembled in a way to buy a call option of underlying assets with a series of excellent prices and to sell the call options on the same property but with a higher strike price. The success of this type of spread depends on the increase in asset prices and the fall in prices, which will cause a loss. In this way, possible gains and losses are limited.

The preparation of the strategy of a bull put spread starts from the same position as for the various strike prices, so the bull call spread consists of purchasing put options with a lower price and a put option with a higher cost. In the case that the price increases, one will achieve limited gains, while the price drop will cause limited losses. A great price depends on the price of the put option. An investor who has a strategy bull put spread has a range of credit because he earned money on the difference in price. The investor buys an option at a lower price but sells another option at a high price. That's why we talk about credit range. If prices rose above most strike prices, investors with bulls put spreads strategies will achieve the greatest profits. But in a case of price drops below the lowest strike prices, this spreads strategies will achieve a limited loss of premiums.

Bear Put Spread is a combination of purchasing put options on certain underlying assets with the higher strike price, as well as drawing up a put option on the same property with a number of strike prices. This strategy gain is realized in the event of falling prices since the investor has the bear's expectations. Maximum height loss and gain are limited. As in the above ranges, the price of the put option depends on a strike price, and the option increases with the strike price. Since the put option makes a profit in the case of prices drop, profits will be higher if the strike price is higher. This is why the bear put spread is a debit range. Specifically, the investor loses the difference between the price at which he buys and sells options. Given that the maximum loss is limited, the worst that can happen is that, at the moment of maturity, the share price is to be above the most of the strike prices. In this case, both of the put options are worthless and the loss is limited to the amount of the premium.

As always, this trade can be reversed to deal with falling prices. It can also be implemented in both directions with both puts and calls. You have to determine the entry point based on the current price and how much you are willing to lose, your expected direction of the stock, and the possible profit, which is capped.

Butterflies

This one is even more complicated, and it requires three components. The basic idea is to buy one low, in-the-money call, selling two at-the-money calls and finally buying a high, out-of-the-money call. This is a strategy for when you expect the market to move sideways, for the highest profit is in the middle and you can maintain a profit within a range. As with most of these strategies involving more than one component, the risk and reward are both limited.

The profit is highest when the spot price is equal to the two written calls. You keep the premium for both written (short) calls, but lose the premiums paid on the two purchased (long) calls. The higher long call is going to cost much less than the short call premiums, as it is far out-of-the-money, but the lower long call is going to cost more since it is either in-the-money or at least closer to being so. The risk is capped at the premiums paid for the long calls. If the underlying is below the lower strike or above the higher strike on your longs, you will incur the maximum loss. From that, you can easily see this strategy is for range trading. You can make big spreads, but keep in mind the profits will be based on how far into the money you are. You can make this more complicated, but you must retain symmetry. Notice that the long and short positions have equal numbers of shares at stake and you should keep your expiration dates the same. Otherwise, you will either open yourself up to a huge risk or diminish your possible profits.

This spread is not directed to increase or to decrease the price of the underlying assets. The investor who chooses a strategy of short butterfly trading expects a significant change in the price, in any direction, regardless of whether it is rising or falling, of the underlying assets. The short butterfly spread is possible to draw up the buying and selling options. If a short butterfly is made up of put options, the trader sells one option with lower and one with the higher exercise price and buys two put options with an average exercise price. Butterfly range can be made in four different ways, which points to its complexity. This includes:

1. The Purchase of a Call Option with the Highest and Lowest Reasonable Price and the Simultaneous Sale of Two Call Options at an Average Price.

2. The Purchase of a Put Option with the Highest and Lowest Exercise Price and the Simultaneous Sale of Two Put Options with High Prices

3. The Purchase of a Call Option at the Lowest Exercise Price, and Selling Call Options at an Average Price Along with the Purchase of Put Options at the Highest

Price, and Sell Put Options at an Average Exercise Price

4. The Purchase of Put Options at the Lowest Exercise Price and Selling Put Options at an Average Price with the Purchase of a Call Option at the Highest Exercise Price and Sell Call Options at an Average Exercise Prices

Condor Spread

Condor spread consists of two horizontal spreads of conflicting expectations and includes four options on the same underlying assets with the same due date. Four different exercise prices for each option show the complexity of the Condor spread.

Condor Spread with Call Options

The similarity of the condor spread with the butterfly spread is inevitable, but the difference is that in the condor spread, there are two different medium exercise prices and the butterfly spread has only one. To perform the long condor spread with the call options trader must buy a call option with a range of exercise price, sell a call option with a slightly higher exercise price, sell a call option with an even greater exercise price, and buy a call option with the highest exercise price.

Vertical Spread

The simultaneous purchase and sale, purchase or sale of options on the same underlying assets, and the same exercise price, but in different maturities, is resulting in the vertical spread. The vertical spread is referred to as the calendar spread due to the use of different maturities. We can distinguish calendar put spread and calendar call spread. These types of neutral strategies can be focused on the growth and drop in asset prices. Combining the different times of maturity in the compiling spread, the investor combines intrinsic value, and time value, of occupied positions in a particular option. In this way, in a case of the option with less time, the investor is set to its intrinsic value, while with the options with a longer time to maturity; the investor puts in the time value of options as a primary goal.

Neutral Calendar Spread

If prices rise or fall in relation to the strike price, the composer of the vertical spread is faced with limited loss. The compiler spread can achieve only limited losses. The main purpose of the assemblers of a neutral calendar spread with call options is to close before expiration of the call option with a shorter expiration time and, at the same time, to expect price stability relative to the price of the call exercise.

Bulls' Calendar Spread

These are aggressive calendar spreads that have bull's expectations, therefore, focused on the increase in share prices or other property. Bull's calendar spread is within a certain range, also neutral, it is compiled with the current market price that is below the strike price of the calendar spread. The advantages of such spread are lower initial cost and a good chance of making the profit, but with significant risk.

To compiler of the bull calendar spread, achieved profits are required in two events. First, he will make a call option with a shorter time to maturity (short option), which should expire worthlessly. Therefore, the range and draw up options go beyond - because the money is likely to call option with a shorter time to maturity. In this way, the investor is left with a call option with a longer time to maturity (longer optional). Secondly, it is necessary to increase the prices of the underlying assets in the strike price range, after the maturity date of options. If the price increases, the investor will make a profit.

CHAPTER - 12

Options and Leverage

As with any investment, your brokerage firm will likely offer leverage, that is, money loaned to you to be invested. While this greatly increases your ability to enter into potentially profitable positions, it obviously increases your risk as well. A quick refresher on leverage is in order, but we assume you have a good understanding of the concept, so we'll keep it brief. The reason leverage is so frequently used in all types of trading is that individual traders frequently lack the capital to make meaningful moves in the market. If your broker offers leverage of 3:1, for instance, that means that for every dollar you put in of your own money, your broker will loan you three dollars to enlarge your investment.

Of course, this money must be paid back, but because of the nature of investing, your profits will still be increased. Let's look at an example. You have found a stock that you think is attractive. You buy 100 shares at $1 per share. Your brokerage gives you leverage at 3:1, so you are able to invest $300 of their money as well. So, in total, you hold 400 shares of the stock. The stock doubles in price the next week, and you are able to sell all 400 shares for a total of $800. After you pay your broker back their

$300 investment, you're left with a profit of $500. Without leverage, if you had only been able to invest your original $100, you would have been able to sell those 100 shares for $200.

Your profit with leverage is $300 greater than it would have been. This is clearly a very dramatic example for the sake of clarity, but the increased percentages in profits using leverage are very real. You can never forget, however, that the opposite is also true. If your stock in the above example had tanked, you would still be on the hook to your broker for the $300 investment that is now lost. So, instead of just losing your own $100, you would have multiplied your monetary loss by a multiple of three.

Now that we're all on the same page, we'll look at special considerations that are important when trading in options.

Options are, as we've talked about before, derivatives. Most derivatives are, by their nature, riskier than simply buying the underlying asset outright. Because of this, brokers require traders who are seeking leverage to buy options to sign a form stating that they understand the risk of using leverage in options trading. This has contributed to the reputation options have as being an especially, even unacceptably risky investment. Don't let this scare you away, though. Risk is often thought of as the "boogeyman" in investing, but let's thinks critically for a moment. If you were completely averse to risk, you'd put all of your money in T Bills, or bury it in the back yard. Risk is simply the other half of the opportunity coin.

In a way, options function as their own kind of leverage.

You may not have the cash on hand to be able to buy 100 shares of some stock. The option will be much cheaper than the stock itself, so you may want to buy the option and then, when it's proven that it will be possible, use the leverage from your broker to exercise your option. With trading strategies that have as many steps as most options trades have, an example is usually helpful. Note that in these examples, we've eliminated brokerage fees for the sake of clarity.

Let's say shares of Spatulas R Us stock are trading at $40 per share. You have looked into the spatula industry and expect it to boom in the upcoming months. SRU is a leader in its industry, so you're pretty confident they will rise in price. All but $4000 of your investment capital is tied up in other ways at the moment though, so if you were to buy the shares outright, you could only buy 100 shares. Let's look at two paths: buying outright and using an option as leverage.

In the first instance, you would buy your 100 shares. Then, just as you predicted, the spatula boom caused the price of your SRU stock to rise to $42 per share. You sell them, making a $200 profit. This is a 5% profit of your total investment. Not bad!

In the second instance, you look up the price for an SRU stock option and see that it's $50. You go ahead and buy 4 options, meaning you have the opportunity to buy 400 shares during the duration of your contract. The same boom happens, and SRU goes up to $42 per share. You exercise your option, and either by liquidating other assets or borrowing from your broker, buy those 400 shares for the $40 price you locked in when you purchased your option. You immediately sell them for the new price of $42, giving you an immediate profit of $800. Of course, you still spent $200 on options in the first place, so your real profit is $600. That might not sound like a shockingly big difference, but look at the percentages! Your profit, in this instance, is 15% of the original investment.

Of course, there is the possibility that the spatula boom you foresaw does not actually happen. Let's take a look at what happens in the above situations when you are wrong. (We are going to assume that you're not a terrible trader and have your stop losses in place. You do, right?)

Alright, let's say you're sitting there, the proud owner of 100 SRU shares that you paid your $4000 for. The stock price drops, and you dump the stocks at $36 (a 10% drop, which is a common point at which to set your stop loss). You've realized a loss of $400, or 10% of your investment.

In the example where you bought the options instead of the stock outright, your investment was only $200. You simply decide not to exercise the option when you see that the stock is dropping. You do lose the money you paid for the premiums, but your total loss is only 5% of what you would have invested had you exercised the option.

Now let's look at how leverage can stack up with the natural leveraging effect of options. As you've seen, leverage can be used to exercise an option that you might not have the capital to otherwise. But what about using leverage to purchase the option itself? Many experts avoid this for any reason because the risk that the option will never pay off is just too high. That's a determination you'll have to make for yourself. When you do, make sure that you are doing the math correctly and clearly, and know what your potential gains and losses are on the deal before you enter into the position. Let's look at an example of what the above situation would have looked like had you used leverage to purchase the options.

First, let's look at the sunnier prospect: you were right about the spatula industry, and the stock jumps up. Let's say your broker offered leverage at a rate of 3:1. You decide that with that rate, you can buy many more options. You purchase 16 options instead of 4, but your initial input is still only $200 because your brokerage supplies the other $600 in the form of leverage. The stock rises as before, you exercise your options, and then immediately sell the shares for a profit of $2 per share. That nets you $3200! After subtracting the $600 you have to pay back to your broker, you're still left with $2600, a whopping 1300% increase on your initial outlay of $200.

Now let's look at what happens if the spatula boom does not pan out and you don't end up exercising any of these options. Your total loss is $800, your $200 plus the $600 you have to pay your broker back. That's a loss of four times as much just buying the smaller amount of options and having them not work out, and twice as much of a loss as buying the stock outright (assuming you don't let your losses run out of control.)

You will rarely have to calculate the delta of an option on your own anymore because almost every investing software or website will do it for you. It's still valuable to know what it is because you will see it from time to time. If an option has a delta value of 1 which means that the option and underlying asset are moving in lock-step, a delta value of 0 means that they are moving independently of one another. The delta value is an important value indicator because it indicates whether an option is "in the money," "at the money," or "out of the money." These phrases mean whether the option's strike prices are above, even to, or below the current price of the underlying stock. For put options, the same phrases are used, but they indicate negative movement rather than positive.

Intrinsic Value

The intrinsic value of an option is the difference between the asset price and the strike price. For a call option, it is calculated by subtracting the stock price from the strike price. For put options, it is the opposite. An intrinsic value of zero indicates that the difference calculated in these equations is negative.

Extrinsic Value

This is also known as the "time value" of an option. It is the difference between the market value, i.e., what the market is willing to pay for the option, and the intrinsic value. In the case of a call option, if the current market price is below the strike price, then the only value the option has is its extrinsic value. For put options, it is the opposite. The time before the expiration date is the main factor determining extrinsic value. The more time there is before an option expires, the more time there is for it to move in a profitable direction, so this makes sense. An option that is out of the money (the current stock price is below the strike price in the case of call options, above the strike price for puts) with an expiration date several months away is going to have a higher extrinsic value than one that expires in a few days.

The other main factor in calculating extrinsic value is the volatility of the underlying asset. The more implied volatility the asset has, the higher the extrinsic value will be. This will shift over the life of the option as the market shifts. Just as buying an option at a low price when you suspect the price will rise is the goal of successful options trading, so is buying one with low volatility that you expect to rise.

CHAPTER - 13

Options Trading Mistakes to Avoid

Option trading can be challenging to master, and you may find yourself going through a frustrating period of trial and error in an attempt to get it right. This is especially likely if you are completely new to options trading, and attempt to view it from the eyes of regular stock market trading. Options trading follow its unique set of rules, and not being conversant with these rules is what can lead you to make some time consuming and costly mistakes.

To save you time, these are the mistakes you are likely to make before getting it right. With this information, you can avoid these mistakes and fast track successful options trading.

Mistake #1 – Applying One Strategy in Every Situation

Different market conditions require differing unique approaches. Sometimes, an options trader will apply the only strategy he knows to every option purchase he makes. This can lead to loss of money and disaster on your portfolio. Buying spreads should be considered as a solution to this problem, and they will fix the mistake. Buying spreads allow you to trade effectively in a range of market conditions. A spread means that you purchase a myriad of options and adopt different strategies to suit these options. In a way, you could say that you are effectively spreading your risk. When you buy several spreads, you adopt a 'long spread' position.

The long spread position has two options – a high-cost option which is bought and a low-cost option which is sold. These options will have some conditions for security, expiration and type of options, which will make it easier to choose the strategy. You can then evaluate the values to make a decision as to when to hold on to your options, or when to sell them. The only thing to watch out for is that using a spread approach may lead to multiple options traded that incur multiple commissions, which may mean higher expenses.

Mistake #2 –Buying Out Of the Money Call Options from the Onset

Most people attempt new ways to invest with a little trepidation because they want to avoid loss, especially a large loss. For that reason, when some opt for options trading, they start with buying call options, as this allows for "testing the waters." It allows for buying low and selling high. Unfortunately, this method is not consistent in the long run and may lead to losing money. Therefore, one needs to consider at least one other strategy to go hand in hand with call options when purchasing. The reason for this is when you buy options, you need to be right about the direction of the move and the timing. A mistake on either of these factors may result in completely losing the option premium paid.

Mistake #3 – Breaking Your Own Rules

When you start trading and you move into your rhythm, you are likely to create specific rules to follow, so as to avoid compromising or loss leading situations in the future. These rules may include 'never selling in the money options' or 'never buying out of the money options.'

When you are faced with an option trade that is going against you, you will definitely be tempted to break all your own rules. This happens when you give in to panic and start reasoning from your emotions, rather than from your options plan. Although when trading in the stock market, you can justify changing your own rules by "doubling up to catch up" for example, this is not possible in the options trading setting.

To evaluate your position before you do something irrational, look at the situation and ask yourself whether you would have made the same move you are now contemplating when you first opened your options. If your answer is a resounding no, do not break your own rules. Consider an alternative game plan.

Mistake #4 – Not Planning Your Exit

It is important to remember that options are decaying assets, and the rate of decay quickly accelerates as the expiration date approaches. In any type of investment you make, you need to have an exit plan in case things go awry. This is also very applicable if things appear to be going well with your options. For options trading, this plan should include your upside exit point and your downside exit point, and your proposed timeframe to complete your exit. As much as possible, you should avoid giving in to greed, particularly if it seems like the options are within your upside exit point as you may be tempted to hold on to them in the hope of gaining more profit.

A plan will stop you from leaving your option too early due to panic, which would mean that you miss out on possible high returns. It will also help you make the right decision when you are experiencing an upswing, as holding on for too long can suddenly lead to extreme loss. An exit plan helps you conceptualize your worst-case scenario on the downside and how it is; you would deal with it once it occurs. It also helps you set upside goals that establish your position for when you want to take your profits and move on.

Options trading requires serious scenario concentration and planning, and should not be driven by emotions. As with any investment, when you purchase options, you should keep in mind that there always exists the possibility that you will completely lose your investment. This is why it is important to have a plan ready.

Mistake #5 – Trading Illiquid Options

A quote options form the market will have a different bid price and ask price. They do not show the actual value of the option, as the value is somewhere in the middle of the bid and ask. The distance between the bid and ask prices depends on the options liquidity.

At the money and near the money options which have near term expiration are usually the most liquid, meaning that if the need arises, they can quickly be converted to cash. As your strike price moves further from the at the money strike price or expiration date goes further into the future, the options are less liquid.

There is the point in trading in options that cannot be easily liquidated when the need arises. Illiquid options can lose you a lot of money as if you are trying to save them suddenly, their prices can drop significantly. You should focus on purchasing liquid options that have an active number of buyers and sellers. Illiquid options are most prevalent with smaller stocks, causing the bid and ask prices to get artificially wide.

Mistake #6 – Wasting Time When Buying Back Stock Options

You should be ready and willing to buy back stock options you may have sold. This can help you save on commission charges and make a little more profit from the trade. You could also consider buying back your options immediately if you are able to keep 80% or more of your initial gain.

Take, for example, you had a contract that spans a period of four months. Within the second month, you are lucky and have already realized an excellent profit. Rather than waiting, you should see your stock options to cash in on your profit, and immediately reinvest your 'principal' in some more of the same options. It could be possible that you will get more profit before your contract end date comes up again.

Mistake #7 – Not Understanding Implied Volatility

You must take time to understand the intricacies of option pricing and volatility. Implied volatility helps you gauge whether an option is cheap or expensive based on past price action in the underlying stock. It is very important when pricing options.

If you understand implied volatility, you can consistently make money when trading options. The less volatile an option is, the more liquid it becomes, and the easier it is to sell your options so that you can realize your profits.

Mistake #8 – Ignoring Powerful Compounded Small Gains

The most successful options traders will have steady profits as they use a range of strategies and set goals like attaining a monthly gain from 2-4%. Options traders should avoid taking extreme risks, as you could be up 100% in one month, and then down 70% in the next month. Although there is room for speculation, you should pick your options spots carefully.

It is far better to put together the small profits which can be gained from a spread than to hold out in the hope that you will make one big return from a single option. The gains from a range of options are likely to add up and offer more than what one option could provide in the long run.

Mistake #9 – Not Understanding Time Decay

Options can easily be a wasting asset. A trader needs to keep in mind the price of an option until the time of expiration. So purchasing puts or calls outright with the underlying stock moving in your direction slowly may means the option does not gain in value. Also, the nearer an option gets to its expiry date, the more important it becomes to sell that option so that you can avoid losing your investment.

Mistake #10–Not Paying Attention to Market Moving Events

If you create an options trade based on a quiet market condition, you will profit as long as the underlying assets stay docile. You need to keep an eye out for market-moving events that might affect your stock during the time frame of your trade. An earnings release could increase volatility and change market conditions, putting a stop could change your quiet time plan.

Your strategy should be able to accommodate such changes and as an options trader, you should be aware of what is occurring in a range of financial markets, whether or not you believe that you will be affected.

CHAPTER - 14

Options Trading Account

Your trading account is where all options trading activities will be done. Basically, an options trading account is a system or platform used by an investor to purchase and buy financial securities such as stocks, indexes and many others. The trading account is held by the brokerage firm and used to manage trading activities on your behalf. With an online trading account, you can hold cash, stocks, and other type of securities.

Technology has made it easy for managing trading accounts. To start using your trading account, you must first of all fund it. Many people think they can use a bill from a friend to fund their options trading account. Well, that is not allowed. Your bank account will be connected to the trading account. Through bank wire or transfer, you can transfer funds into the brokerage account through your savings or checking accounts.

Another factor to consider is a tax. Your trading account can be taxable or tax-deferred like a 401 (k). You can also decide if your trading account will be taxable or simply a non-retirement account. You can choose to open an individual account or brokerage account for your business to trade. These are just forms of trading account, but there are two main types based on their functionality: margin and cash trading account.

Margin vs. Cash Trading Account

Margin Trading Account: A margin account is simply a brokerage account that provides you with a line of credit to buy options, stocks and other securities. Are you planning on using leverage for your trading? Through a margin trading account you can borrow money to buy stocks or options. This gives you a form of leverage if you don't have cash at hand to purchase securities.

What you need to know about the margin trading account is that all margins come with an interest. All the money borrowed to you for trading has an interest associated with it. That means for each that trade you are successful with; the brokerage account has to deduct taxes, fees and interests used in purchasing the securities.

The typical rate is 2% over the prime interest rate. An Intraday Margin Account, for instance, works on a 4:1 leverage ratio. That means for every amount of equity that you have, you will be granted access to credit four (4) times that amount. Let's say that you have a cash amount of $ 1,000 through an intra-margin account you can borrow as much as $ 4,000 for your trading activities.

Cash Trading Account: A trading account deals with only cash. There is no line of credits for you to borrow the securities you deem feasible for you. All trading transactions in your account will be done via the cash you have transferred into the trading account via your savings or checking bank account. This account means you have no form of leverage for all trading decisions.

For instance, when you placed $1,000 into your cash trading account, the only money available for you to spend in buying and trading securities will be that $1,000.00. If you don't close any position in your trading account, you will not have any line of credit to provide you with purchasing power. The settlement date for cash accounts varies, but they can be as short as the day of the transaction and the following one.

Steps to Open a Trading Account

1. Providing Personal Information

To open a trading account, the brokerage firm will require you to provide certain personal financial information. This financial information helps the broker to track, manage and handle your account. You need to be careful you provide the right details to facilitate smooth trading activities. The sign-up process for a brokerage account varies from one broker to another, but the personal information required to run the account is almost the same.

2. Providing Additional Information

The following information must be provided: Your legal name, email address, social security number, employment status, approximate annual income, and others. Some brokers want to know your experience level in trading underlying securities like stocks, index funds, and options.

Are you a registered broker-dealer? Are you managing

a brokerage account on behalf of an individual or an institution? Are you a shareholder in a company assigned to manage the brokerage account for the company? All this additional information will be asked to enable the broker to tailor their services to you. A special disclosure obligation will also be provided to authenticate and protect the information provided.

3. Idle Cash Management

If you have idle cash in your brokerage account, how will it be managed? Your broker would want to know how you intend to handle or manage the account. For example, you have invested and earned $16,500 worth of money. You have decided to trade in other securities with $10,000, what would you like the idle 6,500 to do? You might want to instruct the broker to push it into interest-bearing accounts such as treasury funds, mutual funds or even the money markets.

4. Trading Account Suitability

There are various kinds of trading styles. Your broker would want to know the best way you want to handle risk and manage trading activities. It is the goal of the broker to know the customer and provide the best support and services to be successful in trading activities. Some of the trading styles can be: aggressive growth (more risk-taking in volatile securities), Simple Growth (gain money while preserving original capital), Income Risk Level (using income generate from profits for further trading) and Conservative (capital preservation and using the account of only one thing to protect existing assets).

5. Signing Account Opening Agreement

Before the trading account is opened, the broker would ensure that you sign and approve all the information provided. You might want to check all the information provided as well as read the contract statement to know the terms, policies and conditions used by the broker in managing the trading account. Once you are done, you can then confirm to agree with the terms for the trading contract. An electronic signature, print & sign or mail & sign will be used.

7 Easy Steps to Start Options Trading

To Begin Options Trading, the Following are Some Things to Get Started with:

1. Initial Preparation

2. Choosing an Online Broker

3. Finding your Options Trading Niche

4. Finding Option Trades Opportunities

5. Planning Individual Trades

6. Risk and Money Management

7. Monitoring your Trades

Initial Preparation

It all starts with your mindset. Before you begin options trading, you have to make sure that you have the right mindset of successful options traders. Are you afraid of risk or are you a risk lover? What is your attitude towards winning and losing? What is your approach to trading in the financial market? Analyze yourself and see if options trading is for you, looking at your deep-seated values.

You also need to develop a trading plan. You've got to develop a trading plan that outlines your entry and exit strategy. If you don't have a long-term plan for options trading, chances are that you will give up in the first three or six months. Have profits targets and income ceiling to hit for options trading.

You might also choose to trade in companies that you are comfortable or understand what there are doing. That depends on your trading plan. But to find good options trading opportunities you have to make good use of your trading account and then also dedicate a certain amount of time to study the trade. The more you devote your time to studying the stock market or index trading market, the easier you begin to spot opportunities that are good for you.

While you have to focus on your options trading plan, you need to avoid being urgent. You don't have to be under any repulsion to trade in something you don't understand. All options trading opportunities must be validated through research, evaluation and analysis. If you begin each trade by doing your analysis, you will limit your risk and increase your gains.

Planning Each Individual Trades

When it comes to options trading, the first thing you need to know is how to analyze the market. When you have a good trading opportunity that you are happy about, the next step should be planning each trade. You have to make a calculated risk and manage your risk. You are the CEO of your options trading as well as the chief risk officer.

To minimize your risks in options trading, you have to take research and evaluation very important. You must do your technical analysis. Learn how to analyze stock price movements using moving average, supports and resistance, charts and probability graph. Sometimes, just doing the technical analysis is not enough. There can be fundamental factors that will impact stock price movements.

Risk & Money Management

Every trade involves an amount of risk and capital investments. The better the trading plan and money management skills, the better you will be in managing your risk with each trading capital investment. You must avoid putting all your trading capital into one deal. Limit options trading capital to 10 to 15%.

Learn to control your budget and plan you're financially very well. When you begin to make profits in options, avoid spending the money. Invest the money into your long term-investment account so that it can compound and grow more. Budget your trading capital in such a way that you don't get wiped out in the game.

When it comes to money, many people tend to be emotional. Don't be emotional about stock trends and analysis. Follow the facts and manage the risk. Each capital disbursement should be followed with careful analysis of the option and the underlying strategies to use. Sometimes your analysis can be good, but where the problems come is using the right strategies.

Monitoring Your Trades

You have to keep track of your score. The main focus of every investor is to increase their return on investment (ROI). You want to make sure that you get your money back with much more returns on it. The wind may not go in your favor all the time, but you have to make sure that you have more wins than losses. That is why you have to be conservative about options trading.

What is your initial trading capital? How much did you use to start the trading year? How much profit have you made? What are your average wins? Use the trade performance metrics to measure, track and improve your position. If you measure, evaluate and keep track of progress, you will do well in the long term with your trading.

Finally, look for ways and means to improve. Invest more time into learning about options trading. Learn new strategies, new skills and new ways of analyzing the financial market. Plan each trade wisely, give your best in each trade and manage your trading capital well. Look at how other options traders are doing and learn from them. You might even want to join options trading groups, forums and masterminds.

CHAPTER - 15

How Can You Make Money from Stock

Do you know that you can make money from stocks in two ways, which are dividends and capital appreciation?

Dividends refer to the portion of a corporation's net income for the year that the Board of Directors decides to distribute to the owners, i.e., the shareholders. Dividends may or may not be declared every year because it will depend on whether the corporation earned a good income for the past year and if there are no upcoming projects or activities that need to be funded by retained income or earnings. The only exception to this is cumulative preferred shares, which is a breed of preferred shares that are guaranteed dividend payments every year. If a corporation's Board of Directors doesn't declare dividends for a specific year, the dividends due to such preferred shares are accumulated or treated as dividends payable to be settled as soon as dividends are declared.

There are two reasons why you shouldn't look to dividends for successful stock market investing. The first one is that often, dividends represent a minuscule amount of the market price of stocks. You'd be lucky to get a dividend that's about 10% of the price at which you bought your stocks. The second reason is dividends are very contingent on the financial plans and performance of a company. In other words, they're not even guaranteed, unless you invest in cumulative preferred shares. And given the relatively low number of dividends you may expect, it's just not worth it.

Capital appreciation is where the money's at. This is also referred to as the buy-low-sell-high strategy for making money in stocks. Capital appreciation refers to an increase in the market price of stocks that you buy, and you will surely hit the mark when you sell them on at a much higher price than which you bought them for. For example, you can buy shares of stock of a publicly listed company for $2 a share, and if after five years its price goes up to $4 per share, you'd have doubled your money in just five years! Many people - especially during very good times for the stock market - go agog over initial public offerings or IPOs, which is when shares of stock of corporations are first offered for investing to the general public via the major stock exchanges. Often, the prices of such stocks skyrocket within the first trading day or two, especially if the general market sentiment is very good. It's not unheard of for investors to nearly double their money buying stocks through IPOs and selling them immediately when they start to trade on exchanges.

And speaking of buying stocks at a low price and selling them far along at much higher ones.

Factors that Determine Stock Prices

Many factors can affect the prices of stocks in general, but all of those factors converge into one single biggest factor:

investor sentiment. Keep in mind the primary economic law of supply and demand, i.e., the higher the demand vis-a-vis the supply, the higher the price, and the lower the demand vis-a-vis the supply, the lower the price. That's why all serious stock market investors tend to be anal about the news on networks such as CNBC, Bloomberg, or Reuters. Sometimes, even a piece of news that most of the general public doesn't even care about can seriously affect the prices of shares of stock.

It's for the same reason why the average annual rates of return on shares of stocks of the biggest and most established companies (i.e., blue-chip stocks) aren't as prolific as the younger and less-established ones. By being very big already and in relatively mature industries whose average annual growths aren't as exciting, there's not as much room for substantial growth in both asset size and income compared too much younger industries. But because they're already established, they tend to be less risky compared to growth stocks. So, if you're after much higher returns and are comfortable taking on higher risks, growth stocks are the way to go. If your risk tolerance is a bit lower, then blue-chip stocks are the way to go.

Factors That Determine a Stock's Value

Now, that's not to say that there's no way to objectively determine the true value of a particular share of stock. You must bear in mind that there's a difference between the current market price and value. Often, current market price and value don't see eye to eye. The current market price is what investors, in general, are willing to pay and sell shares of stock for, which may or may not be a stock's objective value.

Since we're on the topic of value, how can you estimate a particular share of stock's actual value? Well, there are many ways to go about it, but most of them involve financial data like earnings, capitalization, and average growth in assets and income. But the primary financial data that affect the valuation of stocks is a company's earnings.

And speaking of earnings, some of the most common measures used to value shares of stocks include earnings-per-share (or EPS), return on equity (ROE) or investment (ROI), and price-earnings ratio (PE Ratio), which are determined as follows:

• EPS is computed by dividing net income after tax by the total number of shares outstanding and is expressed in dollar-terms, e.g., $0.50 per share;

• ROE or ROI is computed by dividing a company's net income after tax over average shareholder equity (ROE) or the average, or current market price of a stock and is expressed in percent, e.g., 10% ROE or ROI; and

• PE Ratio is generated by dividing the current market price of a stock over its latest EPS and is expressed as several times, e.g., ten times or 10X. This means that in general, the stock is selling at a price that's ten times more than its annual earnings per share or that investors are willing to pay $10 for the opportunity to earn about $1 per share.

Active and Passive Stock Investing

When it comes to making money from stocks, there are two ways to do it: actively and passively. And it's by understanding the difference between the two that you'll have a better idea of what investing and trading mean.

Active Investing

As you could infer from the term itself, active investing means a relatively high degree of activity. In other words, you'll need to be more active or involved in managing your stock investments. This means that on top of doing your homework in terms of choosing your stocks wisely, you'll also need to monitor its performance regularly, depending on your investment time frame, i.e., short or long term. These are the things you'll need to do regularly if you choose the active investing route:

• Research and Evaluate: What makes investing in the stock market much different from gambling in a casino, which some "geniuses" think is a very apt comparison, is that you don't just pick random stocks to trade or invest in and expect success? No, you'll need to research and evaluate stocks based on the information you're able to gather to come up with a candidates' shortlist. And from such a shortlist, you'll pick the stocks in which to trade or invest.

• Take Positions: All the research and evaluation in the world will be for naught if that's where you'll end your journey. You'll need to take action based on the information you've gathered and evaluated by taking a position on any or all of the stocks in your shortlist, i.e., buy stocks. Unless you take actual positions, you will not earn anything from stocks. When you buy stocks, you're taking a LONG position. When you're selling stocks that you own, you're taking a SQUARE position. And when you sell shares of stocks that you do not own, you're taking a SHORT position. We'll deal with short positions or short selling.

• Monitoring: When you're after a very quick buck with every stock purchase you make, the more important it is for you to keep track of the price of your stocks frequently. It's because there's a very good chance that you might miss the quick profits boat if you don't check market prices every few hours.

At this point, I'd like to bring to your attention the words "trading" and "investment," in case you're wondering why I'm using them both or interchangeably. Here's the reason: trading is the term often used to refer to very short investment periods. When stock market veterans say they're "trading" stocks, what they're saying is that their investment horizons are very, very short. How short? The longest would probably be a couple of days to a week, while many trades are daily. This means that after they buy, they wait for the price to go up several points within the day of the week and they quickly sell their shares to cash in on the profits. People who "trade" stocks this way have to do it frequently so that over a month or a year, their small profits accumulate into a much bigger total.

However, there's no official barometer for considering whether or not a specific investment holding period's considered as trading or investing so pardon me if I interchangeably use the two terms throughout the volume. It's because when you look at the grand scheme of things, trading and investing are practically the same and the only difference, albeit an arbitrary one, is the time frame. You see, the ultimate goal of trading is the same as buying-and-holding, which is to earn a profit.

Managing Emotions

One of the secrets of the most successful stock market traders is the ability to rein their emotions. In the exciting and frenzied world of the stock market, it can be very easy to be carried away by very strong - and often irrational - emotions such as excitement, anxiety, and greed. Too much excitement can make you buy stocks that are already considered by experts as "expensive." Being too anxious or fearful of incurring losses can cause you to miss out on opportunities to earn very good returns by not buying stocks when appropriate.

Passive Investing

Passive investments are very popular these days, sometimes for the right reasons but mostly for the wrong ones. For one, many personal finance "gurus" have painted passive investing to be the financial savior of every individual on earth who's living in poverty today. For others, many such gurus also make it appear - albeit not purposefully - as if building passive income streams that generate enough passive income is easy. And lastly, the same so-called gurus make it appear that passive investing is passive, i.e., a perfectly inactive form of investing where you do nothing and riches will continue flowing to you. But is passive investing all that? Let's find out, shall we?

Passive investing is taken from the word "passive," which means, among other things, inactive. Therefore, many people have the impression that passive investing means practically waiting for money to just come in. Now, this is where I'll have to shed a bit more light on passive investing.

CHAPTER - 16

Trading Varying Time Frames

Weekly Options Trading

Weekly options are listings that provide an opportunity for short-term trading as well as plenty of hedging possibilities. As the name states, they have an expiration time of exactly one week; in general, they are listed on Thursday and expire the following Friday. While they have been around for decades, in the past, they have primarily been the domain of investors who work with cash indices. This level of exclusivity changed in 2011 when the Chicago Board of Options expanded the number of ways they could be traded, especially to make them more easily acceptable to traders like you. Since then, the number of stocks that can be traded weekly has grown from 28 to nearly 1,000.

In addition to having a short time frame, weekly options differ from traditional options in that they are only available 3 weeks out of the month. They are also never listed in the monthly expiration style. In fact, the weeks that monthly options expire are technically the same as weekly options.

Advantages of weekly options: The biggest benefit of buying into weekly options is the fact you are free to purchase exactly what you need for the exact trade you are looking to make without having to worry about coming up with extra capital or dealing with more options than you currently need. This means if you are looking to start a swing trade, or even an intraday trade, weekly options will have you covered. For those looking to sell, weekly options provide the ability to do so more frequently, rather than having to wait a month between sales.

Weekly options trades are also useful in that they lead to reduced costs for trades that have longer spreads, such as diagonal spreads or calendar spreads, as they can sell weekly options against them. They are also useful to higher volume trades as they are useful when it comes to hedging larger positions and portfolios against potential risky events. Also, when the market is range-bound the weekly options, it can still be utilized through means such as the iron butterfly or iron condor.

Disadvantages: The biggest disadvantage when it comes to weekly options is the fact that you will not ever have very much time for a trade to turn around if you make the wrong choice in the first place. If you are selling options, then you will also need to know that their gamma will also be much more sensitive than it would be with more traditional options. This means that if you are planning to short options, then a relatively small move overall can still lead to an out of the money option entering into the money very quickly.

Buying weekly: Because you are always going to have much less time when it comes to turning a profit with a weekly option, your timing for when to move on a specific decision is going to need to be much more precise than it would otherwise have to be. If you choose poorly at strike selection, time frame or price direction, then you can easily find yourself paying for an option that is generally worthless. You will also need to consider your acceptable level of risk, as the option will be cheaper per unit, but you will need to buy more in a week than you would otherwise.

Selling weekly: Selling reliably for the long-term can generate steady profits if done properly, it only works this way if you are defining your earnings in advance, which means it is important to always know what your options are worth to prevent you from selling yourself short. Selling trades weekly will make it easier to collect the full premium if they guess correctly while still leaving you exposed to unmitigated losses if you choose poorly, which requires an extra margin.

The ideal types of the underlying stock to use for these types of trades is going to be lower priced as they each ultimately consume a smaller amount of your total buying power. This also means it is easier to move forward on trades with lots of implied volatility, as it is more likely to revert to the mean in the allotted time. As a rule, selling a put in the short-term is always better than selling a call as it tends to generate an overall higher return in the shorter period.

Spreads: Spreads are a great way of making a profit in the weekly market. The overall level of implied volatility is going to be much higher in the weekly market than in the monthly variation, so the spread can help you when you find yourself dealing with an unexpected directional change quickly enough that you can actually do something about it. Selling an option against a long option will naturally decrease the role volatility plays in the transaction. The best point to use the debt spread will be near where the price currently is, providing you with a 1 to 1 risk and reward ratio.

Intraday Trades

While options are frequently left out of day trading strategies, this trend is slowly changing. Traders are slowly but surely realizing that they can apply many standard day trading techniques when it comes to selling and buying options successfully.

Intraday trading challenges: When attempting to day trade options, you are likely going to run into some unique challenges that you should be able to best with the proper consideration.

Price movement will decrease value more significantly due to the time value naturally associated with options that are only near the money so close to their period of expiration. Remember, while their inherent value is likely to increase along with the underlying stock price, which will be dramatically countered by the time value loss.

The bid-ask spreads are typically going to be wider than they would otherwise be, which is due to the reduced liquidity that you will typically find with the options market. This will frequently vary by as much as .5 of a point, which can cut into profits if things move at an inopportune time.

Some types of options are naturally a better fit when it comes to day trading than others. Perhaps the most effective is the near month in the money option, which is appropriate for those traders who are a fan of trading stocks with a high level of liquidity. The premium on this type of option is based more closely on its overall value as it is already in the money and getting close to its expiration date. If this occurs, the time value drain is decreased dramatically. This type of option is generally traded most effectively in periods of high volume, which tends to result in a decrease in the gap between asking price and bidding price.

Protective put: The protective put is a type of option that is useful when you purchase put orders along with shares of the related underlying stock. This is a reliable strategy when the underlying stock is likely to experience a high degree of volatility. It is especially effective when used to purchase the same option throughout the day to continue to capitalize on short bursts of positive movement. It is also useful when it comes to providing insurance when purchasing shares of a risky underlying stock, as you will always be limited in your potential losses to the price of the options you purchased.

Protective puts are also useful in a strategy known as bottom fishing. It is common for many underlying stocks to regularly break through existing support levels and continue moving down into an entirely new lower trading range. When this occurs, it is in your best interest to seek out the bottom point of the downturn so that you can catch it before it starts moving back up. This is easier said than done; however, as it is possible for a stock to give off false signs of having hit bottom and buying in at that point will only lead to serious losses. This is where the protective put comes in, however, and limits the possibility for risk substantially.

Directional options trading: The most effective directional strategies when it comes to intraday options trading are those that have the highest overall degree of making it possible to make quick moves over and over again. These moves are typically going to occur at specific retracement levels or around breakouts.

Trades that are based on the Fibonacci retracement on charts for time frames less than 10 minutes can be used to determine reasonable levels of reward/risk, either by selling a credit spread at the level in question or by buying options that are already in money that are likely to rebound at these levels. It is generally going to be in your best interest to look for Fibonacci levels that are likely to overlap at multiple time frames as well as corresponding to the most recent trend experienced by the underlying stock. If you are so inclined, you can also utilize candlestick price patterns as a means of confirming a buy at specific Fibonacci levels.

Alternately, you may find success with oversold or overbought indicators when it comes to range-bound or trendless stocks. You can then sell credit spreads or buy into options that are already in the money and near the current level of resistance and support with tight stops. It is important to keep in mind that a given stock might not move quickly enough to make these levels worthwhile, so it is important to do your research ahead of time to have a reasonable expectation about the future movement.

Indicators that are used to signal lower than average volatility such as Bollinger bands are especially useful when it comes to place trades that you anticipate big moves from. Breakout indicators time, especially for the shorter charts, are also especially useful.

High volatility options intraday strategy: Trading volatility by selling options with high volatility, such as credit spreads that are currently out of the money, will allow you to make a profit when anticipating a volatility drop. This is a commonly used professional strategy to employ when it comes to earning season or other scenarios where the underlying stock has developed a big price gap. The first month's short-term options will have a great deal of volatility that will make it easier to generate a positive reward and risk ratio when selling. The most common way to take advantage of this fact is through utilizing an iron condor with strike prices of the earning move that is expected to be forthcoming.

Then, before the earnings numbers are announced, you look up the premiums of at the money calls and get an early idea of what the major players are expecting when it comes to the earnings. This will allow you to determine where you are going to want to place your put credit spread at along with your call credit spread as well. If the stopgap ends up either too low or too high from the expected range, then you still get to keep the premiums. This strategy essentially allows you to trade the way a market maker would through the use of probabilities.

CHAPTER - 17

Advanced Technical Indicator Analysis

In options trading, technical indicators are used to enable the trader to determine a couple of facts. These include the following:

Duration of Stock Movement

Direction of the Move

Movement Range

There is a difference between trading options and other securities. The main differences are that options are subject to time decay and their value diminishes as time goes. The holding period is, therefore, quite significant. For this reason, the difference between an ordinary trader and an options trader is clearly visible.

An options trader is constrained by time, while an ordinary trader can hold a position indefinitely. This is the major difference between the two and hence the need for additional technical indicators.

Technical Indicators

What are the technical indicators? These are useful indicators that provide information about trends and even possible turning points in the prices of stocks and securities. Technical indicators are among the tools that are used by traders and even analysts to predict the best times to purchase or sell stocks and options. The technical indicators also predict the cycles.

A technical analyst will calculate the essential particulars of a stock. Many of the technical indicators are calculated using data such as:

Closing Price

Highs

Lows

Trading Volumes

And Opening Prices Among Others

Stock prices from the past couple of trades provide most of the raw data required to work out technical indicators. Data mostly used is often from the last 30 days. The data is then utilized to come up with a chart or trend that indicates what has been happening and what will happen to a particular stock. This is because past performances are a great indicator of future trends.

Technical indicators are widely used by options traders to predict the future movement of the price movement of stocks. They also indicate trends within the market. When it comes to technical indicators, there are two main types. These are; leading indicators and lagging indicators

Lagging and Leading Indicators

Most traders appreciate both lagging and leading indicators because they are both invaluable. It is important that as a trader, you are informed about any possible price pullbacks and slowdowns. Ideally, you should never rely on just one of these indicators but on both. This way, your predictions, and trades will always be accurate and reliable.

Most indicators sometimes produce false signals occasionally. Since this is a risk that you want to avoid, then we recommend using at least two or three different indicators. Identify 3 specific indicators that you like, and if they all give you positive information about a stock, then you can feel confident enough to invest in it. There are essentially hundreds of different indicators in use across the world. In fact, most seasoned traders will have developed their own technical indicators so as to predict the markets accurately. You should learn about how to use about 5 different technical indicators. This way, you will have a wide variety of options to choose from.

Top Technical Indicators

We have noted above that there are hundreds of different technical indicators currently in use. However, there are some that are absolutely crucial for options traders. If you can learn how to use about 5 of them, then you will have a strong foundation for your technical analysis. Here is a look at some of the more important ones.

Average Directional Index Indicator, ADX

The ADX or average directional index is a popular indicator that is mostly used for confirmation purposes. It essentially works to confirm the information or signals that are produced by other indicators. This technical indicator works by measuring the strength of any given trend. As an example, you can use the ADX to measure if an upward trend or maybe even a downward trend is slowing down or gaining momentum.

Chart

In the chart above, the +DI is showcased as a green line while the −DI is shown as a red line. The ADX indicator itself is shown as a fat black line. We note that from late February until mid-April, there was a strong stock trend as indicated by the ADX. The stock was trending upwards.

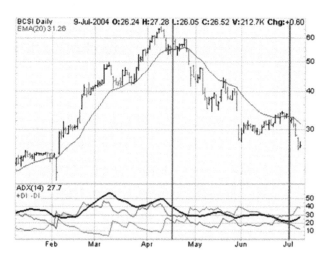

It is possible to notice that the ADX indicator never went

below the 20 marks. This is a clear indicator when the stock ever traded flat. An accurate assessment is mostly visible from the stock price. In general, we notice that this is an accurate assessment as it is visible from the strike price. There was a remarkable uptrend for the first three months and the last three months indicate a downward trend.

Oscillating Indicator

The ADX technical indicator also happens to be oscillating. Its oscillations range from zero to a hundred with zero representing flat trades while a hundred represents a plunging or rising stock. Please note that the ADX indicator showcases the strength of a trend only without pointing its direction.

Bollinger Band Strategies

Another technical strategy that is commonly used to showcase the voracity of stocks is Bollinger Strategy. There will always be an opportunity to learn from the boss. Basically, a Bollinger Band strategy or theory is mostly meant to showcase how volatile the stocks are.

This is a simple technical indicator as it is composed of a simple moving average together with both its upper and lower bands. These upper and lower bands are only about 2 standard deviations away.

Bollinger Band Theory

The Bollinger Band Theory is written in a manner that allows it to resemble a stock's volatility. It is a simple theory that consists of the simple moving average together with its lower and upper bands. These upper and lower bands are about 2 standard deviations apart. We are aware that standard deviations are commonly used in statistics to manage the deviation around the average value. Therefore, whenever you use the Bollinger Band Theory, use it only as a guide, or gauge, together with other indicators.

Application of the Bollinger Band Theory

Any time that the price is too volatile, the Bollinger Bands will be wide apart. This is demonstrated in the chart below. We can observe stock price volatility at the beginning of March, in the middle of April and mid-May. The Bollinger Bands are seen to be a little closer in the absence of price fluctuations. When there is almost no price fluctuation and little volatility, Bollinger bands are observed to be within a tight range. This is clearly observed within the chart below as circled areas. They can be observed in the months of February, in late March and late June.

How to Use Bollinger Band Theory

Historically, we can deduce that stock prices usually do not stay within a narrow, confined, trading range for a long while. You can use strategies such as the relationship between the length and width of the bands. Ideally, the closer the bands are to each other, the shorter the time that will be taken.

Therefore, if a stock begins to trade in a narrow Bollinger Band, like the ones circled in the chart, and then we can deduce that there are going to be large price fluctuations in the coming days. The challenge is that we do not have an idea of the direction that the security will move. This is, therefore, why we should use Bollinger Bands in conjunction with other technical indicators.

It is possible that the stock may turn volatile. When the volatility becomes extreme, then you will be able to note this from the image above. You will notice the stock will approach very close to either the lower or upper Bollinger Bands. The bands will, in turn, widen significantly. We can confidently say that the wider the Bollinger Bands are then, the more volatile the stock prices become.

Relative Strength Index

One of the most useful indicators for options traders is the relative strength index. The RSI is a momentum indicator and is used by traders to compare the size of gains made recently to losses incurred over a time period. Using the RSI, a trader can measure a stock's change in price and speed movement.

These parameters aim to help a trader determine which stocks or securities have been oversold or overbought. This is usually achieved using values that range from 0 to

100. Now any values above 70 indicate that the stock has been overbought while values below 30 simply imply that a stock has been oversold.

Simple Moving Averages

Some of the most important and widely used technical indicators are moving averages. Their main purpose is to smooth out the price pattern and to provide a clear indication of whether a stock is trending or is within a trading range. The moving averages are basically based on the mean stock price, usually the closing price.

Exponential Moving Averages

Apart from the simple moving averages that we have observed, we also have the exponential moving averages. With the simple moving averages, we considered all the 20 days' prices as having the same weight when working out the averages. However, this is not the case when it

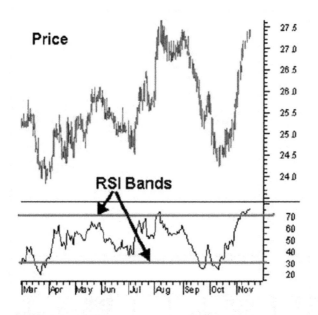

comes to the exponential moving averages or EMAs. In this instance, the latest prices carry more weight compared to earlier ones.

Due to the weighted prices, the EMA or exponential moving averages tend to respond much faster than the SMA or simple moving averages. The EMA also starts to respond and trend upwards much faster compared to the SMA. As a trader, which one of these two moving averages should you consider? Well, both averages have their own merits. The exponential moving average might register false alarms should they occur. The simple moving average resists false alarms and is also resistant to other challenges.

Relative Strength Index

The Relative Strength Index or RSI is another crucial indicator that is popularly used by options traders. It is among the leading indicators and is considered important because it is able to accurately forecast the movement of a stock's price way before it happens.

The RSI is an oscillating indicator and a momentum indicator. As a momentum indicator, it points to overbought stocks whose prices are too high and oversold stocks whose price is too low. The RSI is based largely on gains and losses rather than a stock's closing price.

As an oscillating indicator, RSI fluctuates between 0 and 100. When RSI is at 100, it means that the stock is most overbought while at 0, it is the most oversold. Basically, any amount above 70 is thought to be overbought, while any amount below 30 is considered oversold. While this technical indicator is able to inform us about stocks that have been overbought or oversold, it is valued even more because it can indicate when stocks will exit the oversold or overbought conditions. When stocks exit these positions, they move closer towards the moving averages.

In summary, we can view the RSI or relative strength index as a leading, oscillating, and momentum indicator used to inform traders when a stock exits the oversold and overbought conditions.

CHAPTER - 18

Trading With the Trend

Of course, people only trade one or two contracts at a time and so they aren't risking all that much money. But doing this right is actually pretty tricky. What we are talking about is simply buying to open an options contract and just buying individual calls or puts. So we are not talking about using any complicated strategies of the kind that we are going to talk about.

Buying Calls

So let's get started by considering the most basic strategy of all and that is buying a call option because you believe that the price of the stock is going to increase in the near future. Our consideration here does not involve buying or selling a stock, we are only going to be talking about trading options. Therefore, the goal was buying a call option would be to purchase it at the right moment and then hope that the stock will go up so much that we are able to sell the option for a profit. This all sounds simple enough, almost like something that you could never miss. Unfortunately, in practice, it's actually a lot more challenging than it sounds on paper.

The first consideration is going to be whether or not you

purchase an option that is in the money or out of the money. If this strategy works, maybe that is not really an important consideration provided that it's not too far out of the money. The reason that people decide to purchase out of the money options is that they are cheaper as compared to in the money options. It's also a fact that if the stock is moving in the right direction, out of the money options will gain at price as well.

So if someone tells you that you can't make profits from out of the money options, they are not being completely honest with you. In fact, you can make profits, but it's always going to depend on how the stock is moving and the distance between your strike price and the share price.

Of course, you can always take the risk of putting it a little bit more money upfront and investing in a call option that is already in the money. If the stock price rises, that is only going to solidify your position. You also have a little bit of insurance there. That comes from the fact that if you choose a decent strike price, there is a solid chance it will stay in the money and so even if it doesn't gain much value, you will be able to sell it and either not lose that much, or still make a profit.

Market Awareness

The first thing to keep in mind is what I call market awareness. This involves being aware of everything that could possibly impact the price of the underlying stock. This can mean not only paying attention to the chart of the stock, but you also need to be paying attention to the news and not just financial news. So let's take a recent example by looking at Facebook. In recent months Facebook has been constantly in the news. Some of the news has been good such as a decent earnings report. On the other hand, Facebook has been receiving some pushback from governments around the world. One of the issues that have been raised is privacy concerns. Facebook is also catching a lot of flak over its plan to create a cryptocurrency.

So here is the point. Every time one of these news items comes out, it's a potential for a trend. But there are a couple of problems with this. In many cases, you simply don't know when dramatic news is going to come out. So you have to be paying attention at all times and have your money ready to go. The best-case scenario is purchasing an option for the day before some large event. People are often reacting strongly in the markets when there is a good or bad job report or the GDP number is about to come out. So what you would want to do in that case is first of all pay attention to the news and see what the expectations are of all the market watchers that everyone pays attention to. Of course, they are often off the mark, but it gives you some kind of idea where things might be heading. If a good jobs report is expected, then you might want to invest in an index fund such as DIA, which is for the Dow Jones industrial average. One thing you know is that a good jobs report is going to send the Dow and the S&P 500 up by large amounts. So the key is to be prepared by purchasing your options the day before. But on the other hand, you might be wrong with your guess, which could be costly.

The fact is they don't always work because they are easily misled or maybe it's the human mind that is misled by short term changes that go against the main trend but is temporary. So you can make the mistake while following candlesticks and moving averages of seeing evidence of the sudden downtrend and then selling your position, only to find out that the downtrend wasn't real and it was only a temporary setback soon followed by a resumption of the main trend. So that is something to be careful about.

Setting Profit Goals

If you were going to trade this way, probably the best thing to do is to set a specific level of modest profit to use as a goal. One that I use is $50 per options contract. Some people may be more conservative, so you could set a goal of $30 in profit. Some people might be more risk-oriented. Honestly, I would discourage that kind of thinking because sitting around expecting to make a profit of $ 100 per contract, while possible, can put you in a situation where most of the time you lose money. What might happen is you have to sit around waiting too long to hit that magic number and it never materializes. Options can quickly turn from winners into losers because they magnify the changes in the underlying stock price by 100. So it's very easy to lose money quickly.

Day Trading

For those who are not aware, if you are labeled a patterned day trader, you need to have $25,000 in your account, and you need to open a margin account. So for most individual traders with small accounts, the last thing you want is to be labeled as a day trader. However, since options lose a lot of value from time decay, and many trends are short-lived, you may find yourself in situations where you have to enter a day trade. But if you are doing this, make sure that you only do three per five day trading period. That way you will avoid getting the designation and all the problems that might come about with it. In this case, if you buy a lot of several options that have the same strike price and the same expiration date, those are going to count as the same security. That may result in problems if you need to unload them all on the same day. One way to get around this is to purchase call options with slightly different strike prices instead of getting a bunch with all the same strike price. Of course, if you were going to hold your positions overnight and risk the loss from time decay having to do that may not be something to worry about.

Trading Puts

Trading puts using these techniques is going to be basically the same, with the only difference being that you would be looking for downward trends. This is actually a little bit different because people are accustomed to thinking in terms of rising stock prices means profits. So it might be hard to wrap your mind around the idea of profiting from stock market declines. But you should never ignore the possibility of making money with puts. A successful options trader is going to be versatile. So you should be able to move in between calls and puts pretty easily depending on market conditions. So when bad news comes out, this is a huge opportunity to make money buying put options and then selling them for more money as the price drops. It doesn't matter if the bad news is political, economic, financial, or are related to a specific company. If the bad news is general, then purchase an option for an exchange-traded fund that tracks the entire market. Or a great one to use is SPY for the S&P 500. You can use that one for good or bad news of a general nature. So if it was announced that there was a really good jobs report, buying a call option on SPY, is what you would want to do. On the other hand, if there is some news like China announcing retaliatory tariffs, you would probably want to buy a put option instead.

Range Trading

Some people think that they have to wait for a big stock move in order to make profits. But that's simply isn't the case. You can also look for stocks that are engaged in a pattern that is called ranging. This is a situation where the stock is moving up and down within a range, but it's not breaking out either up or down. This requires a little bit of patience because you have to watch the stock for a while in order to determine what the range is. The lowest price that is reached is called the support level price. You want to see the price Drop down and touch this level two times. When a stock is in range, it will touch that support level price and then rise to a maximum value that represents what is called resistance. So obviously the best time to buy a call option would be when the market price goes down to the support level. Then all you do is whole onto the option until the market price rises back up to the resistance level.

Swing Trading

You can basically swing trade using options. The only difference that has to be taken into account is the fact that time decay may inhibit your ability to hold the position long enough in order to profit. So swing trading would involve looking for our price swing. It's going to have to be something that occurs over a day or two at the most. Otherwise, the price might not move high enough in order to fight against the time decay. So if you're doing this with call options you are going to look for the stock hitting the low price that it's probably going to hit all other things being equal. Then you would buy your call option at that time. From here on out, you just sit and wait until the price rises back to the resistance level. You want to be disciplined about it and don't start hoping that there is going to be a breakout and price. Just take your profits while you can get them and then you can enter more trades later.

CHAPTER - 19

How to Read Options Table like a Pro

Now that you have a better understanding of how you can understand the risks that surround your options through the processing of the Greek mathematical strategy, it's now time to turn our attention to how you can read a modern-day options table. While the Greek methodology is certainly still used today, there are even faster ways to retrieve the information that you need, and as I have already said, the internet is the notoriously easy way that investors are using to access their information these days. While the format on these types of tables can differ depending on the database structure that you're using, the variables are largely the same. Below is an example of a table that you are likely to see when you look up options trading tables on the web:

As should be relatively obvious, some of these terms are probably familiar to you and some of them are probably

	1	2	3	4	5	6	7	8	9	10	11	12
	OpSym	Bid (pts)	Ask (pts)	Extrinsic Bid/Ask (pts)	IV Bid/Ask (%)	Delta Bid/Ask (%)	Gamma Bid/Ask (%)	Vega Bid/Ask (pts/% IV)	Theta Bid/Ask (pts/day)	Volume	Open Interest	Strike
IBM MAR10 110 C	16.25	16.70	0.00 / 0.37	19.77 / 35.15	99.16 / 92.06	0.27 / 1.15	0.007 / 0.053	0.0009 / -0.0279	0	479	110.000
IBM MAR10 115 C	11.65	11.80	0.32 / 0.47	25.37 / 27.68	90.52 / 88.67	1.82 / 1.90	0.060 / 0.069	-0.0227 / -0.0290	47	552	115.000
IBM MAR10 120 C	7.15	7.30	0.82 / 0.97	21.85 / 23.30	79.89 / 78.51	3.53 / 3.45	0.101 / 0.105	-0.0344 / -0.0385	360	1179	120.000
IBM MAR10 125 C	3.40	3.50	2.07 / 2.17	19.04 / 19.75	58.20 / 57.98	5.65 / 5.46	0.141 / 0.141	-0.0431 / -0.0448	1268	5782	125.000
Stock											126.33
IBM MAR10 130 C	1.10	1.14	1.10 / 1.14	17.41 / 17.73	28.66 / 29.04	5.40 / 5.33	0.123 / 0.124	-0.0249 / -0.0338	1868	5947	130.000
IBM MAR10 135 C	0.23	0.25	0.23 / 0.25	16.73 / 17.08	8.45 / 8.91	2.56 / 2.61	0.056 / 0.058	-0.0154 / -0.0164	666	6529	135.000
IBM MAR10 140 C	0.04	0.06	0.04 / 0.06	17.04 / 18.12	1.82 / 2.47	0.72 / 0.88	0.016 / 0.021	-0.0045 / -0.0062	80	4284	140.000
IBM MAR10 145 C	0.00	0.03	0.00 / 0.03	0.00 / 21.03	0.00 / 1.17	0.00 / 0.40	0.000 / 0.011	0.0000 / -0.0038	10	1747	145.000

unfamiliar to you. Let's take a look at the terminology for these variables so that you can begin to read these charts like an options trading professional.

Options Trading Table Column 1: The OpSym

The first column at which we'll look is a comprehensive one that combines information for both brevity and efficiency. The OpSym column is pretty straightforward, as it will provide you with the name of the stock via the stock's symbol, both the year of the stock's contract and the month of the stock's contract, the option's strike price, and it will also tell you whether the option is one that is called or put in nature. If we take a look at the first row on the table, we can easily see that the stock is one that's a share of IBM. The contract month and year is March of 2010, and the strike price is set at $110. Lastly, it should be fairly obvious that the option is a call, due to the fact that there is a "C" in the cell.

Options Trading Table Column 2: The Bid Price

The "number 2" column holds the bid price in it. Although

it's already been stated in a book that I've written on the beginner's guide to options trading, the bid price here is the latest price that has been offered by a potential options buyer for that specific stock. This price is usually most interesting to a seller of that option because he or she will then know that if he or she were to sell their share of the option through a market order, they would receive x number of dollars in return.

Options Trading Table Column 3: The Ask Price

Column three holds the ask price, which in this case can be defined as the latest price that has been offered by an investor on the market to sell a particular option. This is basically the opposite of the bid price, so if you as an investor, were looking to purchase a share of this stock, it would mean that you would be purchasing it at that most recent share price. Additionally, it's important to note here that there is a relationship between the bid and the ask price that a market maker (you) needs to be considering prior to conducting in a trade. It's not enough to simply tell yourself that you like the bid price and go from there. No, it's slightly more complicated than that. Typically, you will want to make sure that there is only a small differentiation between the bid and the ask price.

Options Trading Table Column 4: The Extrinsic Bid/Ask

After the bid and ask price columns, this next column will be able to tell you the price of the option based on adding time as a factor to it. You may notice that there are two numbers within this column. This is due to the fact that one number has the bid price in mind while the other one is in reference to the asking price. The extrinsic bid and the extrinsic asking reference number are both useful when figuring out where the option stands in a given period of time. It's a reality that all options are going to lose their time premium as they get closer and closer to their expiration date. Noting the extrinsic bid and extrinsic asking price for an option will give you a clearer idea of how far along the option is in terms of when it's going to reach its maturation date, and this will allow you to determine whether or not you want to personally invest in the stock with this time range in mind.

Options Trading Table Column 5: Implied Volatility for the Bid and Asking Price

The numbers in this column are similar to the numbers that exist in the extrinsic bid and asking column in the sense that there is more than one. This column represents the level of expected volatility in the future for a particular stock. The numbers for this column are calculated based on the volatility equations that we saw, and also takes into account other various volatile pricing factors. Some of these factors include how high the interest rate is, how wide the difference is between the actual stock's price and the strike price, and how long until the option reaches its maturation date. With these types of factors in mind, the numbers in this column can be interpreted as future rather than current volatility indicators. Lastly, it's important to understand that the higher the implied volatility is for a certain stock's bid or ask price, the more time that is going to be built into the premium for the price of the option. It's often a good idea to see if you can find historical data on the volatility of the option.

Options Trading Table Column 6: The Delta Bid and Ask Percentage

Now can you see why we looked at the Greek formulas before moving to this one? Many of the concepts can be found on an options table. The delta bid and asks percentage is one such term. It is rather pointless to go over the topic of delta again since it was already learned at length; however, one important point to make here is that there are ways that as an options trader, you will be able to get numbers on a particular option without doing the math yourself. If the math-intensive discussion intimidated you some, an options table is a great way to avoid crunching the numbers yourself.

Options Trading Table Column 7: The Gamma Bid and Ask Percentage

The gamma bid and the gamma ask percentage primarily look at the number of deltas that an option will lose or gain if the stock price itself rises or falls by an entire point. Again, if you need to go over this concept again, you should consider heading back because it will likely provide you with some clarity.

Options Trading Table Column 8: The Vega Bid and Ask Percentage in Terms of Volatility

Column 8 will provide you with information on how volatile a particular option truly is. It can be argued that the information for volatility is more accessible when it's presented in this way because it's easier to figure out whether or not the volatility is low or high. Remember, it's generally advised that you should be purchasing stock options when the volatility is low and you should be selling stocks when the volatility is high. From the perspective of the table, this is easier to understand when looking at it. For example, when the volatility for an option is low, this also means that the time premium is going to be lower for the option as well, which ultimately indicates that the overall price that you're going to be paying is lower than if the time premium were calculated later along in the cycle.

Options trading Table Column 9: The Theta Bid and Ask Points per Day

We already know that theta refers to time sensitivity. We also already know that time decay for an option moves faster-and-faster the closer the maturation date comes for it. When we look at the theta bid and ask points on an options table, what this generally means is that we are looking at how much the option is going to lose monetarily per day due to the negative influences of time. This is a great way that you can figure out how quickly a particular option is deteriorating, especially in comparison to others that exist on the market. If you look at it this way, maybe you'll be able to understand it better. An option is like buying a car and driving it off of the dealer's lot. Once you invest in it, the clock starts ticking to the point where the car will one day hold much less value than it did on the day that you purchased it.

Options Trading Table Column 10: The Volume

Finally, we find ourselves back to a column that was not already mentioned. The options table's volume refers to how many contracts for the option were traded during the most recent session for the option. It should be fairly obvious, but generally speaking, the larger the volume of contracts, the together the bid and ask spreads will be and the greater the competition will be as well.

Options Trading Table Column 11: The Open Interest

Column eleven is also fairly straightforward, as was column ten. While the name of the column is "Open Interest" it has nothing to do with the interest rate at all. Instead, open interest refers to the number of contracts that have been opened for a particular option, however, they do not yet have an option that can offset it. If you read my beginner's guide to options trading, you might remember that one of the topics that I discuss at length in that book is the concept of the zero-sum game. With options trading, there can only be winners and losers (depending on the number of investors who are negotiating in a single trade). With open interest, this means that these investors are still waiting for their options shares to either be bought or sold. It's as simple as that.

Options Trading Table Column 12: Strike

The last column on the options table is where the strike price is located. As a refresher, the strike price can be best defined as the price that the investor who has the option can either sell or purchase the option at if he or she chooses to do so. Again, this is another column that is pretty self-explanatory, with not much explanation needed. If you need a refresher on how the strike price works, be sure to head back to my beginner's guide to options trading.

Hopefully, this has provided you with a comprehensive explanation of how the typical variables within an options table operate and coexist. One of the greatest advantages that an options table can provide to the options trader is that it is a place where a lot of information exists in one specific spot. If you were to compare the Greek options to this one, you can probably tell that a lot of the information presented is neatly configured for you in an options table.

CHAPTER - 20

Trading Psychology

Now in trading, you have to possess the right mindset to succeed as a trader. Many traders jump into the market without knowing the essence of trading, and all they think about is how to make money.

We understand that the main reason why most people trade is to make money, but this should not be the first thing on our mind when setting out on this business. Starting up options trading like other financial markets will require that you have the right mindset in executing your trade, watching your trade, taking your profit. One of the main reasons traders' losses in financial markets is their attitude.

We are going to discuss some of these factors and how they will help you become a good trader. This will focus on the human aspect of being a good trader and the qualities you have to develop to succeed as an options trader.

Being Patient

Patience is required in the beginning to become a good trader. In learning how to trade, you have to be patient in learning the tricks and tips involved in trading. Trading is a complex process that involves a daily routine that you have to follow with your trade plan. To keep up with this routine, you have to be patient with the process.

The first phase of options trading is learning how to trade and all the requirements you will need to know about the option. Reading this book is part of the process of learning how to trade options, and you have been patient to this point. You should continue with being patient in trading as many traders have lost their investment in an attempt to try and go ahead of the market.

A lot of traders have become wishful in their trader as they abandon their plan to try and take a quick one to make a profit. In the long run, the trade may go against them when they fail to follow their strategy. Whenever you find yourself being controlled by the will to force the market, without a clear signal from your plan, close the computer and walk away, so you do not make an unnecessary trade.

Wishful thinking will never make your account grow, as you cannot wish the market to make your bid. Do your best to stick to your plan and continuously follow that plan until it becomes a habit.

Start Small

The financial market is not going anywhere since it has been around before you started trading, and it will be around if you lose your capital today. So do not be in haste to make money with options trade as you will have enough time to make money as you start slow.

When opening your first account, search for a broker that offers the minimal deposit and register with that broker. Start with the minimal amount required by the broker and watch how you increase your capital with that broker. The reason you should start with a small capital and grow it gradually is to teach you money management and patience in trading with options.

Starting small will remove the pressure of trying to increase your account quickly, so you are more relaxed taking each trade as they come. Too many traders have lost their investment going in with everything they have too fast, so do not make similar mistakes. Reading and practicing with backtesting and the demo account is different from playing the game with real money, so use as little capital as possible to get the real feeling of it before you put in your savings into the market.

Good Money Management

The more you invest in a trade, the more you profit and also the higher the risk of your capital as you can also lose a sustained amount in the trade. You might have $500 in your account and risk $100 on a trade, and in the end, you might gain double that and increase your capital. That would have been a good bargain, but imagine if the trade had gone against you, then you would have lost more than 25% of your capital.

This is a huge risk when you consider how much you are going to lose, and if you lose five trades with the same risk, then you would have blown off the account. Such a terrible money management strategy is too risky, and traders make the mistake of viewing the price they will gain rather than the risk they are taking.

A wise trader will put risk management upfront as the key point in every single trade you will make to safeguard the funds. Imagine risking $50 or less on each trade with a $500 account; you would have had more trades to lose to wipe out completely. And I am sure you are not going to lose five trades without a win if you follow your plans and stick to your objectives as you gradually increase your capital.

Trading is a gradual process, it is not a get rich quick scheme, and you will become profitable in the long run if you stick to your process.

Selecting a Strategy

The strategy is an important aspect if you want to succeed in options trading, as you cannot make options out of the blue. Developing your own strategy will require some years of experience in the market; as a newbie, you will have to rely on strategies like the ones mentioned in this book.

Although there is no guarantee with these signals, some people, especially those too busy to follow the market, another way the trader uses to follow the market is to follow signals delivered by more successful traders as you copy them and do the same. All these are easy ways to trade the market, but it is better to learn how to do it on your own.

Even if you are not going to trade on your own as you may decide to use an expert trader's advice or using a program to predict trades for you, it is better if you have an idea of what is going on in the market.

Take a Break from a Bad Day

You do not have to trade every day, especially when you are having a bad day, when you make three consistent bad trade, go off from your computer and do something else. At times being on the computer, especially when you do not find a good signal, can be frustrating, and instead of staying online, you might decide to do something else, so you are not forced into taking a position.

Frustration can make a trader enter a position when there is no signal based on the strategy they are using. And they enter the trade based on wishful thinking and begin to wish the market goes their way. To be honest, wishing thinking will hardly move the market in the direction you place your trade. More than half of the time traders take a position based on wishes, without following their strategy, the market usually goes against them, and they lose their trade.

When you are feeling the frustration creeping in, just walk away from the computer or take a day away from trading. Don't let frustration lead you to take a position without following through your plan and avoid any wishful trading. If you have been trading for a while, you may have come across some days when everything keeps going bad right from the first day. Any trade you take that day may end up going bad and no matter what you do, nothing will seem to go right, so when a day begins like that, stay away from the market, tomorrow is another day, and the money will still be there to make in the market.

Choose a Timeframe that Suits your Style

I don't get how people can trade using multiple timeframes; it can really mess up my trade plan as the other timeframe will confuse. One key to being successful in trading is to select a suitable time frame that will suit your style and your availability. Some people cannot trade intraday because their schedule will not allow the trader to follow the intraday time frame, so they may end up becoming a swing trader.

If you want to play the intraday game and your schedule will not allow you to focus on the necessary timeframe like the 1-hour timeframe and below, then you will face difficulties. You may end up missing out on opportunities and may be forced to trade whenever you have a chance to look at the chart. This will make you take some calls that do not correspond with your signal, which may affect your trade.

How do You Handle your Loss?

The way traders handle losses in the market is important for the psychology of the trader and how they will perform in the market. Some traders react to losses very badly, and with each loss, they are seeking to change their strategies, feeling that their plan has failed them.

No trading plan is 100% fail-proofs, and if you can get a 70% success rate, then you are in a good place. There are times when the plan will fail you, but that does not mean that you will change the plan. When you lose, do not go on a revenge trade and try to gain back what you lost instantly. Accept the loss and move on while you stick to your plan and wait for the next set up to present itself before you take the next move.

Losses are inevitable in the financial market, and you must take them when they come and do not allow the losses to destabilize you. Because losses are inevitable, you have to employ a good money management strategy, so you don't dent your capital with some of the few losses.

Keep it Simple

You do not need complex strategies or analyses to trade options as the simplest strategies can do the trick. Building strategies with too many technical indicators can become confusing as the indicators might end up giving different readings and signals in the market. This can create conflicting signals that may affect your trade.

In the financial market, the trick is to keep it simple and repeat whatever you are doing. While trading for the first time, I was into technical analysis, and on my charts, I may have not less than three indicators on the chart. It was chaotic and confusing that I do not know which one to focus on, and this causes me some opportunities.

Trading psychology is important for you to get the right mindset when trading the financial markets. There is a course on the financial market that dwells on trading psychology and the mindset that is involved in trading the financial market, and this shows the importance of the mindset.

The right attitude can make a successful or a bad trader, and the wrong attitude can ruin your account no matter the foolproof strategies you employ in the market. While developing your plans and strategies, ensure to develop the right attitude and find ways to maintain them in your lifestyle.

CHAPTER - 21

How to Get Started in Swing Trading

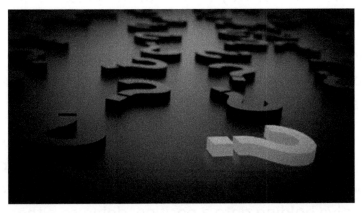

Investing is a great way to take your money and make it grow. And if you get down the right strategy and learn how to make this work for you, you will be able to get some really great return on investment without having to work on it full time. There are actually quite a few options when it is time to invest, and you are sure to find the one that works the best for you in no time. But one of the best options that will help you to earn a lot of money in a short amount of time, but is not as risky or as stressful as day trading, includes a method known as swing trading.

What Is Swing Trading

We first need to take a look at swing trading and what this

is all about. To start, swing trading is a style of trading that we can use to capture the gains that happen in a stock or any other financial security that we want to use, over a period of a few days to several weeks. The traders are going to work with technical analysis to help them find the right opportunities for trading and to help them make some more money. There are times when the fundamental analysis is a better choice for the swing trader because it allows them a new way to look at the patterns and the trends in prices.

Both in this analysis are going to be important. But they do work in completely different ways, so we have to understand when to use each one.

This is just the start of what we need to know to start with swing trading; there is so much more that we can focus on as well. For the most part, the process of swing trading will involve holding onto a position, doing so either long or short, for more than one trading session. This is the difference between swing trading and day trading. The day trader will purchase security and has to sell it by the end of the day. The swing trader is still on a short term strategy, but they can have anywhere from two days to two weeks to decide to hold onto the stock or to sell it for a profit or a loss.

The swing trader gets a little bit more time to work with the stocks than a day trader, but they usually need to get rid of the stocks, either for a profit or a loss, within a few weeks. There are some trades that last for a few months and can follow this option, but it is important that you only hold onto the stocks for a short amount of time before doing this strategy. Holding onto them for months or years turns you out of swing trading and over to some of the other options. Those are great ways to invest as well, and if you want to mix it up sometimes, holding onto stocks for longer can work well too, but this is not swing trading.

In a few cases, a swing trade can start with us planning to use it for a few days, and then we get out of the trade during the same trading session. This is a rare option, and usually, the swing trader will only use it when the conditions are really volatile, and it is hard to know where they will go after this

The goal of working with swing trading is that we want to go through and capture a chunk of a price move we think will happen in the future. While some traders like to look for stocks with a lot of volatility in them, some others like to work with a stock that is more sedated.

Most successful swing traders are only looking to capture a bit of the potential price movement. Then they are ready to get out of the trade before things reverse and then move on to the next opportunity that comes out there. As you learn how to read charts better and understand more about the stock market or the security market that you want to work with, you will get better at handling some of the ups and downs of the market, and you can make some good decisions on how to do your trades.

There are a few things that we can consider when it comes to working with swing trading, and that we need to check before we go through with some more information on swing trading and what we can do with it. These points will include:

This kind of trading will involve the trader taking some trades that will last a few days up to a few months to help the trader make some profits from the price moves that they anticipate.

Swing trading is a good way to trade, but the trader has to be ready to see that there are risks for staying in the market over the weekend and overnight if they choose this strategy. It is possible that the cold price gap and open at a different price by the next day or after the weekend.

Swing traders are able to take some profits with the help of the risk to reward ratio based on the profit target and the stop loss, or they are able to take some losses or profits based on some of the price action movements or the technical indicators along the way.

Swing trading is often seen as one of the most popular forms of trading because there is a lot of potential profit that can be made out of it. This option allows the trader to look for some opportunities that will show up within a few weeks, and then they can capitalize on it. This can make some good money in the short term, without being as risky and volatile as getting in and out of the market quickly with day trading.

If you decide that swing trading is the right option for you, then you should have really good familiarity and understanding of how technical analysis works. We will talk about some of the specifics that come with this option later, but basically, it involves looking at lots of different charts and figuring out the best course of action based on some of the trends that show up in the market. Adding a bit of knowledge about the news and how that can affect the stocks and whether that will keep things following the trends or disrupting them, can make a difference in how much success you can see with this kind of trading.

Swing traders will often take some time to look at the daily charts and see whether there are some good opportunities that they can jump on. It is common that they can look at the hour or the 15-minute charts to see whether there is something for them to jump on, and it can help them to find the right stop loss, take profit, and entry levels that will make them the most money possible.

There are a few benefits and negatives that we can see when we look at swing trading. We will take a look at some of the positives first:

This will require less of your time than day trading and can give you more profits with less work.

It helps us to maximize some of the short-term profit potentials because it is easier to catch some of the market swings that happen.

It is possible to work just with a technical analysis of this one and see some great profits out of it. When we only have to work with one type of analysis, it is a lot easier to trade and can make the process easier.

While there are a number of benefits to working with

swing trading, we also need to focus on some of the reasons why people are worried about using this kind of trading strategy at all. Some of the negatives that come with swing trading include:

Some of the positions that you use will be subject to risks that occur overnight and on the weekends. This can make it a lot riskier to get the work done.

If the market does a big reversal on you, this can create big losses that are hard to work with.

Sometimes a swing trader will miss out on some of the longer-term trends because they are focusing just on the short-term market moves that they see.

How Is Swing Trading Different From Day Trading

If you have spent some time learning about day trading in the past, you may feel like there are a lot of similarities that show up between the two trading strategies. There are a few differences that show up here, but there are also a few things that can make this kind of trading similar, and as a beginner, it is hard to know the similarities and the differences between these two styles of trading.

The main difference that shows up between the swing trading and the day trading is the amount of time you spend in the market and hold your position. With swing trading, you will hold onto the position at least overnight and often for a few days and then you will close out the position. The day trader is going to close out their position before the market has a chance to close on the same day they purchase the security. So, to keep it simple, day traders will purchase and sell their positions in one day, and then the swing trader will hold onto the position for up to a few weeks.

Because they hold onto the position overnight, it is likely the swing trader will have to deal with some form of unpredictability from the overnight risk. This could be things like gaps and a down against the position. By taking on the overnight risk, these trades are made with some smaller position sizes compared to what we see with day trading, assuming that the two traders would have the same sized account. The day trader is more likely to work with position sizes that are larger because they can take that risk out.

A swing trader is going to also have some pass to margin or leverage up to 5%. This means that if the trader has been approved to do something known as margin trading, they would only need to have $25,000 of their own capital to make the trade, but the margin would allow them to trade up to $50,000.

CHAPTER - 22

Forex Trading

The first and most important benefit of forex trading is its liquidity. As you know, the forex market is extremely liquid, meaning you can sell your currency at any time. There will be a lot of takers for it, as they will be looking to buy a particular currency. The highly liquid market can help you avoid any loss as you don't have to wait on your currency to be sold. And all of it is automatic. You only have to give the sell order, and within no time, your entire order will be sold.

The forex market is open 24 hours a day, which makes it a great place to invest in. You can keep trading during the day and also during the night if you are dealing with a country's currency whose day timings coincide with your night timings. You can come up with a schedule that will allow you to conveniently trade with all of the different countries that lie in different time zones. You can also quickly sell off a bad currency without having to wait the whole night or day.

The rate of returns in a foreign currency trade is quite high. You will see that you can invest just $10 and control as much as $1000 with it. All you have to do is look for the best currency pairs and start buying and selling them. The leverage that these investments provide is always on the higher side, which makes them an ideal investment avenue for both beginners and old hands.

The transaction costs of this type of trade are very low. You don't have to worry about big fees when you buy and sell foreign currencies. That is the one big concern that most stock traders have, as they will worry about having to shell out a lot of money towards transaction costs. But that worry is eliminated in currency exchanges, and you can save on quite a lot of money just by choosing to invest in currency.

Non-Directional Trade

The forex market follows a non-directional trade. This means that it does not matter if the difference in the currencies is going upwards or downwards, you will always have the chance to remain with a profit. This is mostly because there is scope for you to short a deal or go long on it depending on the situation and rate of difference. You will understand how this works as and when you partake in it. The main aim of investing in forex is to remain with a steady profit, which is only possible if you know when to hold on to investment and when to sell it off. This very aspect is seen as being a buffer by traders and is the main reason for them choosing to invest in forex.

Middlemen Eliminated

With forex trade, you can eliminate any middlemen. These

middlemen will unnecessarily charge you a fee and your costs with keeping piling up. So, you can easily avoid these unnecessary costs and increase your profit margin. These middlemen need not always be brokers and can also be other people who will simply get in the way of your trade just to make a quick buck out of it. You have to be careful and stave such people off in order to avoid any unnecessary costs that they will bring about. Education is a key here and the more you know, the better your chances of avoiding any such frauds.

No Unfair Trade

There is no possibility of anyone rich investors controlling the market. This is quite common in the stock market where a single big investor will end up investing a lot of money in a particular stock and then withdraw from it quickly and affect the market negatively. This is not a possibility in the foreign currency market as there is no scope for a single large trader to dominate the market. These traders will all belong to different countries, and it will not be possible for them to control the entire market as a whole. There will be free trade, and you can make the most use of it.

No Entry Barrier

There is no entry barrier, and you can enter and exit the market at any time you like. There is also no limit on the investment amount that you can enter with. You have to try and diversify your currency investments in a way that you minimize your risk potential and increase your profit potential. You can start with a small sum and then gradually increase it as you go.

Certainty

There is a certainty attached to foreign currencies. You will have the chance to avail guaranteed profits if you invest in currency pairs that are doing well. These can be surmised by going through all the different currency pairs that are doing well in the market. With experience, you will be able to cut down on your losses with ease and also increase your profits. You have to learn from your experience and ensure that you know exactly what you are doing.

Easy Information

Information on the topic of foreign currencies is easily available on the internet and from other sources. This information can be utilized to invest in the best currency pairs. You have to do a quick search of which two pairs are doing well and invest in them without wasting too much time. If you need any other information on the topic, then this book will guide you through it. You can directly go to the topic that you seek and look at the details to provide there.

Apart from these, there are certain other benefits like minimal commission charged by the OTC agent and instant execution of your market orders. No agency will be able to control the foreign exchange market.

These form the different benefits of trading in the forex market but are not limited to just these. You will be acquainted with the others as and when you start investing in it.

Choosing Currencies to Trade

The U.S. Dollar is involved in some 89% of currency trades, and currency pairs that involved the U.S. Dollar and some other currency from a large, developed economy are called the majors. There are seven major currency pairs. Let's take a look at each one so that you will be familiar with what people are talking about when they mention the majors. A major currency pair can be any of the following.

EUR/USD

The Euro and U.S. Dollar currency pair is the most popular and widely traded of the majors. The Euro was introduced in 1999, and it's a relatively strong currency that represents all the major countries in Europe that are part of the European Union. Although Brexit is dominating recent headlines, even with Britain as a part of the European Union, it has maintained its own currency, the Great British Pound. Hence, the Euro is the currency used by members of the EU on the continent.

When it comes to this currency pair, you are going to want to watch moves by the European Central Bank or ECB, and also the U.S. Federal Reserve. Of course, in any of the majors, you are going to be looking at moves by the U.S. Federal Reserve.

The biggest strength of this currency pair from the perspective of a small retail trader is that it is a highly liquid financial asset that often has substantial volatility. In recent years, the volatility and the magnitude of moves (on average) have decreased somewhat, but it's still a rather strong average pip movement of 200 pips. Since this currency pair is so liquid, getting in and out of trades fast is not going to be an issue. This currency pair is certainly a good choice for beginners, or for a trader of any level.

Professional Forex traders are generally not spending their time focusing on exotic currency pairs.

Some exotics like the Mexican Peso are more stable than others, such as the Iraqi dinar. But the biggest weakness for any exotic currency is that they are not highly desired by traders, and as a result, you might find yourself stuck in trade far longer than you want to be.

The economies of many exotic currencies are also unstable and subject to more political upheaval than the economies of most major countries. This means that volatility can suddenly be sent soaring on some political event. Rapid depreciation can often be seen with exotic currencies, and while this can offer an opportunity to bet against the currency, remember that getting out of a trade is something that can always be an issue. So there are two main weaknesses that you need to consider when thinking about trading exotics–instability and low levels of liquidity.

In any business, the tools are really crucial to how the business operates. In forex trading, this is as well as a similar situation. The new traders or the experienced traders need the tools to master their trade and also make the right decisions to reach their goals.

Nowadays, the trading tools can be with a fee or without it. Many platforms offer free trading tools for traders to use at the basic level. Some platforms offer the subscription. Traders become the members and pay the services monthly or yearly.

The economic calendar is helping the traders get fresh and updated news such as what happens in the future of the market, important related to trading economic data, new policies from the central bank, the elections and monetary policies updated around the world and much more. These are really important for trading, especially in the forex market.

You can get the economic calendar from brokers or financial websites. It will provide a big picture of the economy, such as the events that impact the economy at what level, the unemployment rate, expecting the market conditions. Traders will have to keep close eyes on these things because trading currencies will be effective. Pip is the measuring unit, and it is the most popular and smallest measure unit in forex trading, especially between the currency pair. The pip calculation is convenient to use. Many traders use this forex trading tool easily in exchange for the pair currency. The users just have to enter the detail of their position, the amount of the currency, size of trade, currency pair and also leverage. Forex market has three (3) biggest markets around the world. One market closes, and then another market opens. That is why some traders can trade 24 hours. Besides that, the market also overlaps with each other so the traders can also trade 2 markets at the same time. With the right strategies, traders can get double profit. The Time zone converter helps traders know exactly which market is opening at exactly what time. The experienced traders often trade around 3 or 4 mornings Eastern Time because they can trade in London market, which is the biggest market for forex. It also overlaps with the Asia forex market.

CHAPTER - 23

Why Traditional Investment Strategies Fail

Anyone afraid to lose money investing in the stock market, the real difference between the rich and the poor is that the rich use most of their income for savings (pension and insurance) and education.

With the transfer of wealth, the preservation of assets and the transfer to the next generation as the secret of financial success, it is surprising that at least 20% of Americans have taken out investments or even retirement plans.

The comparison of human behavior is that we are complete believers and can plan important events in life, but this is often forgotten in terms of investment. You will find that a third of investors have a written mindset that determines their investment portfolio and their pension plan.

Why are you interested?

The investment world is a tough forest, a deadly aquatic world; the most demanding and rigorously organized people depend on it for their survival, while others must succeed. A written letter that responds to the end of our response to emotions such as money, this prevents us from meeting our educational and emotional needs.

Rather than following a folding idea that encourages you to make fair investment decisions, it's better to say that it forces you to stick to a rational system created by investment principles.

It is also important to consider the main reasons why investors fall victim to the market and lose their precious funds:

1. Investors ignore facts and calculations of investing in vulnerable companies or financial instruments

2. Increased confidence has led some investors to believe that they cannot invade and can still enter the market.

3. Everyone wants to be considered a hero and a general capable of leading soldiers to victory. This can lead to your investment decision not based on strategic thinking, but on the desire to impress your friends, colleagues or family members.

By developing an investment plan and following the statement, you increase your chances of developing and increasing your savings or investment. Here are steps to make a plan and avoid the spirit of the herds and the addiction issues that would cause us to invest heavily:

1. Identify Specific Ideal Goals

Rather than saying that you want an adequate pension, think about how much money you need. Your specific goal may be to save $500,000 when you are 65 years old.

2. Calculate the Monthly Savings

If you were to save $500,000 at age 65, how much would you save each month? The amount is determined each month. However, you may need to adjust your goals.

3. Choose your Investment Strategies

When you record your long-term goals, you can choose more aggressive and risky investments. If your goal is short term, you can choose a lower risk investment. Or, you may want to balance more.

4. Information on Development and Investment Policy

Create investment policy information to guide your investment decisions. If you have an advisor, the investment policy statement will explain the rules your advisor should follow in the portfolio. Your investment policy statement must be:

Explain your purpose.

Describe the skills necessary to achieve the objective.

Describe your earnings and time forecasts.

Indicate the type of risk you will assume.

Building your Portfolio

What is Investment Strategy?

Investment methods are essential for successful recruiting. The purpose of your investment is to make money. You need to be a savvy investor with the right frame of mind, know what to do, have an idea, and be ready to make the right decision.

Your investment philosophy is the concept of success. It's a good photo of what you want to do. When you choose an investment, you must choose a strategy, otherwise, you risk making the wrong decision and the wrong investment.

Why is Strategic Investment Necessary?

Investment methods are essential to success. Only those who blame them will play and have the chance to find a bad job. Your goal should be to maximize profits. Without an investment strategy, this is impossible.

You also need an investment strategy to track your investment. Why should I buy these vouchers? Why are you trading this? Why choose this strategy? If some of these questions are the questions you are asking yourself, a good strategy should help you answer them.

What is the Structure of the Portfolio?

When you create your own investment plan, it takes time, effort, learning and planning. Consider the steps below to create your investment strategy:

Step 1: Determine your Investment

Before purchasing items, please determine the funds you wish to invest in. Never say "I want the best investment." Be precise. Will you buy stocks, bonds, mutual funds, real estate, stock markets, etc.? Are you going to invest in any type of security or several types of security?

Step 2: Know Exactly What You Are Going to Do

Now that you know the guarantees that can save you money, you can get the most out of them. Download books and tools, find them online and find everything you want to do.

I know you may not be familiar with this area, so please start with the basics. Even if you spend a few months before you start, it's still worth it. It is best to wait a few months and then reach the end or come back immediately to start and lose a lot of money. If you are interested in the experience, please use the free stock market game until you are ready to invest in real money. You can actually find more information about this game in the link below.

Step 3: Develop Diagnostic Procedures

You are now in your investment strategy. Design research methods. Research is very important for all types of investment. You have to know exactly what they are investing your money in to know that it is a good choice.

If you study, you will also do research. Once you know how to do it, you can start planning strategies. Choose the type of expense, financial information and other information you are looking for. Before buying, learn to weigh each stock, bond, or other investment.

Step 4: Determine the Amount to Invest

Basically, the amount you invest depends on the amount you can invest. Obviously, if you trade to pay $3,000 before taxes, you cannot invest $10,000 a month. Distribute the dollar amount or as a percentage of your regular investment income.

Try to give yourself a chance. Make sure you invest more and more. If you think you can make $100 a month, try it first, then make $200 next month. The more you invest, the more you can get. If you invest too much, even a weak investment philosophy can work well.

Step 5: Write your Portfolio

It is time to spend some money, but that is not the way to fail. Buy stocks and build your portfolio. After the research, you know exactly what to buy. Buy as many of these values as possible.

Build a solid product portfolio plan for diversity in your research to reduce risk and maximize your profits. Buy a business that promises future growth or value based on your research.

Step 6: Monitor your Portfolio

The beginning of your investment strategy is not the end. You should continue to monitor and continue to make changes. Invest at least an hour a week. For example, if you buy shares in 5 different companies, you should search for that company at least 5 hours a week.

If necessary, buy or sell stocks or other securities. If you are unsure of a business or think you have spent most of your investment, please continue. Don't waste money

The most important thing is to continue your education and training. Read all the books you can get and get information gradually and regularly. Not all of the information you have read or heard. Use this option to help you develop an investment strategy.

Building your Portfolio

You may have guessed that a fatal investment book requires a lot of preparation and planning. By choosing the right measures, problems can be reduced in the future. It is also a very good way to ensure your capital reaches its full potential.

When creating the best investment portfolio a business can buy, keep the following five things in mind.

(1) Find out What You Want to Achieve

Goal setting is a good way to decide which stocks and assets are best for your portfolio. If you want to accumulate large deposits after retirement, investing in stocks and low-risk assets is a good idea. These fluctuations are small and profits are common. However, if you want to make a lot of money quickly, look for high-risk stocks that can maximize returns in the short term.

(2) Select the Time Range.

Time is always necessary. If the search time is long, other devices can be acquired. Time can reduce the risk because you do not have to recover the funds immediately. However, if you save money faster, you may need to avoid risky investments. You don't want to gamble, if you take risks, everything will be lost.

(3) Calculate your Comfort Zone

Not everyone has the same risk tolerance. Some people can manage venture capital without interruption, while others can stay overnight and rest. You have to be honest with yourself. You can risk venture capital. Since quality is residual income, it is important to create a portfolio that can grow without increasing fear.

(4) Protect your Type of Property

Do not rely on stocks and bonds. Reserve your fortune is affected by the tide and causes fear. You should also consider other assets such as real estate, direct ownership, private equity and commodities.

(5) Take into Account your Energy Needs

If you do not need short-term funds, do not hesitate to invest in real estate, facilities and equipment such as real estate. However, you should consider using more liquid assets, such as stocks. This way, you can quickly withdraw your investment as needed. Lack of fluid means you have to persevere. Please think carefully before choosing assets in your portfolio.

(6) Observe the Direction, but be Confident

Many directions are everywhere. Although you should consider using these models to update your portfolio from time to time, it is important not to drive immediately. Calculate assets or active stocks over time, but if you've done enough research and reliability, invest in it. After this process starts, managing Office should be a little meaningful, but you need to "improve" your services from time to time.

(7) Obtain Technical Advice

A financial planner can help you overcome the most difficult decisions. Find financial advice to calculate many alternative investment tools. Remember to be honest with your own personal thoughts and concerns. A good consultant should be able to take your concerns into account and help you create the best documentation.

Most people expect to build a good investment portfolio but only lose and lose most (if not all) of their wealth. Why does this happen to these people? They may, however, not be capable of getting enough information about the product method to predict what will happen, which will cause them many losses. Furthermore, it makes no sense to compensate or reduce losses.

CHAPTER - 24

Characterizing Your Trade Success through Your Options Trading Strategies

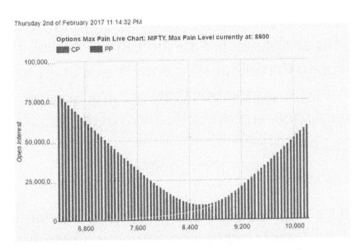

Would you like to make each progression of your trading procedure a beyond any doubt shot towards your trade success? Do you wish to dispense with or, if not, reduce your stresses over your trade commitment and become progressively particular about your trade execution? Is it accurate to say that you are in for something which could enable you to improve as an entertainer in the options trading industry? When you got 'yes' as your response to those inquiries, this part is something for you that will give you a few bits of advice about your trade. With this, you should concentrate on your options trading techniques.

Tossing Sure Shots

A trader's strategy in options trading is incredible assistance in making his trade progress. This strategy could characterize the trader himself when he ends up victorious or not. Having significant procedures resembles having an endowment of foreseeing what will occur later on in which the trader must be set up to stay away from misfortunes concerning his trade. With the assistance of these procedures that the trader utilizes, each progression that the trader will perform will bolster his objectives and set up his arrangements for the future conditions which may happen that will shake his trade execution. With that, there will be an affirmation that the trader will toss beyond any doubt shots and make the most of the scoreboard for him.

Lesser Worries

Choice trading is a simple sort of trade wherein a trader could have lesser stresses concerning misfortunes that he may look amid his trade commitment. The pressure that you may understand because of the business stresses that accidents may give you has alleviation in options trading through your options trading systems. We can't state that misfortunes can be completely disposed of because that will be unthinkable, however, you can make sure that they might be cut down in the event that you have that great strategy since it will give you a few thoughts of what may occur amid your trade commitment which will assist you with becoming much arranged.

Better Performance

To whole it up, having beyond any doubt shots and fewer stresses in your trade execution will help you in up-evaluating yourself as a superior trader and help you acquire from options trading. Your techniques will give you certainty about your success in all commitments that you will make. These successes will open you more opportunities than you may snatch, which will offer you higher benefits than what you anticipate. This is proof that choice trading is a commendable field which is flooding with success opportunities for financial specialists who get into it. Also, this likewise demonstrates trading with methodologies is an extraordinary activity to have a beyond any doubt success,

The Use of Options Trading Strategies

Do you have stresses concerning by what means will you reduce the dangers of your commitment in options trading? If you are wishing of having lesser misfortune and higher benefit, would you like to augment your assets and develop your prosperity rate? If your answer is 'yes,' all you need is a compelling and proficient options trading strategy. This will be such a significant amount of support for novices, specialists, and different dimensions of people who are taking part in the options trading business.

A reason for cerebral pain to consider how much benefit you are missing a result of the misfortunes happening amid your exchanges. The facts demonstrate that dangers are always present in all undertakings, yet a lot of it isn't reliable. You may not dispense with them. However, you can even now accomplish something and that it's to limit them by utilizing strategies.

Strategies to be utilized to develop your trade are resolved as ahead of schedule as you're arranging stage. These are generally insignificant products of a decent arrangement which is embraced all together for a trader to seek after his objectives and targets. In the phase of arranging, you will initially consider "what would you like to do?" at that point, you will figure "In what manner will you do it?" that is how you will decide the ways on the best way to make your trade successful.

Options trading strategies are the determinants of your trade movement. These strategies will enable you to decide whether your alternative will move evenly, vertically, or corner to corner. The inquiry is the thing that strategy is the best.

As a trader who needs achievement in the field of options, trading must resemble a chess player. Options trading, similar to chess, are a battle of strategies; the individuals who will have the beyond any doubt win are the individuals who are having their best options trading strategies. You should remember that your every move will have a significant effect in the entire fight; all things considered, you should turn out to be careful in your every step. Ensure that you will do is dependable for the success and won't be the purpose behind you to misfortune.

Why Develop Options Trading Strategies

Stock market trading opens up the chance to make a

considerable measure of benefit if one is sufficiently educated and practices sound judgment. Stocks and bonds are the runs of the mill sorts of speculations for tenderfoots and the progressively moderate individuals. People who need to risk may choose to go into options contracts. If they do as such, they should utilize one of the outstanding alternative trading methodologies.

There are a few motivations to utilize alternative trading methodologies, and they vary contingent upon the market conditions and whether the individual is buying or selling. For the most part, they are being used by buyers to restrict their misfortunes to the premium paid if the alternative is underestimated and has expanding instability. Sellers use them to confine their troubles in circumstances of enormous credit. At the point when the market is unbiased, utilizing specific choice trading methodologies can give the investor a beyond any doubt approach to make a benefit.

Investors, who are merely beginning, for the most part, utilize a secured call strategy since it is increasingly preservationist. It includes composing a trading contract to buy while owning offers of the stock. In stock choice trading, one options contract gives you authority more than 100 offers of stock. These offers are generally held in a similar brokerage account from which the call contract is composed. The possessions fill in as collateral for the commitment natural recorded as a hard copy of the call contract.

As investors acquire involvement in options trading, the

open call strategy might be something they use. This happens when the investor sells call options on the market without having any responsibility for stocks. It is likewise alluded to as a revealed call or short call strategy. There are more hazards inalienable in this strategy because the potential for benefit is restricted, yet the potential for misfortune is boundless if the stock cost increments over the activity cost for the options being sold.

Options Trading Strategies Help You Become an Effective Option Trader

Do you have a few reserve funds in the bank and still wish to cause it to develop? Do you want to make it work for you as you get ready for your retirement and future endeavors? Would you like to appreciate life to the fullest with your family, companions and friends and family as you resign - having such an effortless, calm and exciting knowledge after years and many years of diligent work? If indeed, you better have a go at contributing and trading options as you can make every one of these things conceivable. Get the compelling options trading techniques today and perceive how these tips could make you push through with your venture and trading endeavors.

Necessarily, options trading methodologies are exceedingly intended to support specialists, experienced financial specialists and traders just as the tenderfoots and even the individuals who are keen on seeking after this art. These systems for options trading are delegated a few devices to enable you to begin and keep up such extreme status of your speculation. Options preparing might be given to any individual who has the energy, intrigue, and excitement over this endeavor.

Learning the upside and the drawback of this speculation and trading adventures is a decent procedure. Like this, you will, in general, diminish the odds of uncovering your well-deserved money to hazard - restricting the likelihood that it would not work for you. By doing some inflexible research, regardless of whether it just takes a couple of snaps at your very own pace and accommodation might be a decent sign that you genuinely have good intentions and would need to truly work more earnestly towards an unwinding and an effortless retirement in time.

Finding an Effective Options Trading Strategy and Succeeding

In case you are one of the people who need to wind up fruitful in the field of options trading? Would you like to know the key to a useful trade? People who were prevailing in this field never make it as a result of karma or shot. They all make the thing in like manner that helped them out to get what they have since you should likewise have to pick up progress. That thing is a successful options trading strategy.

In this modern world, many people are attempting to discover to increase money related efficiency and steadiness. This makes people adventure in different methods for contributing. One of these is options trading. In any case, the way to accomplishment in this field isn't smooth and quick-paced. It would be hard for the individuals who are simply in the beginning line of taking part in this undertaking. That is the motivation behind why a novice must strategize an arrangement after diving in the waters of stock trading.

The web offers different procedures that will be useful for your business if you have no clue on what strategy you will utilize. It would be better if you will search for websites of those people who are additionally wandering in stock trading for you to discover a few hints that are tried compelling by them. These tips may likewise help you in trading. You should broaden your network by finding people who are known in this field and look for assistance from them.

There are likewise locales that offer gatherings called "online courses" and online training in compelling options trading, which may help those people who are new in the field. This will acquaint an amateur all the while and become furnished with methodologies that will support them. It is advantageous for a first-year recruit to have a coach who will fill in as a guide in the field of trading.

In a fruitful trade, you should not play boorish. This is a modern world. The individuals who accomplish triumph have minds that are loaded with strategies and methodologies. On account of options trading, it is a need for a trader to discover a trading strategy that will enable them to achieve triumph. It involves decision and lifting a finger to pick up achievement in your undertaking.

CONCLUSION

So here we are at the end of this guidebook on trading options. They can be extremely profitable, but learning to trade them well takes time. You can choose to use indicators to determine your entry points. I'm all for this approach but remembers that over the long term, you're better served learning the basics of order flow and using them.

There is no shortage of options strategies you can use to dramatically limit your risk, and depending on the volatility levels, you can deploy separate strategies to achieve the same ends. Contrast this with a directional trading strategy where you have just one method of entry, which is to either go short or go long, and only one way of managing risk, which is to use a stop loss.

Spread or market neutral trading puts you in the position of not having to care about what the market does. In addition, it brings another dimension of the market into focus, which is volatility. Volatility is the greatest thing for your gains and options allow you to take full advantage of this, no matter what the volatility situation currently is.

Options can be a bit hard to get your head around at first since so many of us are used to looking at the market as a thing that goes up or down. Options bring a sideways and a different vertical element to it via spreads and volatility estimates. More advanced options strategies take full advantage of volatility and are more math-focused, so if this interests you, you should go for them.

Said that, do not assume the complexity means more gains. The strategies shown in this book are quite simple, and they will make you money thanks to the way options are structured. They bring you the advantage of leverage without having to borrow a single cent.

You can choose to borrow, of course, but you need to do this only if it is in line with your risk management math. Risk management is what will make or break your results and at the center of quantitative risk management is your risk per trade. Keep this consistent and line up your success rate and reward to risk ratios, and you'll make money as a mathematical certainty.

Qualitative risk management requires you to adopt the right mindset with regards to trading, and it is crucial for you to adopt this as quickly as possible. Remember that the implications of your risk math mean that you need not be concerned with the outcome of a single trade. Instead, seek to maximize your gains over the long term.

The learning curve might get steep at times, but given the rewards on offer, this is a small price to pay. Keep hammering away at your skills, and soon you'll find yourself trading options profitably, and everything will be worth it.

How much can you expect to make trading options?

Well, I said that I'm not keen on putting numbers to this sort of thing. Generally, good options trade can expect around 50-80% returns on their capital. As you grow in size, this return amount will decrease naturally. However, to start with these are beyond excellent returns.

Always make sure you're well-capitalized since this is the downfall of many traders. You need to be patient with the process. A lot of people rush headfirst into the market without adequate capitalization or learning and soon find that the markets are far tougher than they thought. So always ensure the mental stress you place yourself in is low and that you're never in a position where you 'have' to make money trading.

I wish you the best of luck in all of your trading efforts. The key to success is to simply never give up and to be resilient. Reduce the stress on yourself, and you'll be fine. Here's wishing you all the success in your options trading journey!

Lightning Source UK Ltd.
Milton Keynes UK
UKHW050709151220
375239UK00007B/140